The Quiet Landscape

Archaeological investigations on the M6
Galway to Ballinasloe national road scheme

The Quiet Landscape

Archaeological investigations on the M6
Galway to Ballinasloe national road scheme

Edited by
Jim McKeon and Jerry O'Sullivan

NRA Scheme Monographs 15

First published in 2014 by
The National Roads Authority
St Martin's House, Waterloo Road, Dublin 4
Copyright © National Roads Authority and the authors

Library of Congress Cataloguing-in Publication Data are available for this book.
A CIP catalogue record for this book is available from the British Library.
Material from Ordnance Survey Ireland is reproduced with the permission of the Government of Ireland and Ordnance Survey Ireland under permit number EN0045206.

ISBN 978-0-9574380-7-1
ISSN 2009-0471

NRA Scheme Monographs 15
Copy-editing: Editorial Solutions (Ireland) Ltd
Cover design, typesetting and layout: LSD Ltd
Index: Julitta Clancy
Printed by: W&G Baird Ltd

Front cover—'The Quiet Landscape' (2011) by Jêrome Hébert.
Back cover—A long-cross silver penny of the reign of King Edward I (1272-1307) (John Sunderland).

Contents

Contents of CD-ROM

1. About this CD-ROM: explanatory note

2. Archaeological excavation Final Reports 2005–2007

Excavations by Valerie J Keeley Ltd in Sector 1		
Filename	**Site description**	**Director**
Doughiska E2052.pdf	Burnt mounds at Doughiska	Liam McKinstry
Coolagh E2435.pdf	Cashel with round-house and lime kilns	Colum Hardy
Carnmore West E2436.pdf	Cashel with souterrain and cereal-drying kilns	Bruce Sutton
Ballygarraun West E2534.pdf	Isolated medieval burial with charcoal and antler	John Lehane

Excavations by Headland Archaeology (Ireland) Ltd (now Rubicon Heritage Services Ltd) in Sector 2		
Filename	**Site description**	**Director**
Newford E2437.pdf	Pyre, post-pits and burnt mound	Brendon Wilkins
Furzypark E2553.pdf	Burnt spread with sherds of possible funerary vessel	Brendon Wilkins
Farranablake East E2352.pdf	Cashel	Tom Janes
Moyode E2353.pdf	Estate tenant's cottage	Tom Janes
Deerpark E2438.pdf	Cremation burial and ring-ditch	Brendon Wilkins
Deerpark E2057.pdf	Kennels of Tallyho Lodge	Tom Janes
Rathgorgin E2439.pdf	Modern burnt spread	Brendon Wilkins
Brusk E2063.pdf	Brick clamps	Brendon Wilkins
Curragh More E2520.pdf	Cremation burial	Tom Janes
Clogharevaun E2056.pdf	Multi-period landscape	Brendon Wilkins
Carrowkeel E2046 Vol 1.pdf Carrowkeel E2046 Vol 2.pdf	Cemetery-settlement enclosure	Brendon Wilkins
Ballykeeran E2440.pdf	Short-cist cremation burial and ring-ditch	Brendon Wilkins

Excavations by CRDS Ltd in Sector 3		
Filename	**Site description**	**Director**
Killescragh 1 E2070.pdf Killescragh 2 E2071.pdf	Burnt mounds and trackways	Ken Curran

Excavations by CRDS Ltd in Sector 3 (cont.)

Filename	Site description	Director
Caraun More E2073.pdf	Prehistoric pits and medieval watercourses	Sheelagh Conran
Caraun More 1 E2074.pdf	Burnt mound	Nóra Bermingham
Caraun More 2 E2055.pdf	Burnt mound	Nóra Bermingham
Caraun More 3 E2072.pdf	Burnt mound	Tamás Péterváry
Cross E2069.pdf	Ring-ditches with cremations and inhumations	Gerry Mullins
Rahally E2006.pdf	Hillfort, ringforts and field system	Gerry Mullins
Rathglass E2121.pdf	Bronze Age cremations, medieval ironworking and cereal kiln	Tamás Péterváry
Treanbaun 1 E2064.pdf	Cremation cemetery and palisaded enclosure	Marta Muñiz-Pérez
Treanbaun 2 and 3 E2123.pdf	Medieval cemetery-settlement enclosure (Treanbaun 2) Prehistoric lead mine and cists (Treanbaun 3)	Marta Muñiz-Pérez
Gortnahoon E2075.pdf	Cereal kilns, storage pits and metalworking	Tamás Péterváry
Newcastle E2076.pdf	Post-medieval house and field ditches	Sheelagh Conran

Excavation by The Archaeology Company for the PPP company (Sector 3)

Filename	Site description	Director
Ballynaclogh E3874.pdf	Chipped stone assemblage, hearths and trackway remnants in peat	Michael Tierney

Excavations by Eachtra Archaeological Projects in Sector 4

Filename	Site description	Director
Cooltymurraghy E2448.pdf	Burnt mound	John Tierney
Coololla E2447.pdf	Spade mill and lime kiln	John Tierney
Urraghry E2449.pdf	Mesolithic tools and Bronze Age burnt mound	John Tierney
Barnacragh E2446.pdf	Burnt mound	John Tierney
Loughbown 1 E2442.pdf	Ringfort and earlier Iron Age features	Nik Bower

Excavations by Eachtra Archaeological Projects in Sector 4 (cont.)		
Filename	**Site description**	**Director**
Loughbown 2 E2054.pdf	Ringfort with souterrain, metalworking, corn-drying kilns and early modern building remains	Nik Bower
Mackney 1 E2445.pdf	Bronze Age hearth, pits and saddle quern	John Tierney
Mackney 2 E2443.pdf	Bronze Age hearth and pits	John Tierney
Mackney 3 E2444.pdf	Ringfort, round-house, souterrain and *cillín* burials	Finn Delaney

3. Other surveys and analyses 2004–2007

Filename	**Survey description**	**Surveyor(s)**
ArchaeoPhysica Vol 1 03R147.pdf ArchaeoPhysica Vol 2 03R147.pdf ArchaeoPhysica Vol 3 03R147.pdf	Archaeological geophysics (recorded magnetometry survey) in 26 sample areas of the road scheme • Main report (text) Vol. 1 • Main report (figs) Vol. 2 • Aughrim sector Vol. 3	Ann Roseveare and Martin Roseveare
Aughrim metal detecting R002.pdf	Metal-detecting survey in fields at 'Luttrell's Pass' on Aughrim battlefield (1691)	David Sabin and Kerry Donaldson
Architectural heritage Vol 1.pdf Architectural heritage Vol 2.pdf	Building surveys at 10 locations of rural buildings directly affected by the road scheme	Sharon Kelly
Loughrea– Attymon Railway.pdf	Architectural survey of the Loughrea–Attymon Light Railway line	George Geddes
Pollen analysis Ballinphuil bog.pdf	Pollen analytical investigations at Ballinphuill bog	Karen Molloy, Ingo Feeser and Michael O'Connell
Suck river survey E1487.pdf	Suck river crossing underwater metal-detecting survey	Eoghan Kieran

4. Inventory of selected artefacts from excavation sites

Inventory of artefacts.pdf compiled by Jim McKeon.

Foreword

Galway is a large and diverse county. It is popularly associated with the rugged mountain country of Connemara and its splendid Atlantic beaches. The city itself has become synonymous with festivals and festivity: from street theatre and the arts to its famous race meetings and—a more recent coup—around-the-world yacht racing. But there is another Galway of low-lying cattle pastures, dispersed rural dwellings and historic market towns, which is less well known. This is the quiet landscape of this book, extending across the rural interior of east Galway, from the outskirts of the city to the town of Ballinasloe.

One measurable benefit of the new M6 motorway is a significantly shorter journey time across this landscape. This is partly achieved by bypassing towns and villages along the old roads: Ballinasloe, Aughrim, Kilreekill, Loughrea and Craughwell on the R446 (the old N6), and Kilconnell, New Inn, Kiltullagh and Athenry on the more winding R348. The quality of life in these places is greatly improved by being bypassed, but some travellers may feel that their enjoyment in the journey is diminished because they no longer encounter the old towns and villages along the way. Of course, anyone who travels in east Galway for leisure is at liberty to leave the main road and visit these places. But if they remain instead on the new M6 motorway they will be pleasantly surprised to discover that it offers them many new vistas of the countryside, revealing the quiet landscape of east Galway on a grand scale.

I was prompted to this meditation on the different experiences of travelling on old roads and new ones when I previewed the contents of this latest book in the NRA scheme monograph series. Just as the motorway has created a series of new vistas across contemporary east Galway, the archaeological investigations that preceded it have opened new windows on the early history and prehistory of the region. The discoveries described in *The Quiet Landscape* are remarkable in their variety, especially in a county where there has been little previous archaeological fieldwork outside its historic towns. Some of these discoveries are of the first importance and a few are unique in the Irish archaeological record. In these pages readers can discover for themselves, among other excavated archaeological sites, a Bronze Age lead mine at Treanbaun, a great prehistoric hillfort at Rahally, an early medieval cashel at Coolagh or an 18th-century spade mill at Coollola—none of them previously recorded, all of them brought to light by investigations on the new road.

The NRA is pleased to have supported Galway County Council in commissioning the investigations that led to this publication. We value the public communication of the work and I would like to congratulate CRDS Ltd, Eachtra Archaeological Projects, Rubicon Heritage Services Ltd—formerly Headland Archaeology (Ireland) Ltd, the Palaeoenvironmental Research Unit at NUI Galway, Valerie J Keeley Ltd and the editors for bringing their work to completion in this book.

Fred Barry
Chief Executive
National Roads Authority

Acknowledgements

Archaeological investigations on the M6 Galway to Ballinasloe road scheme were commissioned by Galway County Council—acting as Roads Authority on behalf of Ballinasloe Town Council, Galway City Council and Roscommon County Council—and were funded by the National Roads Authority. Statutory consents ('Ministerial Directions') for the main investigations were issued by the National Monuments Service, in consultation with the National Museum of Ireland.

The Preliminary Design for the scheme, including the Environmental Impact Statement (EIS), was developed by M C O'Sullivan (afterwards part of RPS Engineering). The Project Directors at Preliminary Design stage were Ger Horgan (MCOS) and Gerry Carty (RPS). The archaeology chapter of the EIS was compiled by Martin Fitzpatrick of Arch Consultancy Ltd. Anne Roseveare and Martin Roseveare, of ArchaeoPhysica Ltd, contributed a supplementary report on archaeological geophysics at Preliminary Design stage, in consultation with Kevin Barton of Landscape and Geophysical Services.

Once the scheme was approved by An Bord Pleanála, the main phase of the archaeological investigations (2005–07) was executed in four sectors by CRDS Ltd, Eachtra Archaeological Projects, Headland Archaeology (Ireland) Ltd (now Rubicon Heritage Services Ltd) and Valerie J Keeley Ltd (VJK). The Senior Archaeologists for the companies were Nóra Bermingham, Richard Clutterbuck and Finola O'Carroll (CRDS), John Tierney (Eachtra), Colm Moloney (Rubicon) and John Lehane (VJK). The investigations were supervised for RPS Engineering by Resident Engineers Tom Prendergast, Niall Healy and Mark Deegan, and by Resident Archaeologist Ross MacLeod. N6 Construction Ltd appointed The Archaeology Company, directed by Michael Tierney, to monitor construction work. This phase of the project was supervised for the NRA by RPS Engineering, under the direction of David Cawley, assisted by Resident Engineers John Heffernan and Tony Gallagher.

Over 150 archaeological fieldworkers worked on these investigations, from a dozen different countries, in the difficult conditions that can often prevail on open-air excavations at all seasons of the year in the West of Ireland. They are too numerous to name here individually but we wish to record our sincere thanks for their contribution to the project. The landowners who facilitated access to the lands acquired for the road scheme, during our investigations, are also too numerous to be named but we hope they enjoy this book.

The editors would like to thank all those in the NRA and at Galway County Council National Roads Project Office (NRPO) for their support throughout the project and especially Project Archaeologist Martin Jones and his colleagues in the NRA Archaeology Section; NRA Inspectors Peter Walsh and John McGuinness; and Galway County Council Project Engineer Ciarán Wynne and former Senior Engineer Jack Eising.

The production of *The Quiet Landscape* was managed by Sheelagh Hughes at Editorial Solutions (Ireland) Ltd in Belfast. The book was designed and typeset by Róisín McAuley of LSD Ltd. The index was compiled by Julitta Clancy.

Chapter 1

Landscape and people

Fair Green, Ballinasloe, October 2011 (Kenneth O'Halloran)

1.1 Landscape

The title of this book was prompted by a conversation with Dr Stefan Bergh, who teaches archaeology at the National University in Galway. Stefan's fieldwork at the time was in the upland areas of Sligo and Mayo. "These are loud landscapes," he told me, "places that speak to me with a strong voice about the way geology and topography have shaped human experience in the past." Then he continued, after a ruminative pause, "but where you and your friends are working now, in east Galway, is a very quiet landscape that speaks in a whisper and, I suspect, has many secrets".

We knew immediately what he meant. In the landscape traversed by the new M6 motorway in east Galway (Illus. 1.1.1) there are no prominent mountains forming barriers or major river valleys offering arterial routeways, and it is easy to become lost in the maze of winding back roads among rural townlands that all very much resemble each other. But Stefan was right to surmise that there are untold secrets in this landscape. The townland names that appear throughout this book are now permanently inscribed in the archaeological record as distinctive places with very particular stories: a hillfort in Rahally, where Bronze Age tribal people congregated in a great enclosure that overlooked the Galway plain; a hilltop in Cross, where early Christians claimed patrimony in the land by burying their dead in an ancient pagan cemetery; a *cillín* in Mackney, where the local people buried their

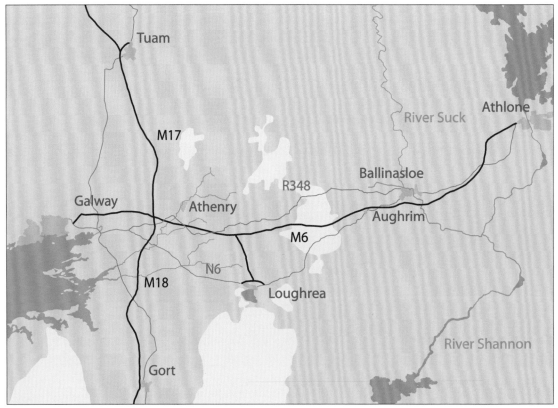

Illus. 1.1.1—Location map of the new M6 Galway to Ballinasloe motorway (red) and existing main roads (green) in the region.

unbaptised infants in an ancient ringfort ditch until their landlord closed it up with rubble; a clay-pit in Brusk, where bricks for Victorian building projects were shaped by hand and hardened in turf-fired clamps.

There are dozens of such stories in this book. Mostly they are told in the spare, empirical language of archaeological field observation and post-excavation analyses. We consider it important to present the primary evidence in this way because it is this that makes the stories real. All of us are marooned in the ever-present. We will never be able to revisit earlier times or speak with earlier peoples. But in discovering, ordering and understanding the physical evidence of their lives we can have a vicarious encounter with them as vivid as lipstick on a cold cup.

One thing we have in common with earlier peoples is the physical landscape inhabited by them and us. In east Galway this was shaped by the last glaciation, beween 110,000 and 11,700 years ago, and especially the retreat of the Irish Sea Glacier between 20,000 and 18,000 years ago (McCabe 2008). Glacial action moulded a gently undulating landscape of low, rounded hills, interspersed with winding, steep-sided gravel ridges known as eskers. Between the hills and eskers are lower-lying areas, typically poorly drained and peaty, and often supporting coarse, rushy meadows where the lands have been drained for livestock pasture. Glaciation accounts for the surface landforms but the limestone bedrock dates to a much earlier time. Everywhere in east Galway there are buildings and fieldwalls in the sober grey limestone that was formed in the Middle and Upper Carboniferous periods, about 350–290 million years ago (Illus. 1.1.2). Along the route of the new road the bedrock is overlain by deposits of the crushed and milled mineral soil known as glacial till or 'boulder clay' (75%), or by glacial meltwater deposits of sand and gravel (20%), or by peat (5%) (Cawley 2004, 347). In the Suck Valley, near Ballinasloe, there are also finely sorted alluvial deposits in the river floodplain but, where the river is crossed by the motorway, in Pollboy, these are overlain by a deep, wide peat bog. All of these deposits are very variable in depth. The deepest peat occurs in raised bogs or peat basins on the watershed between Cappataggle and Aughrim. Elsewhere peat was encountered as a shallow mantling layer 0.5–1.5 m in depth. Glacial tills are up to 15 m deep in places along the route but become quite shallow towards the west, where karst bedrock exposures occur. The topsoils formed on these parent materials are, in the west, shallow, free-draining mineral soils (brown earths and rendzinas); in the east, peaty soils subject to waterlogging (grey brown podzolics, gleys), and with some blanket peat on the higher ground between (Illus. 1.1.3). And here is a word of warning to archaeologists collecting surface finds from topsoil: pasture improvements have been achieved over the years by drainage but also, in places, by importing quantities of soil to raise and level the land surface.

Surface elevation along the route varies from about 20 m (Ordnance Datum) in the west, near Galway City, rising to 120 m between Cappataggle and Aughrim, and descending again to 40 m at the River Suck crossing by Ballinasloe. The highest ground forms a watershed between the Galway plain to the west (Illus. 1.1.4) and the Suck Valley to the east. To the west of the watershed are the small rivers that converge on Galway Bay around the coastal villages of Oranmore, Clarinbridge and Kilcolgan. Linear mounds of grass-grown earth and rubble along the riverbanks are the tell-tales of episodic drainage works since Victorian times. The underlying limestone is soluble and often fissured. Consequently, these watercourses on the Galway plain are shallow, narrow rivers that never accumulate much water, because so much of it is lost to underground aquifers. (The Dunkellin River expands spectacularly into a large turlough at Rahasane in winter but, in general, these seasonal

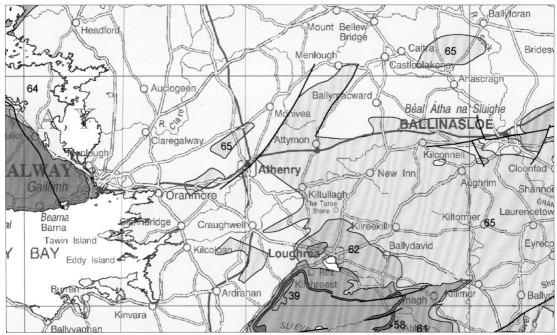

Illus. 1.1.2—Map of the bedrock geology in the region. East Galway lies on Carboniferous limestones (grey, blue) about 350 million years old (Geological Survey of Ireland).

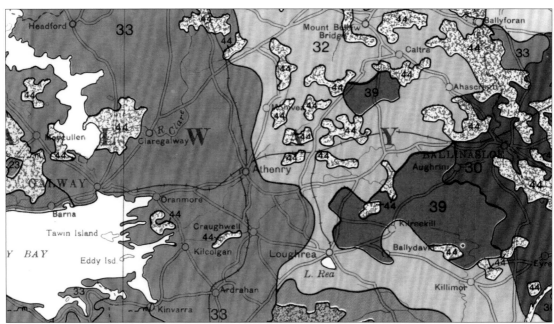

Illus. 1.1.3—Map of the soils in the region. The lands traversed by the new motorway are predominantly on shallow brown earths (orange), grey brown podzolics (yellow, red) and gleys (dark blue), with some blanket peat on higher ground (light blue) (Teagasc).

Illus. 1.1.4—View west over the Galway plain from Rahally hillfort, on a western spur of the Kilreekill Ridge (Studio Lab).

or 'vanishing' lakes are more typical of the karst limestone country in south Galway.) East of the watershed, the town of Ballinasloe lies in the floodplain of the Suck. The Suck is a mature river that forms the county boundary with Roscommon, and is a tributary of the Shannon. Below their confluence, the Shannon forms the Galway county boundary with Offaly and Tipperary.

The changing vegetation cover in this landscape has been influenced throughout the centuries by fluctuations in climate and human population density and by changing farming practices. This is all reflected in the fossil pollen accumulated year-on-year in local peat bogs. As part of the investigations for our road scheme, fossil pollen in a sample core from Ballinphuill bog (Illus. 1.1.5), near Rahally hillfort, was analysed at the Palaeoenvironmental Research Unit at NUI Galway (Chapter 4 and CD-ROM). Crops and livestock were much more important than wild food for most of prehistory and early history. From a relatively early date, large swathes of the landscape were cleared for farming. In the region today farming is dominated by dry cattle, with some sheep and dairying. The average farm size is 25 ha and 74% of farms are in permanent grass pasture (Farrelly 2004, 399). The land is more or less all in freehold now—a gentle revolution hastened by successive Land Acts of 1881–1903—but the 'squared fields' representing estate improvements by the old landlords are still in use everywhere. The field boundaries are most commonly drystone walls, sometimes replaced with post-and-wire fences, but hedgerows on earthen banks occur towards the east, around Aughrim and Ballinasloe. There are very few surviving remnants of early modern demesne woodlands and, where they occur, broadleaf trees have commonly been replaced by commercial conifers. Fewer than 5% of farmers are involved in commercial forestry of any sort (ibid.). A generation ago, dispersed farmsteads dotted the countryside between the towns and villages. In recent years, rural Galway has become extensively 'suburbanised' by the linear development of new houses along local back roads, so that

Illus. 1.1.5—There are several large raised bogs on the higher ground between the Galway plain and the Suck Valley. Ballinphuill bog provided fossil pollen evidence for past vegetation change (Chapter 4).

today's rural communities are typically a mixture of established families from farming backgrounds and newcomers who live in the country but commute to work in the city and the larger towns.

1.2 Old roads and new

Roads have played an important part in the history of east Galway. When gross landforms are formed by glaciers, and lakes and rivers have found their settled places in the landscape, then, from a bird's-eye viewpoint, the next major development is the establishment of major routeways. Cattle go to market on them and armies to war. Monasteries, castles, towns and villages become established along them and, over time, the social landscape takes its order and orientation from them. Historically, two arterial routeways crossed the interior of County Galway from east to west. The old winding north road—or as we know it now, the R348—leaves Ballinasloe and makes its way via Kilconnell and New Inn, passing the walled Norman town of Athenry. Some scholars believe that it perpetuates one of Ireland's oldest east–west highways, the Slí Mór (most recently Geissel 2006). The south road, the old N6 (now the R446), is equally ancient. Between Ballinasloe in the interior and Oranmore on the coast, it passes through towns and villages at Aughrim, Kilreekill, Loughrea and Craughwell. A new motorway is a radical intervention in this settled landscape. It has no pedigree, no slow evolution from cart-track to paved road, and it seeks to avoid, not bisect, the centres of population (Illus. 1.2.1).

The M6 Galway to Ballinasloe motorway scheme was developed by Galway County Council—acting on behalf of Galway City Council, Roscommon County Council and Ballinasloe Town Council—with funding from the Department of Transport via the National Roads Authority. The Preliminary Design and EIS for the road scheme were published in August 2004. After an unusually long and lively oral hearing (in session for 27 days between November 2004 and January 2005) the scheme was eventually approved by An Bord Pleanála in June 2005. Construction commenced in April 2007 and was completed in less than three years. The road was opened in December 2009, ahead of schedule, when the old N6 became impassable because of flooding caused by extraordinary late November rainfall. Thus, the new road had a dramatic baptism that immediately justified its birth.

The new motorway is a tolled road, with a toll station at Cappataggle, and for the first 20 years it will be maintained and operated by a private company, M6 Concession Ltd. It is 56 km long on the mainline with 23 km of side roads and a 7 km link road to Loughrea. The footprint of the scheme extends over a total area of 588 ha. It is intersected by the old N6 on an overbridge at Urraghry. At Ballinasloe it crosses the 'Connaught Extension' of the Grand Canal and then the River Suck. It is

Illus. 1.2.1—The construction of a new arterial route is a major intervention in a settled, historic landscape. At Pollboy, in the Suck Valley floodplain, thousands of cubic metres of peat were replaced with rammed stone and gravel to carry the new road over the bog (Hany Marzouk for Galway County Council).

one of several road schemes that combine to form a network of new national primary routes in the West of Ireland: east–west between Galway and Dublin and north–south between the towns and cities along the 'Atlantic Corridor'.

1.3 Archaeological investigations

The formal approval of a major road scheme by the planning authorities sets in train the 'advance works' that precede construction proper. These can include permanent fencing, scrub and hedgerow clearance, building demolitions and any additional engineering surveys or test-pits required to complete the design. This is also when the main phase of archaeological investigations occurs. Once, this would have been done at construction stage, leaving the opportunity for archaeological discovery more or less to chance, when construction vehicles were milling about and large-scale earthmoving operations were already underway. Now things are better ordained and especially since the implementation of a *Code of Practice between the National Roads Authority and the Minister for Arts, Heritage, Gaeltacht and Islands* (DAHGI & NRA 2000). These days, archaeological investigations on national road schemes are largely completed prior to construction, with an adequate amount of

Illus. 1.3.1—Early maps are an important 'desk-based' source in assessing the archaeological landscape. The early medieval cemetery-settlement at Carrowkeel (Chapter 3) was previously recorded only as a circular earthwork on the first-edition Ordnance Survey map of 1838 (Ordnance Survey of Ireland).

time and resources and, in consequence, tend to be more systematic and more exhaustive than in the old days.

For the M6 scheme the archaeology chapter of the EIS was compiled by Arch Consultancy in 2000–01, based on a walkover inspection of the route and a trawl through desk-based sources that included aerial photographs, pre-existing survey and museum records, and early maps (Illus. 1.3.1). John Cronin & Associates contributed a supplementary EIS chapter for the western end of the route, which was originally to have formed part of the Galway City Outer Bypass scheme. In tandem with the EIS, in 2003–04, there were small-scale test excavations on the known, protected sites (i.e. Recorded Monuments) that would be affected by the scheme, by archaeologists from Galway County Council. Also in 2003–04, the Council commissioned a very extensive geophysical survey, by ArchaeoPhysica, to search for buried soil anomalies of possible archaeological origin. Twenty-six areas were selected for survey amounting to a total area of c. 163 ha or c. 28% of the footprint of the scheme, making this one of the largest archaeological geophysical surveys ever undertaken in Europe. The survey areas were chosen because of good land capability, or known archaeological sites, or neighbouring historic towns or villages. The survey method was 'recorded magnetic gradiometry' (Illus. 1.3.2). Eight of the 39 sites that would eventually be excavated on the scheme were discovered by this method (Table 1.3.1).

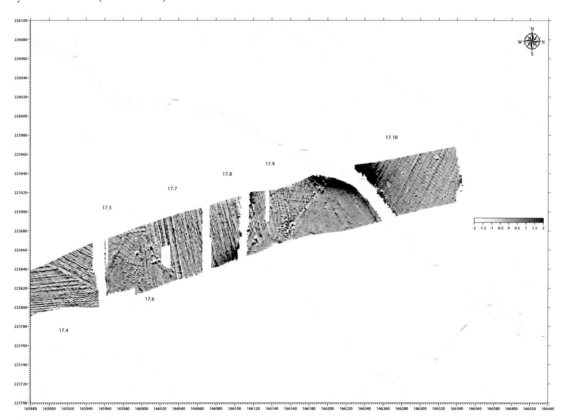

Illus. 1.3.2—Spade-dug cultivation ridges in Cloonycanaun and Rahally were recorded by archaeological geophysical survey. The survey was conducted in 26 areas amounting to 28% of the footprint of the road scheme (ArchaeoPhysica 2004).

Table 1.3.1—Methods of assessment and discovery on the M6 Galway to Ballinasloe road scheme

Extent of road scheme		
Total area of road scheme		588 ha
Length of road scheme (centreline)		56 km
Discovery of excavated archaeological sites	**Area ha (% total)**	**No. sites**
Test excavation by hand and/or machine	56 ha (9.5%)	18
Previously known sites and monuments (RMP sites)	—	6
Desk study (non-RMP sites from maps and other sources)	—	2
Geophysical survey (selected areas)	163 ha (28%)	8
Field inspection	588 ha (100%)	4
Construction monitoring (selected areas)	30 ha (5%)	1
Total number of excavated sites	—	**39**

Following approval of the scheme, the main phase of investigations was conducted in 2005–07. Four archaeological companies were appointed by Galway County Council to carry out surveys, test excavations and full excavations throughout the scheme, which was now divided into four sectors, each about 14 km long. The four companies were Valerie J Keeley Ltd (Sector 1), Headland Archaeology Ltd (now Rubicon Heritage Ltd) (Sector 2), CRDS Ltd (Sector 3) and Eachtra Archaeological Projects (Sector 4). The targets of test excavations included six sites of previously known Recorded Monuments directly affected by the scheme, 49 sites of geophysical anomalies, and numerous surface anomalies (humps and bumps) of suspected archaeological interest, which were identified by field inspection. Testing on Recorded Monuments and other, suspected archaeological sites was by hand in the first instance and then, more extensively, by machine if hand-testing produced a nil result. Testing on geophysical anomalies was generally by machine. Apart from these targeted test excavations, a great deal of other testing was done by machine in greenfield areas of no known or suspected archaeological interest (Illus. 1.3.3). An array of 'centreline and offset' trenches was opened in every field and bog along the route where this was possible, amounting in total to c. 45 ha of 'blind' test trenches or about 8% of the lands acquired for the new road. Topsoil stripping in the environs of known or suspected monuments combined with small-scale hand-testing increased the total amount of test excavations to 56 ha or about 9.5% of the lands acquired.

Excavating topsoil by machine in 'blind' test trenches may seem a crude procedure, but it is also very effective. It is the main means of discovering previously unrecorded archaeological sites on a big road scheme and on the present project accounted for 16 of the 39 sites that were eventually fully excavated. Not all of the lands acquired could be tested at this stage, however, and residual areas of bog or woodland amounting to 5% of the scheme were monitored instead at construction stage. This was done by The Archaeology Company, appointed by N6 Construction Ltd, a subsidiary of the PPP company. One new site was discovered by monitoring, consisting of prehistoric worked wood remnants and chipped stone tools in a peat basin at Ballynaclogh, in Sector 3.

Illus. 1.3.3—Test excavations by machine, under archaeological supervision, were very extensive. This proved to be the most effective means of discovering previously unrecorded archaeological sites in the footprint of the new road. Ronan Jones records the soil profile at Rahally (Jerry O'Sullivan).

In addition to excavations there were several kinds of survey (reports on CD-ROM). Archaeological divers from Moore Group Ltd searched for artefacts in the river bed at the Suck crossing—though with a nil result (Illus. 1.3.4). Archaeological Surveys Ltd made a very detailed metal-detecting survey on part of the 17th-century battlefield at Aughrim—this time with some limited success. The finds included several lead bullets or musket balls, a grenade fragment, assorted buckles, badges and buttons of possible military provenance, and several coins, including at least one of the base metal coins (a gunmoney shilling of 1689) issued by a desperate James II in the absence of gold and silver (Sabin & Donaldson 2004; Shiels forthcoming). In the course of construction monitoring, The Archaeology Company recorded a sectional profile of the Grand Canal earthwork (Connaught extension 1828–1965) (Illus. 1.3.5). Vernacular buildings to be demolished along the route were recorded in surveys by Moore Group Ltd and the buildings of the Loughrea–Attymon Light Railway (1890–1975) were recorded by George Geddes (Illus. 1.3.6). As mentioned already, the Palaeoenvironmental Research Unit of NUI Galway analysed the fossil pollen in a sample core from Ballinphuill bog. And at two of the excavated sites—Loughbown 1 ringfort and Caraun More medieval ditches—small-scale geophysical surveys attempted to map unexcavated features that extended into greenfield areas outside the footprint of the road scheme.

What did we find? The excavated archaeological sites described in this book are very diverse in their type, period, scale and significance. They range from a modest burnt spread at Rathgorgin—

Illus. 1.3.4—At the Suck crossing near Ballinsaloe, where a series of natural weirs formed an easy fording place in antiquity, divers with metal-detecting equipment searched the riverbed for archaeological objects (Moore Group Ltd).

Illus. 1.3.5—Canal bridge on the 'Connaught Extension' (1828–1965) of the Grand Canal. Small pleasure boats now come to Ballinasloe via the River Suck. The dewatered canal earthwork was traversed by the new road in Pollboy near Ballinasloe (Studio Lab).

which turned out to be a relatively recent deposit—to the great Bronze Age hillfort at Rahally, which was declared a National Monument by John Gormley TD, Minister for Environment, Heritage and Local Government, when it was discovered in Sector 3 of the new road. What is striking about these discoveries as a group is that they represent a much greater density of archaeological sites and monuments than is represented in previous records for the region, and also a more diverse range of site types and periods (Table 1.3.2).

The number of previously recorded monuments within 2 km of the road scheme is known from baseline data that includes the Record of Monuments and Places (RMP) and a published archaeological inventory for part of east Galway (Alcock et al. 1999). A corridor extending to 2 km on either side of the new road has an area of roughly 244 sq km. Within this corridor, the total number of sites and monuments that can be identified from previous records is 419, with a density of roughly 1.7 per square kilometre (Shine 2008). Now compare this with the results of our investigations on the road itself. Thirty-seven archaeological sites lay partly or entirely within the footprint of the road scheme, which has an area of 588 ha. Six were Recorded Monuments but there were 31 other, newly discovered sites. From this very large trial trench across east Galway it is possible to conclude that the true density of archaeological sites and monuments is at least six sites per square kilometre (or about four times what was previously indicated) and that roughly five new archaeological sites may be expected in any random greenfield area of 1 sq km in the region.

What also emerges from our discoveries on the road scheme is a more balanced sample of periods and site types (Table 1.3.2). In the same corridor, 4 km wide, the tally of previously known sites and monuments is dominated by early medieval enclosures (33%) and undated sites (42%)—many of which are also enclosures, and probably early medieval too (Illus. 1.3.7). Later prehistoric sites

Illus. 1.3.6—An engine shed of the disused Loughrea–Attymon Light Railway (1890) in Loughrea (George Geddes).

are poorly represented (7%). Early prehistoric sites and multi-period sites are entirely absent (0%). In contrast, the excavated sites within the footprint of the road—despite being a much smaller sample—are more diverse. Early prehistoric sites appear for the first time (3%). Later prehistory forms a substantial horizon in the sample (32%). Multi-period sites form the single biggest group (46%) and include several sites that would have been recorded as early medieval—because the principal identifying features were enclosures—if they had not been excavated. Later medieval sites are the only category where investigations on the road have not added significantly to the existing number of known sites. Some evidence of later medieval settlement was recorded but typically occurred as sporadic finds or isolated features in earlier settlement or burial sites. This is puzzling, as east Galway was certainly not unpopulated in this period and there are some very well preserved rural settlement remains surrounding the standing ruins of churches, tower houses and castles in the county (Illus. 1.3.8). It is a result that underscores the randomness of survival and discovery in pre-development investigations, even on a very large project like a motorway scheme.

Illus. 1.3.7—Aerial view of Bullaun and Cahernamuck townlands, with the disused Loughrea–Attymon Light Railway (left), a tributary of the Dunkellin River (top), and a relict landscape of field banks and earthwork enclosures. Ringforts and other early medieval enclosures dominate the existing record of archaeological monuments in east Galway (M C O'Sullivan for Galway County Council).

Illus. 1.3.8—An extensive relict landscape of field banks and broad ridges surrounds a ruined 13th-century de Burgo castle in Oldcourt (bottom right), c. 600 m from the new road. No later medieval sites were discovered by investigations along the road itself (M C O'Sullivan for Galway County Council).

Communicating discoveries

It has not been possible to describe all of our work in the confines of this book, but the various surveys and scientific reports—as well as the fully illustrated stratigraphic and interpretive reports on the excavations ('Final Reports')—are reproduced in PDF format on the CD-ROM that accompanies the book. We have also communicated the investigation results in other outlets and in a variety of media, including site tours, public lectures and classroom presentations, leaflets, newspaper and periodical articles, and a portable exhibition of poster-boards that was displayed in 16 public venues in Galway City and county in 2009. Publication of *The Quiet Landscape* is the keystone in this programme of public communications.

Table 1.3.2—*Major periods represented by archaeological excavations on the M6 Galway to Ballinasloe road scheme compared with previously recorded monuments within 2 km of the scheme. 'Multi-period' excavations are sites where two or more periods are represented*

All monuments and excavation sites	Early prehist.	Later prehist.	Early medieval	Later medieval	Post-med. /Modern	Multi-period	Undated
Probable period of all previously recorded monuments in the environs of the motorway (< 2 km; total 419) (right)	0 (0%)	28 (7%)	138 (33%)	44 (10%)	33 (8%)	0 (0%)	176 (42%)
Principal periods of excavated sites along the new motorway (right) and periods represented on individual sites (below)	1 (3%)	12 (32%)	3 (8%)	0 (0%)	5 (14%)	16 (43%)	0 (0%)
Excavation sites and Site types	Early prehist.	Later prehist.	Early medieval	Later medieval	Post-med. /Modern	Multi-period	Undated
Doughiska Burnt mounds	—	Yes	Yes	—	—	Yes	—
Coolagh Cashel with round-house and later lime kilns	—	Yes	Yes	—	Yes	Yes	—
Carnmore West Cashel with souterrain and cereal kilns	—	—	Yes	Yes	—	Yes	—
Ballygarraun West Isolated burial	—	—	Yes	—	—	—	—
Newford Pyre site and burnt mound	—	Yes	—	—	—	—	—
Furzypark Burnt spread with pottery sherds	—	Yes	—	—	—	—	—
Farranablake East Cashel	—	—	Yes	—	—	—	—
Moyode Estate cottage	—	—	—	—	Yes	—	—
Deerpark Cremation and ring-ditch	—	Yes	—	—	—	—	—

Table 1.3.2 (continued)

Excavation sites and Site types	Early prehist.	Later prehist.	Early medieval	Later medieval	Post-med. /Modern	Multi-period	Undated
Deerpark Kennels of Tallyho Lodge	—	—	—	—	Yes	—	—
Rathgorgin Modern burnt spread	—	—	—	—	Yes	—	—
Brusk Brick clamps	—	—	—	—	Yes	—	—
Curragh More Cremation burial	—	Yes	—	—	—	—	—
Clogharevaun Multi-period landscape	—	Yes	—	Yes	Yes	Yes	—
Carrowkeel Cemetery-settlement enclosure	—	—	Yes	Yes	—	Yes	—
Ballykeeran Cist burial and ring-ditch	—	Yes	—	—	—	—	—
Killescragh 1, 2 Burnt mounds and trackways	—	Yes	—	—	—	—	—
Caraun More 4 Pits, watercourses and settlement waste	—	Yes	Yes	Yes	Yes	Yes	—
Caraun More 1–3 Burnt mounds	—	Yes	—	—	—	—	—
Cross Ring-ditches, cremations and inhumations	—	Yes	Yes	—	—	Yes	—
Rahally Hillfort, ringforts and field system	—	Yes	Yes	Yes	Yes	Yes	—
Rathglass Cremations, iron-working and cereal kiln	—	Yes	—	Yes	—	Yes	—
Treanbaun 1 Cremations and palisaded enclosure	Yes	Yes	—	—	—	Yes	—

Table 1.3.2 (continued)

Excavation sites and Site types	Early prehist.	Later prehist.	Early medieval	Later medieval	Post-med. /Modern	Multi-period	Undated
Treanbaun 2 Cemetery-settlement enclosure	—	—	Yes	—	—	—	—
Treanbaun 3 Lead mine and cists burials	—	Yes	—	—	—	—	—
Gortnahoon Cereal kilns, storage pits, metalworking	—	—	Yes	Yes	—	Yes	—
Ballynaclogh Worked wood, chipped stone tools	Yes	—	—	—	—	—	—
Newcastle Enclosure, house and field ditches	—	—	Yes	—	Yes	Yes	—
Cooltymurraghy Burnt mound	—	Yes	—	—	—	—	—
Coololla Spade mill and lime kiln	—	—	—	—	Yes	—	—
Urraghry Chipped stone tools, burnt mound	Yes	Yes	—	—	—	Yes	—
Barnacragh Burnt mound	Yes	Yes	—	—	—	Yes	—
Loughbown 2 Ring-ditch, ringfort	—	Yes	Yes	—	—	Yes	—
Loughbown 1 Ringfort with souterrain, metalworking and kilns; modern building	—	—	Yes	—	Yes	Yes	—
Mackney 1 Hearth, pits and saddle quern	—	Yes	—	—	—	—	—
Mackney 2 Hearth and pits	—	Yes	—	—	—	—	—
Mackney 3 Ringfort with souterrain, round-houses and later *cillín* burials	—	—	Yes	Yes	Yes	Yes	—

1.4 People

Mesolithic period (8000–4000 BC)

Who do our discoveries represent? At some point in their family history, everyone who lives in Galway is descended from an 'incomer'. Some are here longer than others. In our excavations we glimpse the very first arrivals. A campsite on the margins of a peat basin at Ballynaclogh was littered with chipped stone tools that included blades, scrapers, arrowheads and hammerstones, as well as the debitage of tool-making, amounting in total to 2,839 pieces of Late Mesolithic/Early Neolithic date (c. 6500–3400 BC) (Illus. 1.4.1). A few early prehistoric chipped stone artefacts were found in Barnacragh and Urraghry too. These were even older (c. 8000–6500 BC) and represent the very first hunter-gatherers in the region. All three sites are in the River Suck catchment. This suggests that the earliest people used the rivers as routeways, spreading out from the Shannon basin along its tributaries and finding their way into east Galway via the Suck. The landscape at this time was dominated by mature woodland, with pine, oak and elm the commonest species.

Illus. 1.4.1—An early prehistoric campsite was discovered on the edge of a bog at Ballynaclogh. Worked wood and chipped stone artefacts were recovered on the site (The Archaeology Company).

Neolithic period (4000–2200 BC)

In the Early Neolithic period the pollen record clearly signals the arrival of a more sedentary people, who cleared the woodlands to make way for pasture and possibly tillage. The houses and tombs of these first farmers are well known from archaeological fieldwork elsewhere in Ireland but did not feature in our investigations on the M6 route. Instead, we encountered remains of the people themselves, at Treanbaun. On a low, broad knoll, contained within the confluence of two streams, quantities of chipped stone, charcoal, pot sherds and burnt bone were found in a group of small, shallow pits. A few fragments of bone could be identified as human. It seems this was a simple cemetery where only token amounts of cremated bone were deposited, 'seeding' the ground with remains of the ancestors.

Bronze Age (2200–500 BC)

The knoll between two streams at Treanbaun remained in use—or was intermittently used—throughout the Neolithic period and the Bronze Age. Most of the activity on this site cannot easily be categorised as either 'domestic' or 'ritual', and this is probably not a distinction that would have been understood in prehistoric times, where ritual was pervasive in daily life. Nonetheless, a big, circular timber structure that was erected in the Middle Bronze Age can be interpreted with some confidence as a purely ritual structure. This was almost certainly some sort of temple or sacred enclosure, with a screen wall inside the entrance to restrict visual access to the interior.

The interweaving of ritual in all aspects of prehistoric life is seen again at a second site in Treanbaun townland. Here, in the Early Bronze Age, a large circular pit was excavated through layers of bedrock to expose a seam of lead and silver-bearing galena in its base. The mine pit was cut through an earlier cist burial and another cist was inserted into it when it was backfilled. Thus, burying people in the earth and extracting minerals from it occurred on the same spot. This is unlikely to have been coincidence and the second cist burial may have been intended to 'close' the mine or secure it in some way. Later post-holes, stake-holes and occupation debris indicate an episode of habitation on the site. Bronze Age mining on a large scale is well attested by research, in south-west Ireland especially (e.g. O'Brien 1994 & 2004), but this single pit at Treanbaun, closed with a cist burial, is a unique site in the Irish archaeological record.

Illus. 1.4.2—A newly discovered Bronze Age hillfort at Rahally (outlined) was designated a National Monument. Now c. 60% of the enclosure is preserved in farmland to either side of the new road (CRDS Ltd).

Cremation was a preferred means of disposing of human bodies in Irish prehistory. Inhumation was also practised at different times. (It is harder to identify excarnation in the archaeological record—i.e. exposing the body to carrion and the elements—but there is some evidence for this too in early prehistory.) The excavation site at Newford affords a rare glimpse of a Bronze Age cremation pyre. The pyre was constructed over a large pit and evidently collapsed into it, leaving multiple fragments of human bone in a dark layer of charcoal.

East Galway was a populous place by the Late Bronze Age, when a semi-open landscape is represented for the first time in the pollen record beginning c. 1050 BC, with evidence for extensive pastoral farming and some tillage. The hilltop enclosure at Rahally suggests this was the economic basis for a structured, hierarchical society, with a central authority. There are over 200 large hilltop enclosures in Ireland but only about 80 of these can be classified as 'hillforts' (Grogan 2005, 111–29). Only six of these are larger than Rahally, which consisted of concentric earth-cut ditches with an overall diameter of 450 m (Illus. 1.4.2). The evidence suggests that Rahally was not primarily a 'fort' or a settlement site and it was probably built for public assemblies at royal inaugurations, or fairs or religious festivals or some combination of these. Its setting on a spur of the Kilreekill Ridge gave it commanding views to north, west and south-west. The ridge itself is neither elevated (at c. 100

m OD) nor steep, so that the hillfort would not have been conspicuous from the plain. Yet it would probably have occupied a prominent position in the worldview of the people who lived in its hinterland.

Iron Age (500 BC–AD 400)

Around AD 1–200 the tide of human life seems to recede for a while in east Galway. Our pollen evidence points to regenerating hazel scrub, followed by an increase in elm and ash. In our excavations, Iron Age society is mostly glimpsed in stray features found on sites that are chiefly of some other period: an early mealworker's bowl furnace at Caraun More; a La Tène artefact at Rahally; or cremated human bone at Cross. Despite this apparent lull in the continuity of settlement in the Late Iron Age, later generations were keenly aware of the prehistoric monuments they saw in the landscape around them and they

Illus. 1.4.3—The Turoe Stone, about 2 km south of the new road, is an enigmatic masterpiece in La Tène sculpture (Con Brogan, Department of Arts, Heritage and the Gaeltacht).

frequently reused them. The enigmatic Turoe Stone, with its swirling La Tène decoration (Illus. 1.4.3), stands about 2 km south of the new road. It must have seemed as impressive to early medieval eyes as it is to us today. Excavations at Cross, Carrowkeel and Treanbaun reveal how early medieval communities sited their cemeteries on older, prehistoric burial grounds. Perhaps the older monuments gave them a borrowed pedigree that would have enhanced their claims to tenure on the land.

Early medieval period (AD 400–1200)

The outstanding example of appropriated patrimony is the hillfort at Rahally. The concentric ditches of the Bronze Age hillfort were already very ancient when they were crowned in the early medieval period by a cluster of ringforts. By now east Galway and south Roscommon formed the territory of Hy Many or Uí Máine—a subkingdom of Connacht of the O'Conors. The Uí Máine are the first people in this story for whom we have a name and their territory is mapped out in a medieval document that was translated and published by John O'Donovan (1843). The Uí Ceallaigh were the dominant sept among the Uí Maine. They were named after *Ceallach*, a pseudo-historical ancestor. The excavation director at Rahally, Gerry Mullins, suggests that Rahally derives from *Rath Uí Ceallaigh*. Thus the ancient hillfort was not only reoccupied but also renamed by these new lords of east Galway, who evidently appreciated its importance as the tribal capital of a much earlier population.

By this time the plain was once again well populated and was evidently prosperous too. Ringforts and cashels appear in great numbers in the Irish landscape from about AD 500. Ringforts are especially numerous in east Galway and include an unusually high number of bivallate or double-banked enclosures (Stout 1997, 112). Essentially these were farmsteads. The large enclosures excavated at Loughbown 2 and Mackney were certainly inhabited: they contained round-houses and souterrains (stone-built underground chambers) as well as occupation debris. But there is little evidence for human occupation of the smaller enclosures at Loughbown 1 and Farranablake and these may simply have been stockyards. The cashel at Coolagh was unusually large and contained only a single round-house, perhaps a herdsman's house. The cashel at Carnmore West was more complex, with a souterrain in the interior, and corn-drying kilns and at least two annexed outer enclosures.

The daily life of these farmsteads is glimpsed in the artefacts found in them: iron blades, quern-stones, spindle whorls and loom weights, bone combs and pins, metal slag or furnace fragments. These objects represent, variously, butchery and leatherworking, cereal processing, textile-making, bone-carving and metalworking. The farming economy of the period is seen in quantities of animal bones and charred plant remains from kilns, hearths and waste-disposal pits. Then as now, livestock husbandry was more important than tillage and cattle were dominant over sheep, goats and pigs. But cereal cultivation became more important as the period advanced and is strongly attested in pollen evidence beginning at c. AD 600. There were cereal kilns at Carnmore West; the stone-lined ditches at Caraun More West are interpreted as mill-races; and the large, stone-lined pits at Gortnahoon were possibly sunken grain silos (Illus. 1.4.4). Apart from an unusual assemblage of wild bird bones from Loughbown 1, there is little evidence that wild creatures contributed to the pot. Hunting was a privilege of the aristocracy. All this is mirrored in an early medieval documentary source that describes the education appropriate to different social ranks (*Cáin Iarraith*: Kelly 1998, 452). Girls of noble

birth learned to sew and embroider
while boys were taught board
games, hunting and weapons
skills. Children of common rank
had a more practical education.
Girls learned to use the quern and
kneading-trough and to care for
lambs and kids. Boys were taught to
dry grain and split firewood, to care
for livestock and wool-combing. No
doubt the heavier manual work was
done by slaves.

Illus. 1.4.4—Recording an early medieval, semi-subterranean drystone structure—possibly a grain store—at Gortnahoon (CRDS Ltd).

The remains of the people
themselves were found in early
medieval sites at Carrowkeel and
Treanbaun. These were two large
earthwork enclosures with evidence for human occupation, but they were not typical farmsteads.
At each of these sites the eastern quadrant was reserved for the dead. In Carrowkeel there were
remains of 132 individuals, most of whom were buried between the seventh and 12th centuries.
At Treanbaun there were 31 individuals, buried between the seventh and 13th centuries. At both
sites the skeletons mostly lay west–east in shallow grave pits, in conformity with Christian tradition.
Once, it was tacitly assumed that all early Irish Christians were buried in the consecrated burial
grounds of churchyards or monasteries. Carrowkeel and Treanbaun are among a growing number of
'cemetery-settlement' sites that show this was not the case. It seems that many ordinary folk in this
period were buried in extended family burial grounds, within an enclosed settlement space, shared
by the living and the dead over many generations.

Later medieval period (AD 1200–1550)

The Normans looked jealously across the Shannon at the kingdom of Connacht. An invasion was
inevitable and in 1235 Richard de Burgo crossed into the West with 500 heavily armed knights
and a royal charter that dispossessed the Irish of most of their territory. De Burgo granted lands to
his supporters in the newly conquered Lordship of Connacht. What was taken by knights and foot
soldiers was consolidated by masons and carpenters. Walled towns and rural manors were established
at strategic locations throughout the Lordship. Loughrea had been a royal centre of the Uí Máine
(Illus. 1.4.5). Richard de Burgo built a castle there and made it his main seat (Illus. 1.4.6). A wet
ditch still surrounds the town centre in Loughrea, but Athenry is the outstanding surviving example
of a Norman walled town in Ireland, with its market cross, priory and parish church all guarded
by Myler de Bermingham's stout castle (Illus. 1.4.7 and 1.4.8). In time, the Uí Ceallaigh reasserted
themselves in east Galway. Former Uí Máine territory became known as 'O'Kelly Country' and the
Kellys—and to a lesser extent the Maddens, who were also of Uí Maine descent—sought to rival
the Clanricarde Burkes with their lands, church endowments and the construction of tower houses
(Illus. 1.4.9).

Illus. 1.4.5—Several crannógs on Lough Rea bear witness that this was already a royal centre of the Uí Máine before Richard de Burgo built a walled town on the lake shore (Jerry O'Sullivan).

Illus. 1.4.6—Richard de Burgo led the Norman invasion of Connacht in 1235. He built a castle in the town he founded at Loughrea, making it the caput of his newly conquered Lordship of Connacht (Jerry O'Sullivan).

Illus. 1.4.7—Myler de Bermingham built a castle at Athenry overlooking the walled town he founded on the Clarin River (Jerry O'Sullivan).

Illus. 1.4.8—Norman earthworks and mortared stone walls surround Athenry. The Dominican priory was a Norman foundation but also received endowments from several Gaelic families, including the O'Conors, O'Heynes and O'Kellys (Jerry O'Sullivan).

Illus. 1.4.9—A friary at Kilconnell was endowed by the O'Kellys c. 1400, at a time when resurgent Gaelic families began to rival their Norman overlords in lands and castles (Jerry O'Sullivan).

Although the new road skirts Loughrea and Athenry, and traverses the heartland of the Norman Lordship, we found very little direct evidence for the colony in our excavations. What we did find, however, was tantalising evidence for a working accord between the indigenous Gaelic people and their new overlords. Outside the towns and nucleated burgh settlements, it seems that ringforts and cashels continued to be occupied in east Galway after the Norman invasion, in the high medieval period (c. AD 1200–1350) and beyond. At Caraun More, Carnmore West and Gortnahoon, radiocarbon date ranges from excavated features extend into the 13th century. This might be construed as evidence that these settlements were extinguished or at least abandoned around the time of the Norman invasion. This was not the case of other early medieval settlement sites—at Carrowkeel, Coolagh, Loughbown 1 and 2 and Mackney—which produced radiocarbon dates extending beyond the invasion years and well into the later medieval period (c. AD 1350–1550). There is evidence from finds too as these sites produced, variously, coins of Edward I, Henry III and Henry VIII, and a miscellany of arrowheads, combs, pot sherds, knives and fishhooks of later medieval type.

Post-medieval period (AD 1550–1700)

The evidence from Newcastle may represent re-occupation of an older site rather than continuous occupation from medieval times. Here, a little stone house was built over the infilled ditch of an earthwork enclosure that most resembled an early medieval ringfort. Pottery, clay pipes, glass bottle fragments and a coin weight dated 1683 all attest its occupation or re-occupation in the 17th and 18th centuries. The records show that by the end of the 16th century a lease of Newcastle was held by one Ffarrdorogh Ó Ceallaigh—Blackie Kelly, if you like; Laughlin Kelly had succeeded to the lease by the mid 17th century (details in Chapter 4). These are the first named individuals to be associated with one of our excavated sites and they are the heralds of the modern period in our journey across east Galway.

In Blackie Kelly's time, the biggest landowners in the county were still the Clanricarde Burkes, the lineal descendents of Richard de Burgo. By Laughlin Kelly's time radical changes were underway in the countryside. Following the Confederacy and Cromwellian Wars of the mid 17th century (1641–52), Connacht was being colonised again, this time by a mixed population of demobbed Cromwellian army officers (winners), Catholic gentry transplanted from the east and south of the country (losers), and the old English merchant families of Galway (the 'tribes'), who were now expanding their interests to include rural estates and planted demesnes across the county (Cunningham 1996; Melville 1996) (Illus. 1.4.10). These changes were accelerated at the end of the century by the 'war of the two kings' (1689–91) between James II and William of Orange. In east Galway, the Jacobite army suffered a heavy defeat in a decisive battle at Aughrim in July 1691 (Illus. 1.4.11). William's accession to the

Illus. 1.4.10—The gentrification of the countryside—with Jacobean houses replacing or augmenting older tower houses—began in the later 17th century. Wallscourt, near Kilreekill village, is visible from the old N6 and is about 6 km south of the new M6 (Jerry O'Sullivan).

Illus. 1.4.11—The old order was swept away at Aughrim battlefield in 1691, where William of Orange achieved a decisive victory over James II (detail from Müller's print in the Danish Royal Library).

Illus. 1.4.12—Garden urn and obelisk at Garbally House in Ballinasloe, a seat of the Trench family, Earls of Clancarty. Frederick Trench shared his knowledge of the local terrain with William's officers at the Battle of Aughrim in 1691 (Jerry O'Sullivan).

Illus. 1.4.13—Excavation of an 18th-century 'spade mill' or water-powered forge at Coololla, by Aughrim. The period 1650– 1850 saw a peak in tillage in Ireland with a corresponding increase in the demand for agricultural tools (Ross MacLeod).

throne saw the commencement of the Protestant Ascendancy period in Ireland and with it the development of a more structured landscape of wooded demesnes and great houses (Illus. 1.4.12), enclosed fields and developments in agriculture that would include a tremendous increase in tillage (Illus. 1.4.13).

Early modern period (AD 1700–1900)

We encountered the world of the new landed estates most vividly at Moyode House and Tallyho Lodge, which were both houses of the fox-hunting Persses. The story of this family is told by James Charles Roy (1997; 2001). The Persses were first granted lands in Galway and Roscommon in the 1670s. Two hundred years later they would own almost 20,000 acres and over a dozen country houses, as well as a house and distillery in Galway City. Roxborough became their principal seat in the county (this was the birthplace of Lady Augusta Gregory, née Persse, of the Abbey Theatre and Coole) but Tallyho Lodge was one of their first houses. According to local tradition, Tallyho Lodge was also the first home of the famous 'Galway Blazers' hunt, with the kennels located in neighbouring Deerpark townland. Our geophysical survey identified the site. Subsequent excavation discovered a cobbled yard and building remnants and a quantity of well-gnawed animal bone! By the early 1800s the hunt had moved to nearby Moyode, where Burton Persse was developing a new estate on 3,000 acres (Illus. 1.4.14). An excavation at Moyode recorded the cottage, kitchen garden and haggard of a herdsman on that estate. The herd's house was a well-built, mortared stone cottage. It was certainly superior to the one-roomed *bothán* that was the typical dwelling of the rural tenantry living beyond the demesne walls at the time. Evidently a landscaped demesne in the early 1800s was an oasis of order and prosperity for all its denizens, high and low—landlord, herdsman and hounds.

Over the next 100 years the orderly world of the rural estate—and the cheap agricultural labour that sustained it—was swept away by famine and rural depopulation, industrialisation and urbanism, freehold farming and, ultimately, by political independence. But some things stayed the same. The clay bricks made at Brusk were possibly used in the construction of buildings on the Loughrea–Attymon Light Railway (1890–1975) but, otherwise, the primitive simplicity of the brick-makers' methods had little in common with the noisy energy of the new railways. The bricks were shaped by hand from local clay, dried in the sun and fired in clamps fuelled by mounded smouldering peat. The

Illus. 1.4.14—A muster of the hounds at Moyode House c. 1900. The house was embellished in Romantic style by Burton de Burgh Persse c. 1850 and burnt by locals in 1922 (Architectural Archive of Ireland).

materials were all sourced locally. Nothing was imported. Nothing was mechanised. And nothing remained when the work was done except ashes and some spoiled bricks (Illus. 1.4.15). The people who made the prehistoric pottery found at Treanbaun or Rahally would have been familiar with the materials and understood the technique. The landscape is a constant in our affairs, both in how it constrains us and in what in provides. Layered rock, clay and peat form the blank pages for all the archaeological discoveries recorded in this book.

Illus. 1.4.15—Excavation of the Victorian brick-making site at Brusk (Chapter 3) (Rubicon Heritage Services Ltd).

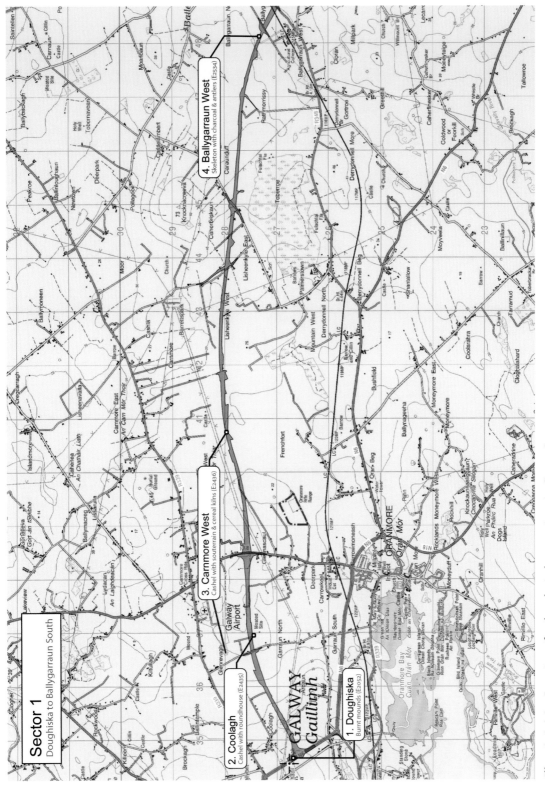

Illus. 1.4.16—Location of archaeological excavations in Sector 1.

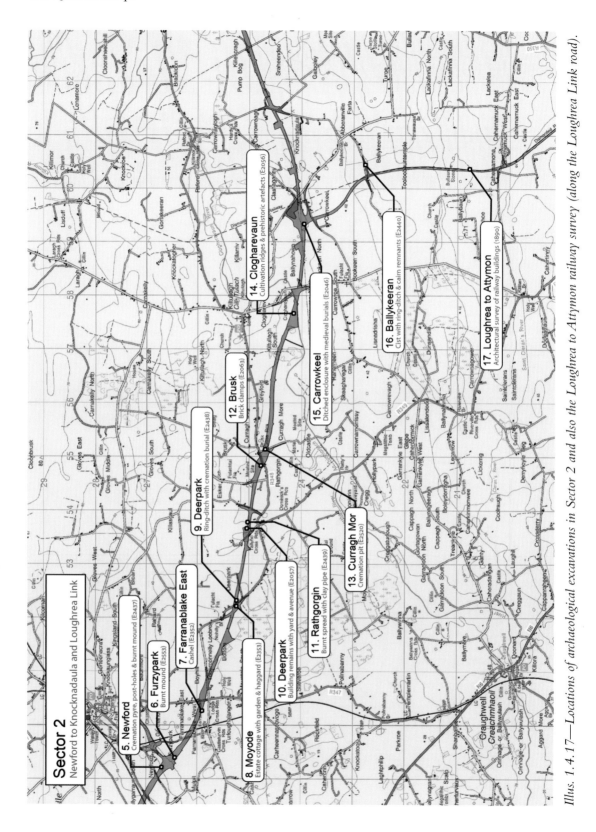

Illus. 1.4.17—*Locations of archaeological excavations in Sector 2 and also the Loughrea to Attymon railway survey (along the Loughrea Link road).*

Sector 2
Newford to Knocknadaula and Loughrea Link

5. Newford
Cremation pyre, post-holes & burnt mound (E2437)

6. Furzypark
Burnt mound (E2553)

7. Farranablake East
Cashel (E2352)

8. Moyode
Estate cottage with garden & haggard (E2353)

9. Deerpark
Ring-ditch with cremation burial (E2438)

10. Deerpark
Building remains with yard & avenue (E2057)

11. Rathgorgin
Burnt spread with clay pipe (E2439)

12. Brusk
Brick clamps (E2063)

13. Curragh Mor
Cremation pit (E2520)

14. Clogharevaun
Cultivation ridges & prehistoric artefacts (E2056)

15. Carrowkeel
Ditched enclosure with medieval burials (E2046)

16. Ballykeeran
Cist with ring-ditch & cairn remnants (E2440)

17. Loughrea to Attymon
Architectural survey of railway buildings (1890)

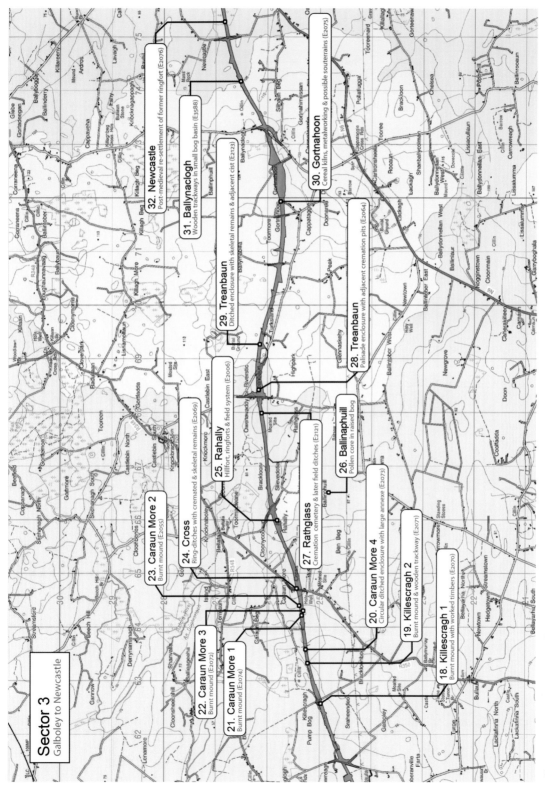

Sector 3
Galboley to Newcastle

18. Killescragh 1
Burnt mound with worked timbers (E2070)

19. Killescragh 2
Burnt mound & wooden trackway (E2071)

20. Caraun More 4
Circular ditched enclosure with large annexe (E2073)

21. Caraun More 1
Burnt mound (E2074)

22. Caraun More 3
Burnt mound (E2072)

23. Caraun More 2
Burnt mound (E2055)

24. Cross
Ring-ditches with cremated & skeletal remains (E2069)

25. Rahally
Hillfort, ringforts & field system (E2006)

26. Ballinaphuill
Pollen core in raised bog

27. Rathglass
Cremation cemetery & later field ditches (E2121)

28. Treanbaun
Palisade enclosure with adjacent cremation pits (E2064)

29. Treanbaun
Ditched enclosure with skeletal remains & adjacent cist (E2123)

30. Gortnahoon
Cereal kilns, metalworking & possible souterrains (E2075)

31. Ballynaclogh
Wooden trackways in small bog basin (E3588)

32. Newcastle
Post-medieval re-settlement of former ringfort (E2076)

Illus. 1.4.18—Locations of archaeological excavations in Sector 3 and also Ballinphuil Bog, where a peat core was taken for pollen analysis.

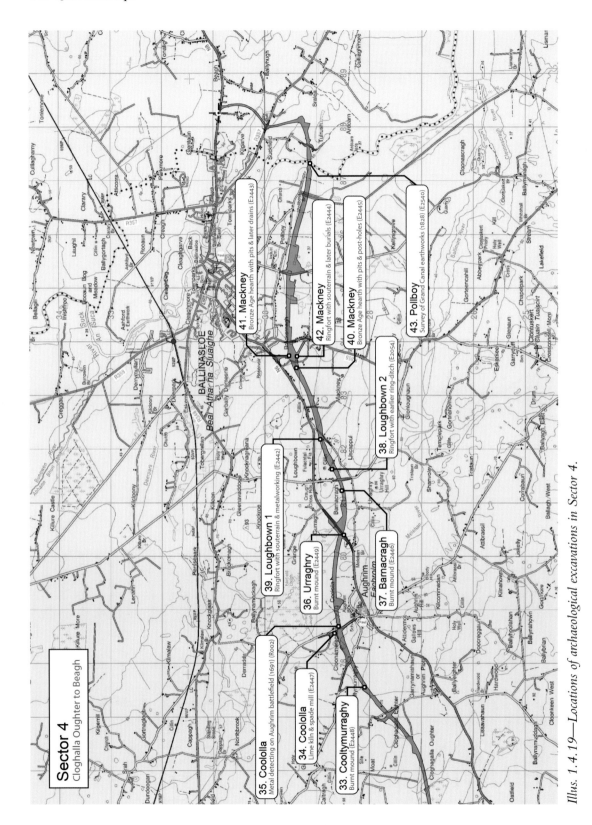

Sector 4
Cloghalla Oughter to Beagh

41. Mackney
Bronze Age hearth with pits & later drains (E2443)

42. Mackney
Ringfort with souterrain & later burials (E2444)

40. Mackney
Bronze Age hearth with pits & post-holes (E2445)

43. Pollboy
Survey of Grand Canal earthworks (1828) (E2540)

38. Loughbown 2
Ringfort with earlier ring-ditch (E2054)

39. Loughbown 1
Ringfort with souterrain & metalworking (E2442)

36. Urraghy
Burnt mound (E2449)

37. Barnacragh
Burnt mound (E2446)

35. Coololla
Metal detecting on Aughrim battlefield (1691) (R002)

34. Coololla
Lime kiln & spade mill (E2447)

33. Cooltymurraghy
Burnt mound (E2448)

Illus. 1.4.19—Locations of archaeological excavations in Sector 4.

Chapter 2

The Windswept Plain (Sector 1)
Doughiska to Ballygarraun

Field system in Frenchfort (Galway County Council)

2.1 Burnt mounds at Doughiska[1]

by Liam McKinstry

The tell-tale sign of a Bronze Age burnt mound is charcoal-stained soil intermixed with heat-shattered stones. This represents a place where water was boiled in wood-lined troughs or pits by immersing heated stones. How was the heated water used? Nobody knows for sure, though hundreds of these sites have been investigated in Ireland. Plausible interpretations include cooking, dyeing, bathing, leatherworking and brewing, or perhaps some combination of these, and hence the waterfilled troughs have been called the 'kitchen sinks of the Bronze Age' (Quinn & Moore 2009, 53).

A group of burnt mounds at Doughiska was located in rough pasture at the foot of a west-facing slope. Natural springs erupted across the site, forming pools of standing water in winter. The mounds were previously known and are described in the *Archaeological Inventory of County Galway* (Vol. 1: Gosling, 1993, 27) as 'a large kidney-shaped grassy mound' with four smaller outlying mounds. In the 1990s one of the smaller mounds and part of the large one were excavated in advance of construction of the existing N6 dual carriageway (Fitzpatrick & Crumlish 2000).

The Doughiska excavation site was at the junction of the existing dual carriageway and the new motorway and this allowed the remainder of the burnt mound group to be investigated. Our excavation recorded one large mound (Mound A), surrounded by three smaller mounds (Mounds B–D), and a small stone spread (Illus. 2.1.1 and 2.1.2). All of the mounds consisted of dark, compact soil with frequent inclusions of shattered/burnt stone and occasional charcoal. Only one mound (Mound D) had a pit or trough beneath it, and this was a simple earth-cut feature with no lining. It is not clear how water was contained and heated at the other mounds. Buckets or leather bags may have been used but no trace of anything like this survived.

The earliest radiocarbon date from the site is from a tree root (Scots pine), from beneath Mound A, dated to 2861–2491 BC (UB-7580).[2] There were other tree roots under Mound A, representing a scrubby pinewood that grew on the thin peaty soil on this site in the Late Neolithic or Early Bronze Age period. Charcoal from Mound B produced a broadly similar date range of 2566–2342 BC (UB-7860). Mounds A and C produced later dates, in the Middle to Late Bronze Age, ranging from 1494–1397 BC (UB-7856) to 904–802 BC (UB-7581). Surprisingly, Mound D and the pit underlying it produced much later dates, in the early medieval period, from AD 897–1025 (UB-7877) to AD 1024–1182 (UB-7874). Although burnt mounds are mostly dated to the Bronze Age in Ireland, there are dated examples from other periods; 'hot stone' cooking is mentioned in some early medieval Irish saints' lives (Ó Driscéoil 1990, 157). Though most of the mounds at Doughiska were prehistoric, Mound D seems to be an early medieval example and the explanation is simply that a site with natural springs would have attracted anyone seeking a reliable groundwater source in all periods.

---

1 Excavation No. E2052; Excavation Director Liam McKinstry; RMP No. GA082: 043; NGR 134700 226660; height 35 m OD; civil parish of Oranmore; barony of Galway.

2 The radiocarbon dates quoted throughout this book are calibrated calendrical dates at two sigma degrees of probability (95%). The accompanying numbers in brackets are radiocarbon lab codes for each date. A full list of the dates is given in Appendix 1.

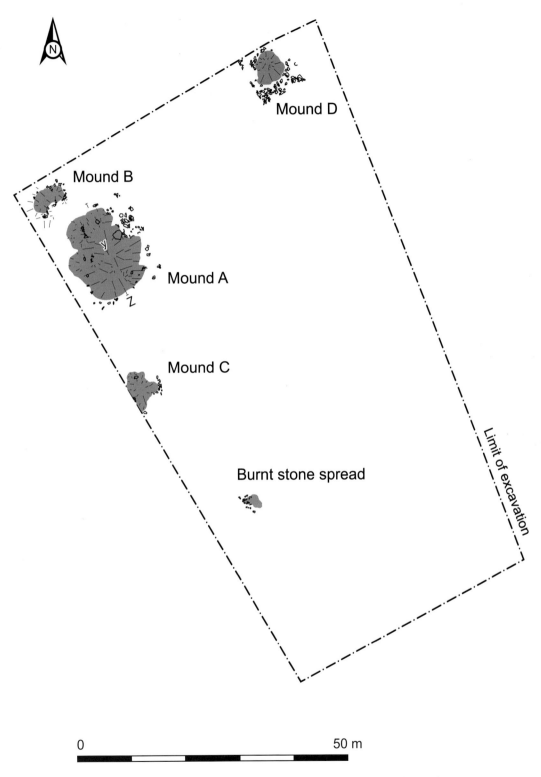

Illus. 2.1.1—Doughiska. General plan of the burnt mound group (Valerie J Keeley Ltd).

The previous archaeological investigations at Doughiska concentrated on a smaller mound to the south of the present excavations and part of the large mound (our Mound A). Again, this excavation produced dates ranging from the Late Neolithic period to the Middle Bronze Age, prompting the excavators to say that Mound A was 'among the earliest known burnt mounds in the country' (Fitzpatrick & Crumlish 2000, 139). With hindsight, however, it seems likely that the Late Neolithic date from that excavation was from a pine root underlying Mound A and not from the mound itself.

A wide variety of wood species was identified on the site. Scots pine roots were found beneath Mound A. Charcoals of alder, ash, elm, hazel, holly and the family of small fruiting trees known as Pomoideae (e.g. rowan, whitebeam, hawthorn and crab apple) were recovered from various Bronze Age deposits. Charcoals of alder, ash, hazel and wild cherry/blackthorn type (*Prunus* sp.) occurred in Mound D, which was dated to the early medieval period. Scots pine and elm are representatives of a tall-canopy woodland environment that largely disappeared in early prehistory in Ireland. The other species probably represent wood collected from the higher, dry ground in the environs of the site in later periods. Some of them, alder in particular, are tolerant of wet (though not waterlogged) conditions and may have been growing on the lower ground around the burnt mounds in antiquity. The *Prunus* species that appear in the early medieval samples are typically early colonisers of cleared woodland areas.

Illus. 2.1.2—Doughiska. Aerial view of the excavation site with winter waterlogging. The cruciform cutting (left) indicates Mound A (Hany Marzouk for Galway County Council).

We still do not know how the burnt mounds at Doughiska were used. There were no food remains or industrial materials of any sort. A contiguous group of large stones, some of them edge-set in the topsoil, ran across the site from west to east, forming a relict field boundary of unknown date. South of the dual carriageway, large edge-set stones flank a remnant trackway of unknown date, known locally as Bóthar na Caillighe (the Hag's Road; Gosling 1993, 177). Apart from these undated relics in the surrounding landscape, there is no known settlement or habitation site that can be associated with the Doughiska burnt mounds.

2.2 Cashel with round-house and lime kilns at Coolagh[3]
by Colum Hardy

Cattle had an importance in early medieval Ireland that is seen today only among some African peoples who live cheek by jowl with their livestock. The circular enclosures in stone or earth that occur throughout Irelandknown variously as cashels, ringforts, cahers and raths)—were primarily homesteads but were also stockyards. That certainly seems to be a plausible interpretation of a large, early medieval cashel discovered at Coolagh, in farmland east of Galway City.

Illus. 2.2.1—Coolagh. Aerial view of the cashel from south. The round-house is in the western part of the interior (left) (Hany Marzouk for Galway County Council).

---

3   Excavation No. E2435; Excavation Director Colum Hardy; NGR 135890 227188; height 20 m OD; parish of Oranmore; barony of Dunkellin.

The cashel stood at the junction of three townlands: Coolagh, Doughiska and Ardaun. It was partly concealed by scrubwood at the margins of improved pasture fields and was bisected by a farmtrack and a drystone field wall (Illus. 2.2.1). The topsoil on the excavation site was thin, and gave directly onto deeply fissured, karstic limestone bedrock, but there were deeper soils in the environs so that the surrounding land was of better quality than the site itself.

Some stray prehistoric finds hint at Late Bronze Age activity on the site. These include a sherd of handmade pottery, pieces of struck flint and chert, and a chert thumbnail scraper. Also, a charcoal sample from a post-hole at the entrance to the cashel returned a date in the Late Bronze Age. The cashel was reused in the post-medieval or early modern period when two small lime kilns were built in the interior. But the main period of interest is the early medieval period, when cashels and ringforts were the dominant features in the human landscape.

Cashel and round-house

The cashel was a large oval enclosure, up to 60 m in overall diameter, with a wall up to 2.6 m wide at the base. The wall had outer facings of large stones with a core of smaller rubble and soil, but most of the stone was robbed for use elsewhere so that only the base of the wall survived. The entrance was in the east. It was roughly paved with flat stones, and flanked by a kerb of large,

Illus. 2.2.2—Coolagh. An entrance on the east side of the cashel was paved with flat stones and flanked by post-holes, forming a gateway (Valerie J Keeley Ltd).

edge-set stones (Illus. 2.2.2). Two post-holes on either side suggest a wooden gate. (The Bronze Age date from one of these post-holes can be assumed to represent much older, residual charcoal.) Another rubble wall adjoined the cashel on the south side, forming part of a large curvilinear annex. (This lies outside the lands acquired for the new road and was not excavated.)

There were remains of a small, circular stone building or 'round-house' inside the cashel, near the enclosure wall on the west side (Illus. 2.2.3). Again, the walls of this building had large facing stones with

Illus. 2.2.3—Coolagh. The single round-house in the interior of the cashel had a narrow, porched doorway, opening to the east (Valerie J Keeley Ltd).

a core of smaller rubble. The entrance was a simple, narrow porch on the east side. (This was blocked with rubble, possibly for reuse of the house as an animal pen in some later period.) The building was about 5.3 m in internal diameter. There was no evidence for roof-support posts internally, and no hearth. Evidently, this was a very simple round-house, probably with a conical roof of thatch or sod resting directly on the walls, much like buildings recorded at Oghil, on Inishmore in the Aran Islands (Jones 2004, 185).

There are radiocarbon date ranges for four samples from Coolagh (Appendix 1). One is prehistoric and the other three are early medieval—ranging between the mid sixth and later 10th centuries. The Late Bronze Age date of 975–814 BC (UB-7692) is from a post-hole in the gateway to the cashel but is probably from residual charcoal, unrelated to that feature. However, it does hint at prehistoric activity on the site, corroborating the evidence of flint and chert objects. Charcoal from a layer of foundation rubble beneath the round-house was dated to AD 651–771 (UB-7690). Charcoal from a post-hole inside the entrance was dated to AD 688–882 (UB-7691). A date of AD 779–973 (UB-7693) was obtained from charcoal in a layer underlying one of the lime kilns (below) but, as suggested above, the lime kiln itself is likely to be much later than this date.

Most of the finds at Coolagh were recovered from topsoil. They include some prehistoric pottery sherds and chipped stone pieces (above), but also several other finds of probable early medieval date. These include two fragments of bracelets carved from shale, a perforated jasper bead, two whetstones or 'hone stones' (Illus. 2.2.4), and several other coarse stone tools used for pounding, polishing and rubbing. Although shale bracelets can date to the prehistoric period, early medieval examples can be distinguished by their D-shaped section, and this can be seen in at least one example from Coolagh. There are sources of jasper, for the perforated bead, some 30 km to the north, towards Cloonfad, and 30 km to the south, in the Slieve Aughty range. Some later medieval and modern material also occurred on the site and this included a medieval long-cross penny (from some time between 1279 and 1509), a George III Irish halfpenny (1769) and clay-pipe fragments of 18th- or 19th-century date.

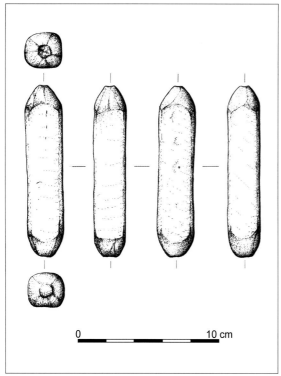

Illus. 2.2.4—Coolagh. Whetstone (E2435:001:010) of probable early medieval date (Valerie J Keeley Ltd).

A small volume of iron slag was found and also some clay crucible fragments. This is clearly evidence of metalworking on the site. The iron slag included some small 'smithing hearth cakes' (the solid mass of slag that accumulates in the base of an iron-working furnace). Their small size indicates blacksmithing rather than 'bloomsmithing', which means that they were probably used in the manufacture and repair of iron objects, and not in the primary extraction of iron from ore or bog iron. The crucibles may represent a finer sort of craftwork. Overall, in this limited evidence we can glimpse a visiting journeyman smith at work, carrying out repairs on site or making tools and weapons on demand, rather than a dedicated, full-time metalworking establishment.

The animal bones recovered at Coolagh were dominated by cattle (28% of 893 fragments), with smaller numbers of sheep/goat (9%), pig (5%), horse (1%), dog (1%), red deer (< 1%) and bird (< 1%), but over 50% of the bones could not be identified. The only evidence for butchery was a single chop mark to a fragment of cattle mandible. Almost all of the bone came from topsoil or from rubble spreads. Consequently, it is impossible to say that it exclusively represents the early medieval economy of the cashel and some of it could have been dumped here in other periods. Similarly, only a few excavated features provided secure, uncontaminated soil samples. No charred cereal remains were recovered from these, and no quern-stones were found, so there is no evidence for early medieval tillage or crop processing.

How was the cashel at Coolagh used in early medieval times? The enclosure was approximately twice the average size recorded for early medieval cashels in the region (Stout 1997, 16). Despite this impressive fact, very little was found in the interior. Livestock was consumed and possibly slaughtered on site. A visiting smith worked there from time to time. There was a single, compact round-house. Early Irish law tracts record the house, goods and livestock appropriate to each social rank in the early medieval period. In particular, the early eighth-century *Críth Gabhlach* prescribes that the *ócaire* (a 'small farmer') should have had a house measuring 19 ft (5.8 m) in diameter (Kelly 1988, 362; MacNeill 1923, 287–90). This corresponds roughly with the diameter of the round-house recorded at Coolagh. But cattle were the premier measurement of wealth and status in this society. With its shallow, free-draining bedrock, and large open interior, the cashel would have made an excellent stockyard and could have held quite a big herd of cattle. In this light, perhaps the real significance of Coolagh is indicated by the large size of the cashel rather than the small size of its single dwelling house.

Lime kilns

Apart from the early medieval round-house, the only other structures in the cashel were two small lime kilns, and these are likely to be much later in date. The kilns had small round bowls, with internal diameters of 1.2 m and 1.6 m, and were built with limestone rubble (Illus. 2.2.5). Both kilns had three, small, stone-lined flues in radial positions. The kiln bowls and flues were filled with burnt limestone fragments and charcoal.

Illus. 2.2.5—Coolagh. One of two lime kilns of probable post-medieval or early modern date in the interior of the cashel (Valerie J Keeley Ltd).

Lime kilns begin to appear in the rural Irish landscape from at least the early 18th century and some earlier examples are recorded. The roasted, crushed product was used for a variety of purposes, which included construction and building maintenance (mortar and lime-wash), but especially fertilising the land. Medieval examples were most probably associated with major building projects, rather than agriculture. For instance, a late 13th-century kiln excavated in Drogheda was probably used in the construction of the town wall (Walsh 1997, 62); and a kiln at Cullenagh More, in south County Galway, which gave a date range of AD 1469–1633 and may have been used in the construction of nearby Drumharsna Castle (Delaney & Tierney 2011, 159–60). In general, most rural examples are later than this and the ones at Coolagh are probably post-medieval or early modern kilns that produced roasted, crushed lime fertiliser rather than builder's lime.

2.3 Cashel with souterrain and cereal-drying kilns at Carnmore West[4]
by Bruce Sutton

The cashel at Carnmore West was not a previously recorded monument. This may seem surprising, because the enclosure and associated features extended over quite a large area. The remains were very denuded, however, and lay concealed at the margins of pasture land, on one side, and the rough, heathy expanse of an army shooting range on the other—roughly halfway between Galway City and Athenry. Only a stump of the cashel wall was upstanding, but this tell-tale feature was enough to ensure the site was identified by fieldwalking before the construction of the new road, leading to the discovery of an extensive early medieval estate landscape.

---

4   Excavation No. E2436; Excavation Director Bruce Sutton; NGR 140720 227970; height 20 m OD; civil parish of Claregalway; barony of Dunkellin.

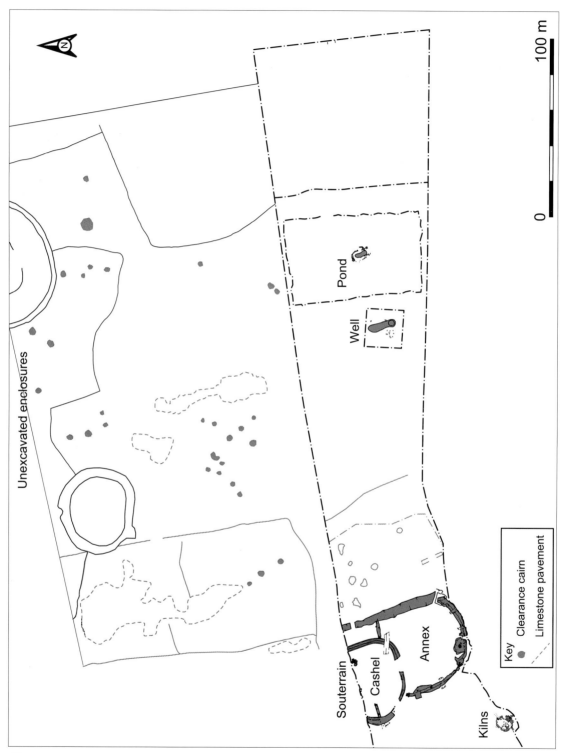

Illus. 2.3.1—Carnmore West. General plan of the excavation site (lower left) with neighbouring field walls and enclosures of probable early medieval date to north-east (Valerie J Keeley Ltd).

Like the cashel at Coolagh (above), this enclosure was located at the junction of three townlands: Carnmore West, Glennascaul and Frenchfort. The excavated features included the remains of the cashel, a souterrain inside it, an adjoining annex and adjacent corn-drying kilns, outside the annex. Further east along the road corridor there were remains of a stone-lined well and a clay-lined livestock pond (Illus. 2.3.1), but as these are modern features or undated, they will not be considered further here. There were other elements of this relict landscape beyond the boundaries of the road scheme including tumbled field walls and remnants of at least two other circular enclosures of probable medieval date, about 200 m north-east of the present one.

Cashel, annex and souterrain

The cashel was about 55 m in overall diameter. The wall was mostly robbed out but had originally been at least 2 m high and was built with large limestone blocks with a core of smaller rubble. (On the east side the wall core included a third, central row of large blocks.) The entrance was in the south. It was flanked by a stout kerb of large, edge-set stones, with a rough pavement of small rubble around the outside (Illus. 2.3.2). There were rock-cut post-holes on either side of the entrance, suggesting a wooden gateway. Charcoal from one of these was dated to AD 576–655 (UBA-7866).

The entrance opened to a large outer enclosure or annex, which extended around the south and east sides of the cashel. (On the east side it was incorporated in a modern field wall.) Again, this was

Illus. 2.3.2—Carnmore West. Edge-set stones flanked the entrance to the cashel and small rubble formed a rough pavement outside it (Valerie J Keeley Ltd).

built with large stones forming outer wall faces and a smaller rubble core. The annex had a narrow entrance on the west side, by the cashel wall, with post-holes for a wooden gate or barrier. Charcoals from these post-holes were dated to AD 676–869 (UB-7684) and AD 688–883 (UBA-7869).

Inside the cashel, a souterrain or underground chamber was discovered at the northern limit of the site. Only the entrance was visible. This was a simple 'pit drop' with roughly built steps on one side. A sturdy iron nail was embedded in the wall and another was found on the floor, suggesting a timber-framed doorway. The entrance was blocked with rubble and with the bones of a pony or donkey—presumably dumped here as a carcass (Illus. 2.3.3); radiocarbon dating showed that this occurred in the modern period (Appendix 1). Beyond the entrance, the remainder of the souterrain extended beyond the boundary of the road scheme, beneath the adjoining pasture field, and thus beyond the permitted limit of excavation. Nonetheless, because the souterrain was perfectly intact it was possible to fully record its fabric and extent from within (Illus. 2.3.4). The entrance passage descended into a spacious, stone-lined tunnel, up to 2 m high and almost 3 m wide. This extended north for roughly 15 m before turning east (right) for another 5 m. The side walls were mostly built with rubble but were partly rock cut towards the base. Here and there, clay was used as a bonding agent, possibly for repair work. The ceiling was formed by large flat slabs up to 3 m long. Charcoal from the souterrain entrance was dated to AD 662–856 (UB-7688).

Only a few other features were recorded inside the cashel. There was a small, rock-cut hearth pit, very close to the souterrain and this hints at a house that may have stood over the entrance. There were

Illus. 2.3.3—Carnmore West. The souterrain entrance was blocked by soil and rubble including the skeleton of a small horse or donkey (Valerie J Keeley Ltd).

Illus. 2.3.4a—Carnmore West. Souterrain entrance passage (Valerie J Keeley Ltd).

Illus. 2.3.4b—Carnmore West. Souterrain passage showing daylight in the entranceway (Valerie J Keeley Ltd).

Illus. 2.3.5—Carnmore West. Quern-stone fragments from the cashel, with concentric grooved decoration (E2436: 001: 023) (Valerie J Keeley Ltd).

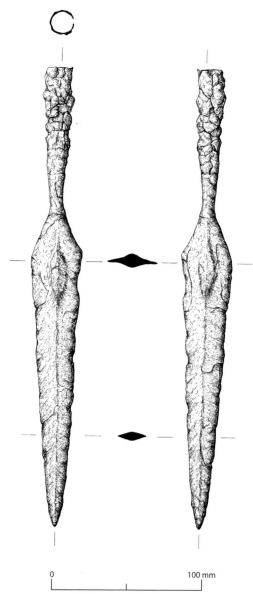

isolated post-holes scattered across the interior, forming no pattern. Some concentrations of rubble on the inside face of the cashel could have been remains of buildings or animal pens abutting the wall face, but these features were very poorly defined so that the available evidence does not make a convincing case. As stone was the main building material, and most of this was robbed, there may once have been several buildings in the interior for which no evidence survives. Charcoals from the rock-cut hearth were dated to AD 720–948 (UB-7686) and AD 772–965 (UB-7687). Charcoal from a pit underlying collapse from the cashel wall was dated to AD 710–889 (UBA-7865).

Illus. 2.3.6—Carnmore West. A spearhead (E2436:50:30) of probable early medieval date was found beneath a rubble spread from the collapsed cashel wall (Valerie J Keeley Ltd).

The finds from Carnmore West represent several different periods. Finds of probable early medieval date include a lump of iron slag (possibly from bloomsmithing), two baked clay fragments with quartz temper (possibly associated with metalworking), a bone peg, a shale bracelet fragment, four quern-stone fragments from at least two quern-stones—one decorated (Illus. 2.3.5), an iron knife and an iron spearhead. This last find was recovered from the base of a spread of rubble at the outer wall face of the cashel, suggesting that it was most likely left here during the occupation of the enclosure. Its long, straight-edged, tapering form resembles Viking spearheads (Illus. 2.3.6). Later finds include three iron knives and a copper-alloy buckle, all of later medieval date, and a James II (1690) 'gunmoney' Irish half-crown.

Crops, livestock and food processing

About 30 m south of the cashel, a group of corn-drying kilns was located outside the annex. There were two earth-cut kilns of keyhole or dumbbell shape, truncated by a later, L-shaped kiln, inserted over them. This later kiln had a stone-lined drying chamber and a flue constructed with stone lintels set on upright slabs. There were remains of a small, subcircular stone building adjacent to the L-shaped kiln (Illus. 2.3.7). This appeared to be c. 7 m in overall diameter with an entrance on the east side but, again, the evidence was very incomplete.

Charcoal samples from the earlier two kilns gave dates of AD 665–859 (UB-7689), AD 687–881 (UBA-7867) and AD 988–1152 (UBA-7864). Charcoals from the later, L-shaped kiln were dated to AD 641–723 (UBA-7868), AD 657–865 (UBA-7870), AD 723–972 (UBA-7872) and AD 1045–1258 (UBA-7871). This 'staggered' sequence of dates from the kilns suggests an extraordinarily long period of use but also reflects a degree of cross-contamination in the dated deposits. This probably arose from digging and re-digging around the kilns, with charred kiln waste becoming incorporated

Illus. 2.3.7—Carnmore West. Cereal-drying kiln complex with remains of a roughly built stone building (right) (Valerie J Keeley Ltd).

in the backfilled soils, as the structures were maintained, rebuilt and replaced over a long period. Later disturbance by burrowing animals may also be a factor.

Most of the charred plant remains identified at Carnmore West were from samples taken from the kilns. Taken in aggregate, the main cereal crop was oats (42%), followed by barley (36%), with smaller amounts of wheat and rye. This is a typical distribution for an early medieval kiln site. Weeds were less common in samples from the cashel, suggesting that cereals were first dried in the kilns and then cleaned before being taken into the cashel.

An assemblage of 2,577 animal bones included the main domesticates, in the following proportions: cattle (23%), sheep/goat (10%), horse (7%) and pig (2%). There were also small quantities of bone fragments from dog (< 1%), red deer (<1%) and house mouse (<1%). Butchery marks were present on the cattle, sheep/goat and horse bones but not on the pig bones. The value of this assemblage in understanding the economy of the cashel is limited: about 57% of the fragments could not be identified, more than 40% came from topsoil, rubble spreads and other disturbed deposits—so that they could not be assigned confidently to the early medieval period, and the minimum number of individuals represented for any one species is small.

A limited assemblage of mollusc shells was collected. Predictably, this included several species of naturally occurring land snail but some marine molluscs were also recovered from inside the cashel and from the cereal-drying kilns, including periwinkles, cockles and mussels. The cashel is over 5 km from the sea at Oranmore. Shellfish could easily have been transported this distance for food, in early medieval times, but they may also have been imported to the site as accidental passengers on seaweed used for manuring, in later times.

Who lived and worked at Carnmore West?

On typological grounds alone the cashel could be dated to the mid or late first millennium with a high degree of confidence. (Souterrains typically belong to the later part of this period.) This is very strongly endorsed by a large suite of radiocarbon dates and, to a lesser extent, by the finds. Several dates from the cashel and kilns converge on a period between the sixth and eighth centuries, but taken all together the date ranges from the site extend from the late sixth to the mid 13th century. There are several metal objects of later medieval date among the finds—including three scale-tang knives and a copper-alloy buckle—so the site may well have continued to be occupied into the high medieval period.

The size of the cashel at Carnmore West, its corn-drying kilns, souterrain, annex, and the neighbouring enclosures north of the road corridor, all combine to suggest that it was a place of some local importance during the early medieval period. The site is located today on the boundaries of three townlands and these land divisions may have existed since early medieval times. It is plausible, therefore, to see it as part of an estate centre rather than an isolated farmstead—where crops were brought for processing and perhaps animals for slaughter. However, our cashel was not likely to have been the dominant enclosure in this estate: the excavation recovered no high-status finds, such as ornate brooches or imported pottery and one of the neighbouring enclosures, outside the lands acquired for the road, is a much larger bivallate cashel. It is very likely the occupants of that cashel were members of the lordly class (*flaith*) and our cashel was occupied by dependent members of the same kin group, settled on the estate lands as 'clients' of the lord.

2.4 Solitary burial at Ballygarraun West[5]
by John Lehane & Patrick Randolph-Quinney

Isolated burials are uncommon in the archaeological record of early medieval Ireland. Mostly the dead were buried around churches or in family burial grounds. The solitary grave of an adult woman at Ballygarraun West is doubly unusual because the body was laid on a bed of charcoal and was accompanied in the grave by a piece of worked red deer antler and other animal bones. Who was this woman and what was the symbolism of this strange burial?

The grave was found in a pasture field, about 2 km south-west of Athenry, within an area identified by geophysical survey as having archaeological potential, because of a concentration of anomalous soil magnetic characteristics (ArchaeoPhysica 2004, Vol. 1, 21–2 and CD-ROM). The field was intensively investigated by test trenches and topsoil stripping but nothing else was found apart from this one burial. The grave itself was a simple, shallow, oblong pit (Illus. 2.4.1). It was unmarked, but an unusually high proportion of large stones was observed in the base of the topsoil round about it, which may have contributed to the anomalous magnetic readings.

Within the grave the skeleton was disturbed, with only 35% of the bones present. Nonetheless, it was clear that the body had been laid on its back, fully extended with the head in the west. The

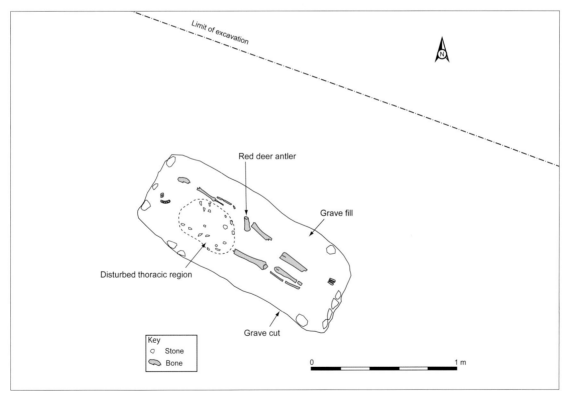

Illus. 2.4.1—Ballygarraun West. Plan of the grave showing the disturbed, poorly preserved skeletal remains and red deer antler (Valerie J Keeley Ltd).

5   Excavation No. E2534; Excavation Directors Dermot Moore (testing) and John Lehane (excavation); NGR 148207 227273; height 45 m OD; civil parish of Athenry; barony of Athenry.

arms were probably folded over the torso. The individual was a woman at least 50 years old and only 1.41 m (4 ft 6 in) in estimated height. She had osteoarthritis in the spine, and heavily worn teeth with poor oral hygiene, indicated by plaque and surrounding bone inflammation. A piece of worked red deer antler lay on the pelvis. This was from a naturally shed antler. It was very weathered and had several cut and chop marks where a tine had been removed. There were no other grave goods. The lower limbs of the skeleton were lying on a bed of carbonised plant material. This contained charcoals of hazel and alder, and very small quantities of seeds including barley (17 grains), wheat (1) and black bindweed (1)—a weed commonly found growing in cereal crops. There was no evidence of *in situ* burning so that this material must have been burnt elsewhere, then gathered and placed in the grave. Two cattle teeth were found at the interface between the topsoil and the grave fill, and two other tooth fragments, of cattle or deer, were found in the disturbed grave fill, near the skull. A bone sample from the skeleton was dated to AD 432–661 (UBA-7683); charcoal samples from the burnt deposit beneath the skeleton were dated to AD 432–600 (UBA-7863) and AD 578–659 (UBA-7862).

Was the Ballygarraun West burial pagan or Christian? The body was oriented (roughly west–east), extended and supine, all in accordance with Christian tradition, and the radiocarbon dates indicate that the woman died some time after Ireland's Conversion. On the other hand, burning grain to spread it beneath the body was condemned by the early Church as a pagan ritual (O'Brien 2003 and 2010; Randolph-Quinney 2007, 30–1)—so the people who buried the woman at Ballygarraun West were not much concerned with approved Christian practice it seems. A pagan ethos is also suggested by the piece of deer antler placed on the woman's pelvis. This is paralleled in other female graves, of similar date, at Eelweir Hill, Co. Offaly, and Collierstown, Co. Meath (Ó Floinn 1988; O'Hara 2009, 94–5). The large stones found lying about the grave, in the base of the topsoil, may be remnants of a cairn or mound, which would also hearken back to pre-Christian burial practices. All in all, there are several elements of this strange burial that speak of an older, pagan world and its traditions and it may be that the adult woman in the grave at Ballygarraun West was a 'wise woman' in that world.

Chapter 3

Heartland (Sector 2)
Newford to Knocknadaula

Market Cross, Athenry (Jerry O'Sullivan)

3.1 Pyre, post-pits and burnt mound at Newford[6]

by Brendon Wilkins

After food and water, fire was probably the most important resource in prehistory. It was the essential agent in many sorts of transformation. Excavations in Newford offer glimpses of fire at work in two very different facets of life in prehistory: the mysterious passage from life to death on a cremation pyre and, nearby, the mundane challenge of capturing and boiling spring water in an earth-cut pit.

The excavation took place in two areas by the Lavally River, 1.5 km south-west of Athenry (Illus. 3.1.1). A large group of pits and post-holes on level ground above the river valley (Area A) included the remains of a Late Bronze Age cremation pyre; elsewhere, on the bank of the river (Area B), a burnt mound and hot-water trough were probably used for some sort of subsistence or craftwork. The burnt mound produced an unusually early radiocarbon date, in the Neolithic period.

Cremation pyre, pits and post-holes (Area A)

A dispersed group of 73 pits, post-holes and stake-holes was recorded in Area A. Among their fills were a small piece of shell-tempered pottery, several fragments of struck chert, burnt and unburnt animal bone fragments, burnt plant remains including hazelnut shell and cereal grains (barley and wheat), and abundant charcoal. Two of the biggest pits are interpreted as the footings for a pair of stout marker posts, set 4 m apart. There is some evidence that these posts did not decay *in situ* but were removed in antiquity, and that a burnt deposit containing animal bone was placed in the resulting voids. Charcoal from the pits and post-holes produced several dates, ranging from 1114–1009 BC (UB-7400) to 1048–936 BC (UB-7401), in the Middle to Late Bronze Age (Appendix 1).

One especially big pit was interpreted as the draught-pit for a cremation pyre (Illus. 3.1.2). It contained a variety of fills, including soil and stones, burnt and unburnt animal bones (pig, sheep/goat and deer antler) and charcoal (oak, ash, hazel and willow). One of these fills was especially rich in burnt material, including cremated human bone. It seems likely that a funerary pyre was built over the pit and collapsed into it as the wood was consumed by flames.

The burnt bone fragments recovered from the pyre pit amounted to 685 gm. Only 72 gm of this could be identified as human, but there is a high likelihood that some or all of the other pieces are human too. The identified fragments represented parts of the skull, teeth, arms, hands, ribs, spine and legs of an adult at least 21 years old. A modern adult cremation produces between 1,200 gm and 3,000 gm of burnt bone (McKinley 1993, 285). What happened to the rest of this individual's bones? The small amount of bone overall, and the absence of many fragments from larger bones, suggests that much of the cremated bone was gathered carefully from the ashes of the pyre for burial elsewhere. Two bone samples gave dates of 791–569 BC (UB-7406) and 803–674 BC (UB-7484).

These radiocarbon dates show that the cremation pyre was a much later event than the other pits and post-holes in Area A. So what sort of activity do they represent? Only 14 of these pits and post-holes contained burnt bone fragments (total 25 gm) and none of this could be identified as human.

---

6   Excavation No. E2437; Excavation Director Brendon Wilkins; NGR (Area A) 149079 226736 at 37 m OD and (Area B) 149254 226485 at 26 m OD; parish of Athenry; barony of Athenry.

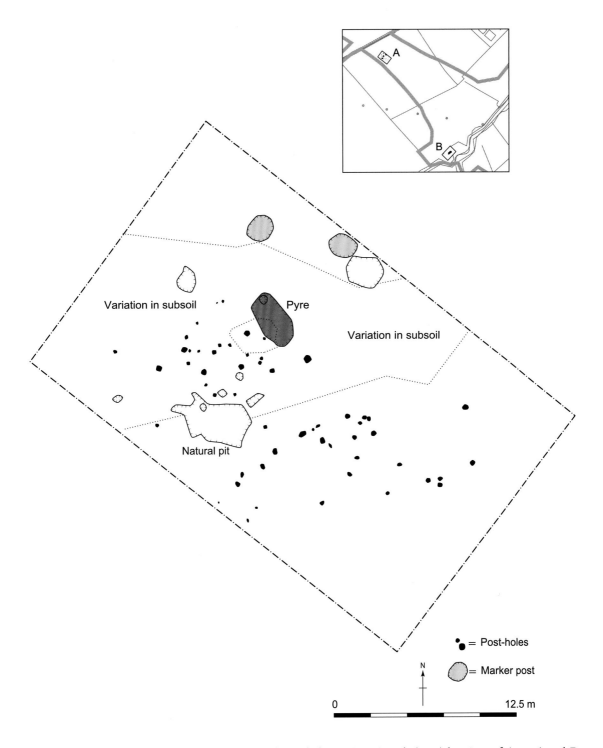

Illus. 3.1.1—Newford. Plan of the pyre, pits and post-holes in Area A with (inset) locations of Areas A and B (Rubicon Heritage Services Ltd).

Illus. 3.1.2—Newford. North-facing section of the pyre pit in Area A (Rubicon Heritage Services Ltd).

There were no domestic hearths or identifiable buildings, but there were animal bones, cereal grains, chipped or work chert and pottery—albeit in very small quantities—and this could reasonably be interpreted as evidence for a settlement site in this earlier phase at Newford. On the other hand, the fills of some of these pits and post-holes were quite rich in charcoal and it may be that the burnt bone fragments in these features were placed there deliberately, in a 'cemetery' with only token burials. There is also a middle-ground interpretation that recognises human bones as 'social artefacts', used in a variety of ways relating to religious beliefs, ritual practice and an active relationship between the living and the dead (Cleary 2005, 32–4). Thus, the earlier phase at Newford may have been a living settlement site in which the dead were also present—for whatever reason, represented by token burials of minute quantities of bone.

Burnt mound (Area B)

The burnt mound was discovered in a meander of the Lavally River under a thick layer of silty alluvial topsoil. There was an exceptionally large, square trough beneath the mound (4 m wide by 1.35 m deep), cut into the pale, sandy clay subsoil of the river bank. Natural springs in the base of the trough would have ensured that it was continuously filled with fresh water. The burnt deposits that eventually accumulated in the base of the trough included two animal vertebrae, one from a red deer, which suggests these animals were butchered and perhaps cooked on site. A burnt hazelnut shell from the mound gave an unusually early date of 3634–3520 BC (UB-7404), in the Early Neolithic period. The land in Newford is good and slopes gently towards the river on this west side. It would have been an attractive place for human settlement in all periods and hence the sporadic human presence in the archaeological record of this site over a span of roughly three millennia.

3.2 Furzypark: a burnt spread and a disturbed burial?[7]
by Brendon Wilkins

A spread of burnt material was found in Furzypark, in a pasture field on the south bank of the Lavally River (not illus.). This originally consisted of heat-shattered stone and dark, charcoal-flecked

---

7   Excavation No. E2553; Excavation Director Brendon Wilkins; NGR 149388 226470; height 28 m OD; parish of Athenry; barony of Athenry.

clay soil, but had been disturbed by ploughing so that topsoil was mixed through it. There was no underlying trough. In the field, the excavation team believed this was another Bronze Age burnt mound site. Radiocarbon dating seemed to corroborate this when a charcoal sample from the spread was dated to 1611–1443 BC (UB-7407), which is consistent with the known date range for this site type. But pottery sherds from beneath the spread are of a type more often associated with burials and hint at a different explanation.

The pottery sherds found beneath the burnt spread appear to represent a single vessel, probably a bowl or food container. This was decorated with two panels of vertical scores, bordered top and bottom by two or more horizontal lines. The upper part of the bowl was more thin-walled than the lower part. These details suggest the vessel was an Early Bronze Age 'bipartite bowl'. The absence of a smooth finish on the internal face of the pottery indicates that the vessel was not for domestic use. As bipartite bowls like this have only rarely been recorded in non-funerary contexts, it is more likely that the Furzypark bowl was from a disturbed burial or was intended for use in a burial.

Could this burnt spread represent a funerary pyre? This seems unlikely because no cremated human remains were found. It is more likely that pottery sherds from a disturbed burial were incorporated in the spread, though we have no way of knowing now whether this was deliberate or accidental.

3.3 Cashel at Farranablake East[8]
by Tom Janes

The cashel at Farranablake East is another of those curious archaeological monuments where nobody was at home when we called. The cashel was a well-preserved drystone enclosure, standing in farmland about 1.5 km south of Athenry. It is entered in the statutory Record of Monuments and Places as RMP GA096:089. The northern half of the enclosure (about 40% of the whole) lay within the lands acquired for the new road and was fully excavated, but with very little return.

The cashel was a circular enclosure about 50 m in overall diameter. There was no visible entrance. The wall was well built with large, rough limestone blocks forming the outer faces and a core of smaller rubble—which is typical of early medieval enclosures in the region (Illus. 3.3.1). Rubble spreads at the foot of the wall probably represent collapse. A broad bank of earth and stone divided the northern half of the interior into two roughly equal areas. This bank abutted the inner wall face and is probably a secondary feature. A single sherd of later medieval pottery, from a locally made 13th- or 14th-century jug, was the only hint of a human presence in antiquity, but there were many more sherds of early modern and modern ware, dumped in the cashel from a nearby household. An assemblage of 404 animal bones included cattle, sheep/goat, pig, horse and dog, but these did not come from secure contexts and may also have been dumped from elsewhere. There were no hearths, building remains or other occupation features recorded either inside or outside the cashel, and no early medieval artefacts, craftwork evidence or other industrial debris.

The Record of Monuments and Places shows 15 other enclosures within 1 km of the cashel at

---

8   Excavation No. E2352; Excavation Director Tom Janes; NGR 150270 225914; RMP No. GA096:089; height 30 m
     OD; parish of Athenry; barony of Athenry.

Illus. 3.3.1—Farranablake East. Cashel wall, looking west (Rubicon Heritage Services Ltd).

Farranablake East, including one exceptionally large circular earthwork about 250 m north-west of it. Most of these were early medieval settlement enclosures, no doubt, but there is no evidence to show that Farranablake was inhabited in that period, or that it was ever occupied at all. On present evidence, we must consider the likelihood that it was built as a livestock yard, and no more than that, with a related settlement in some other enclosure in the vicinity.

3.4 An estate tenant's cottage in Moyode[9]
by Tom Janes

The Persse family estate of Moyode was in the heart of east Galway, on lands about 4 km south-east of Athenry. (We shall hear more of them presently at the site of their kennels in Deerpark, below.) The adjoining townlands of Moyode and Moyode Demesne formed their demesne lands, surrounding Moyode House. A small building group appeared in a roadside setting, on the northern

---

9   Excavation No. E2353; Excavation Director Tom Janes; NGR 152210 225264; height 35 m OD; parish of Athenry; barony of Athenry.

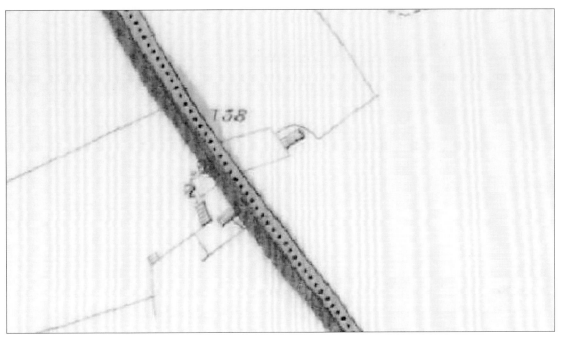

Illus. 3.4.1—Moyode. The excavated cottage was part of an L-plan building group (left) on the Persse demesne lands in Moyode (Ordnance Survey of Ireland).

Illus. 3.4.2—Moyode. The grass-clad remnants of the buildings could be seen in pasture south of the road. Modern houses, opposite, provide a contrast in scale with cottages of the 18th and 19th century (Galway County Council).

boundary of Moyode townland, on the first edition Ordnance Survey map of 1841 (Illus. 3.4.1), but was absent from the second edition map of 1895. Field inspection found the grass-clad building remnants (Illus. 3.4.2) and the site was fully excavated.

The excavation recorded the wall remnants of a three-roomed house with overlying spreads of building rubble and roofing slates. The walls were well built in mortared limestone rubble with a lime-based render on the interior. The internal partition walls were also in mortared rubble and rendered. The doorway, facing the road, had a cobbled threshold and gave access directly to the main or central room. There was a large fireplace, with limestone flags, in this central room, and a smaller fireplace in one of the end-rooms. A common flue within the partition wall served both fireplaces, indicating there had been a chimney on the roof ridge.

The first edition of the Ordnance Survey map showed a second building, gable end to the roadside, immediately east of the house. This was represented in the excavation site only by a spread of rubble with mortar fragments.

There was a small garden enclosure near one end of the house, by the road, with traces of hand-dug cultivation ridges. To the rear of the house, the haggard was a much larger enclosure. Two cells incorporated in the thickness of the wall were possibly for poultry. A smaller, rougher building incorporated in the outer wall face of the haggard may have been a pigsty or store. There was a more substantial building within the haggard, in the furthest corner from the house. No roof slates or timbers were found here but there were residual traces of lime mortar and a lime-based render on the walls. This was probably a byre or possibly a storage shed. Again, there were traces of spade-dug ridges throughout the haggard.

A small assemblage of animal and bird bones was recovered (193 bones). The numbers are too small to be statistically significant and a quarter of the bones were too fragmentary to be identified. The ones that could be identified represent a typical rural menagerie of sheep/goat, pig, cattle, horse, cat, chickens, geese and even a crow.

Artefacts from the site included iron tools and fixtures, clay tobacco pipes and modern or early modern pottery sherds. The pottery is a mixture of utility vessels such as storage jars and chamber pots, along with finer items including a teapot and matching cups, and also a fragment of Staffordshire pottery from an ornamental figurine (a cat). There were fragments of an iron cauldron and a teapot around the fireplace, suggesting the house was not cleared of its contents, and three large iron padlocks from the rubble layer suggest that the doors and windows were secured after it was last occupied.

This house on the Moyode estate was the home of one of its tenants (Illus. 3.4.3). The total area enclosed within the garden and haggard was about quarter of an acre. The typical plot of land apportioned to a 19th-century estate tenant was between a quarter and one acre (Mitchell & Ryan 2001, 331–8). This would have contributed to the subsistence of the tenant and his family, while paid employment was provided by the estate. The dimensions and internal layout of the house are typical of an 18th- or early 19th-century estate cottage, and even the domestic ware is what one would expect to find in such a household (Doyle 2007, 5; Zilic 2002).

Griffith's *Valuation* (1853) records the cottage as a 'herd's house and land' leased from Burton Persse, the owner of the Moyode estate and one of the more affluent landowners of east Galway. A 'herd' was a superior sort of tenant responsible for his landlord's cattle and allowed to keep some of his own among them. We do not know the tenant's name or why the cottage was eventually

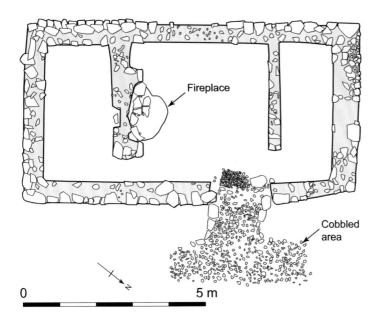

Fireplace

Location map

Cobbled area

0   5 m

Illus. 3.4.3—Moyode. Plan of the cottage (top) and a scene from the tenants' home life (reconstruction drawing by Eavan Ó Dochartaigh for Rubicon Heritage Services Ltd).

abandoned, but we do know that none of Burton Persse's tenants were evicted or forced into the workhouse during the Famine (Roy 2001, 219). Nonetheless, the teapot and cauldron are poignant symbols of a life interrupted or perhaps displaced and it may be that the last tenants of this cottage at Moyode became emigrants, like so many others of their time.

3.5 Cremation burial and ring-ditch at Deerpark[10]
by Brendon Wilkins & Susan Lalonde

In the Iron Age, burials were commonly placed within small circular ditches, often with a covering mound, an enclosing bank or both. Upstanding examples can still be seen in the countryside in east Galway but, in the archaeological excavation record, these 'barrows' often occur as ploughed-down sites where only the circular ditch survives, concealed beneath the topsoil. One of these levelled barrows, or 'ring-ditches', was found by test excavations in Deerpark, 2.7 km south-east of Athenry.

The ring-ditch was 4 m in diameter with a small gap to the south (Illus. 3.5.1). It was filled by soil with red flecks of burnt earth, charcoal and burnt bone fragments. Two charcoal samples from the ditch were dated to 363–113 BC (UB-7451) and 808–558 BC (UB-7452) and two bone samples were dated to 362–111 BC (UB-7486) and 345–45 BC (UB-7485). Three of these dates point to a cremation burial some time between the mid fourth and mid first centuries BC. There is no obvious explanation for the much earlier date as the excavation record does not indicate repeated use of the site over a long period. The sample may have been old or residual material accidentally incorporated in the ditch fills.

A large pit near the ring-ditch had burnt sediment and abundant charcoal in its fill. The excavation team thought this might be a cremation pyre pit but a charcoal sample dated to AD 905–1148 (UB-7450) indicates that it was a much later feature, unrelated to the ring-ditch.

Less than 90 gm of cremated bone fragments were recovered from the ring-ditch, which represents only a small fraction of the total amount that should result from the cremation of an adult body (1,200–3,000 gm). The rest was evidently gathered up from the ashes. The charcoals were dominated by various small fruiting trees (Pomoideae).

The ditch fills were all sieved and this yielded, in addition to bone fragments, three tiny beads—in blue glass, green stone and amber (Illus. 3.5.2). They were not heat damaged and are unlikely, therefore, to have been worn on the cremated body. Probably they were left by mourners, having a symbolism we cannot now decipher. A broken, abraded chert blade was recovered from a tree-hole (i.e. the disturbed area where a tree had afterwards grown on the site) and a chert scraper was found outside the ditch.

---

10 Excavation No. E2438; Excavation Director Brendon Wilkins; NGR 152286 225265; height 38 m OD; parish of Athenry; barony of Athenry.

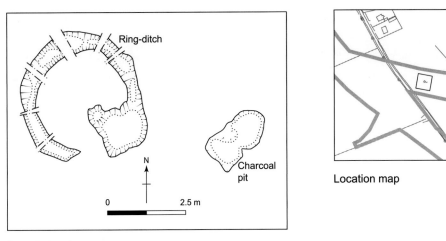

Overall site plan

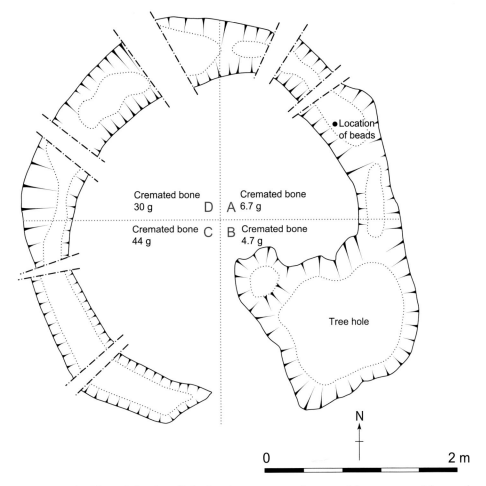

Illus. 3.5.1—Deerpark. Plan of the ring-ditch showing amounts of cremated bone recovered by quadrant and the find spot of the three beads (Rubicon Heritage Services Ltd).

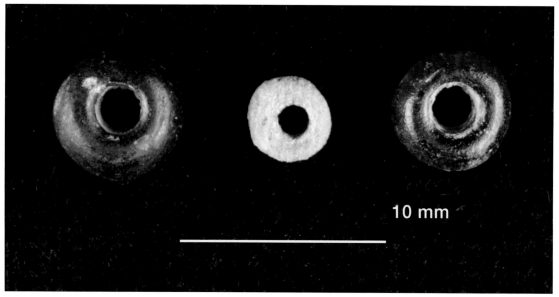

Illus. 3.5.2—Deerpark. Three beads in stone (green), glass (blue) and amber from the ring-ditch. Scale 2:1 (Rubicon Heritage Services Ltd).

3.6 Kennels of Tallyho Lodge at Deerpark[11]
by Tom Janes

Tallyho Lodge was a small country house in Deerpark townland, about 4 km south-east of Athenry, and was an early seat of the fox-hunting Persses, a family especially associated with the Galway Blazers hunt. (We already met them, above, on the site of an estate tenant's cottage in Moyode, associated with another of their houses.) The house at Tallyho Lodge is shown on the first edition Ordnance Survey map of 1841 (Illus. 3.6.1) but today the site is occupied by a modern farmstead and, of the original house and demesne, only remnants of a walled garden survive. A stone in the entranceway to the garden is inscribed with the date 1712 and probably records the construction date of the house. In a pasture field near the site of the house, our geophysical survey detected a strongly defined anomaly that seemed to represent building remains (ArchaeoPhysica 2004, Vol. 1, 31–3 and CD-ROM) and the site was consequently targeted for total excavation.

The excavation uncovered a cobbled yard, flanked by the wall footings of small, mortared stone buildings and enclosed by a mortared stone boundary wall (Illus. 3.6.2). A building on the west side had red ceramic floor tiles bedded in mortar and traces of render on the walls (Illus. 3.6.3). Access to the yard was from the south, along a metalled track with flanking drains, between low earth banks. These banks could be seen prior to the excavation, leading away from the site, and are the only trace of it depicted on the first edition Ordnance Survey map. One of the ditches contained dumps of animal bone, including sheep, goat, horse and cattle. There was no evidence of butchery on any

---

11 Excavation No. E2057; Excavation Director Tom Janes; NGR 153600 22500; height 40 m OD; parish of Athenry; barony of Athenry.

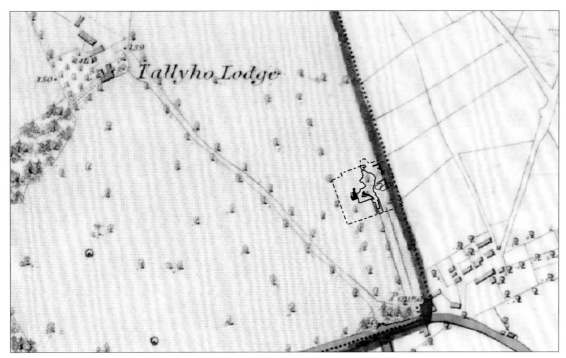

Illus. 3.6.1—Deerpark (Tallyho Lodge). The parallel low banks flanking the approach to the former kennels can still be seen (bottom right) in this extract from the first edition of the Ordnance Survey map (1841), though the kennels themselves were no longer extant (Ordnance Survey of Ireland).

of the bones but a number of them (17%) were gnawed by dogs. Artefacts included clay tobacco pipes, pottery sherds (Table 3.6.1), glass and various metal objects—including a George I coin of 1738. Beyond the walls, on the east side, there was a rectangular, stone-lined well or cistern. There was a lump of pine pitch in the base of the well. This can be used as a sealant or a fire accelerant but was used in the past to repair damaged horses' hooves. There were broken pot sherds dumped into the well and these dated to the 17th or 18th century. Although the assemblage is small, this is the strongest indication of an early date for the building group.

Table 3.6.1—Pottery recovered from the yard at Deerpark arranged by type, form, date and origin. MVR = minimum number of vessels

Type	Sherds	MVR	Form	Date range	Origin
Fine black glazed red earthenware	1	1	Jug/mug	17th–18th cent.	Ireland/Britain
Westerwald	1	1	Tankard	17th–18th cent.	Germany
North Devon gravel-tempered ware	1	1	Dish	17th–18th cent.	England
North Devon gravel-free ware	18	3	Handled jar, bowl	17th–18th cent.	England

Table 3.6.1 (continued)

Type	Sherds	MVR	Form	Date range	Origin
Tin-glazed earthenware	14	6	Plate, dish, mug	17th–18th cent.	Ireland/Britain
Slip-trailed red earthenware	2	1	Dish	18th cent.	Ireland/Britain
Manganese mottled ware	1	1	Tankard, mug	18th cent.	England
English stoneware	14	5	Tankard, chamber pot	18th–20th cent.	England
Black glazed red earthenware	5	1	Storage pot	18th–20th cent.	Ireland/Britain
Brown glazed red earthenware	1	1	Storage pot	18th–20th cent.	Ireland/Britain
Unglazed red earthenware	1	1	Storage pot	18th–20th cent.	Ireland/Britain
Creamware	3	1	Plate	19th–20th cent.	Ireland/Britain
Transfer-printed ware	1	1	Plate	19th–20th cent.	Ireland/Britain
Spongeware	1	1	Plate	19th–20th cent.	Britain
Porcelain	3	2	Saucer	19th–20th cent.	Britain
Total	**67**	**27**		**17th–20th cent.**	

Despite the presence of kitchen and table wares, this yard in Deerpark was unlikely to have been primarily a domestic place—though some estate workers may have had their quarters here. It is more likely to have been a kennels, or perhaps a kennels and stables, and this is supported by the gnawed animal bones and pine pitch. This interpretation answers very nicely to a local tradition that Deerpark was the first home of the Galway Blazers hunt. However, the combined evidence of artefacts and maps indicates that the yard and buildings on this site had fallen out of use and were levelled by the time the hunt was formed in 1839. They were probably the kennels of nearby Tallyho Lodge and may well have been associated with an earlier hunt.

The Persses were among the wealthier families in east Galway by the late 18th century, when 'Old' Burton Persse settled at Tallyho Lodge (Lane 1996, 403). He later moved to nearby Moyode and built Persse Lodge there. Burton Persse's son, Burton de Burgh Persse, inherited Persse Lodge in 1829 and replaced it with a neo-Gothic house in baronial style, which he named Moyode Castle (Roy 1997, 194). The house became the nucleus of a 3,000-acre estate. It is very ruinous today but its gate lodges and avenues survive. Moyode merited a mention in the *Topographical Dictionary* compiled by Samuel Lewis in the 1830s, though Tallyho Lodge did not (Lewis 1837, 449). Perhaps the house at Tallyho Lodge was in decline by that time or, at least, was no longer the residence of a prominent gentleman landowner and a pillar of east Galway society.

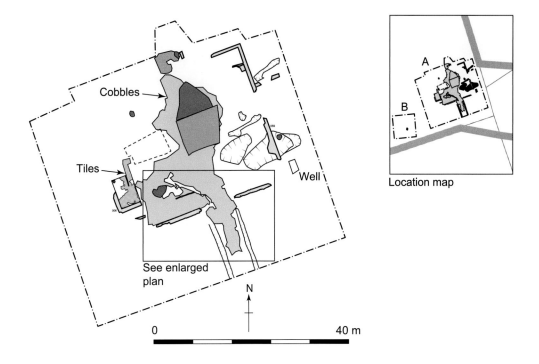

Cobbles

Tiles

Well

See enlarged plan

N

0   40 m

Location map

A

B

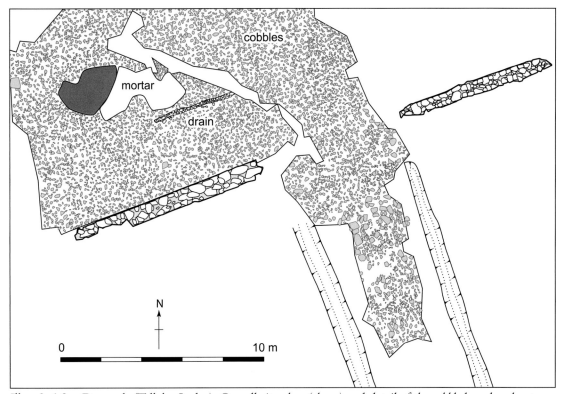

cobbles

mortar

drain

N

0   10 m

Illus. 3.6.2—Deerpark (Tallyho Lodge). Overall site plan (above) and detail of the cobbled yard and entrance avenue to the kennels (Rubicon Heritage Services Ltd).

Illus. 3.6.3—Deerpark (Tallyho Lodge). One of the buildings flanking the yard had red ceramic floor tiles (Rubicon Heritage Services Ltd).

3.7 A deceptive burnt spread at Rathgorgin[12]

by Brendon Wilkins & Amy Bunce

The archaeological investigator must always have an open mind and can expect received wisdom to be overturned by the facts sometimes. A burnt spread at Rathgorgin is a case in point. It was identified by test excavations in pasture (not illus.). The excavation team at first believed it was another ploughed-down burnt mound of the Bronze Age. First impressions were proved deceptive, however, when sherds of Victorian pottery and a clay-pipe bowl stamped 'Home Rule' were discovered among the burnt sediments, which were no more than modern rubbish. And thereby hangs a cautionary tale for our prehistorians.

---

12 Excavation No. E2439; Excavation Director Brendon Wilkins; NGR 153811 224988; height 40 m OD; parish of Athenry; barony of Athenry.

3.8 Brick clamps at Brusk[13]

by Brendon Wilkins

In the 21st century almost all of our manufactured goods come from factories in distant places and most of them are made from synthesised materials. It is easy to forget that, early in the modern period, many products were still made by hand using locally sourced materials.

Brusk is a rural townland about 4.5 km east of Athenry. The area is low lying and poorly drained in places. Underlying its improved grass pastures and shallow loam topsoil are subsoils consisting of deep, compact, glacially deposited clays with gravel inclusions, which would have provided excellent raw material for bricks. Some form of pyrotechnic activity was strongly indicated in a field in Brusk by our geophysical survey (ArchaeoPhysica 2004, Vol. 1, 36–7 and CD-ROM; Illus. 3.8.1). Test excavations found three concentrations of brick, ashes and burnt soil, surrounded by embanked redeposited natural subsoils. Further investigation confirmed that these were the remains of three brick-making 'clamper' kilns.

Kiln 2 offered the most complete evidence of the three examples (Illus. 3.8.2). This measured 11 m by 6.5 m and consisted of 12 rows of predominantly red bricks or 'benches'. The 10 benches in

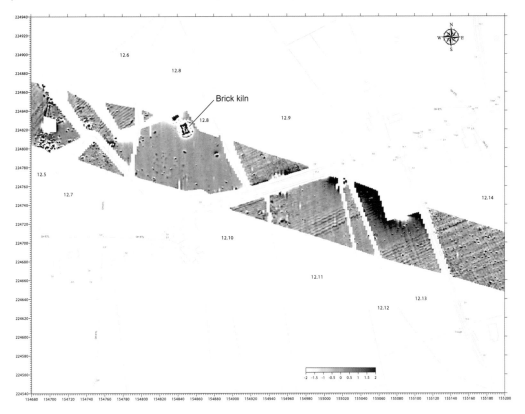

Illus. 3.8.1—Brusk. The brick kilns were strongly defined in geophysical survey imagery based on recorded magnetometry (ArchaeoPhysica 2004, Vol. 2, 40).

13 Excavation No. E2063; Excavation Director Brendon Wilkins; NGR 154875 224784; height 36 m OD; parish of Kiltullagh; barony of Athenry.

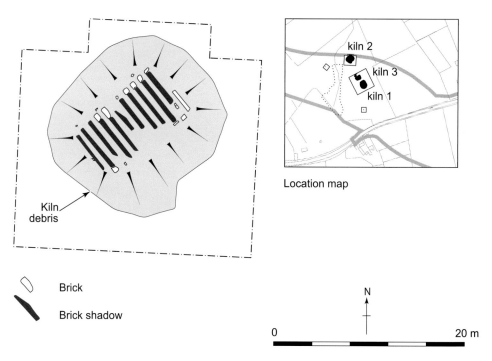

Kiln debris

Brick

Brick shadow

Location map

kiln 2

kiln 3

kiln 1

N

0   20 m

Illus. 3.8.2—Brusk. Location map and plan of Kiln 2 (top) and detail of Kiln 2 during excavation (photo) (Rubicon Heritage Services Ltd).

the centre of the kiln were of double-brick thickness, with the bricks laid transversely, so that the benches were faced by 'headers' (i.e. the end faces of the bricks). The two outer benches, flanking the kiln at either end, were of single-brick thickness and, again, were laid transversely, with headers facing the benches. The ends of the benches were sometimes finished with bricks laid on edge. The basal bricks in all the benches were also laid on edge. These end and basal bricks, being partly fired and sometimes fused or misshapen, were left *in situ* when the main mass of the bricks was harvested from the kiln after firing. Bricks fired in the centre of a kiln would have been exposed to higher temperatures and lower oxygen. The bricks in the central benches of Kiln 1 were yellow, and harder but also more brittle than the other bricks it produced. Evidently the yellow bricks had a higher value, as the ends of the yellow benches were finished with red bricks that would become wasters. The remnant bricks found *in situ* were overlain by a pile of brick rubble. Beneath the kiln remnants was a layer of coarse yellow sand—probably redeposited from a nearby watercourse. This would have insulated the kiln and also provided a clean, level bed for the basal courses. The underlying subsoil was scorched and, in places, contained carbonised roots (these were the only charcoals observed on the site and therefore the kiln fuel was probably peat). The bricks themselves were red or yellow and typically measured 0.24 m long, 0.1 m wide and 0.07 m thick.

Apart from the three kilns, the excavations at Brusk did not find evidence for any ancillary buildings or activities, such as brick-working, storage and drying, or on-site accommodation for the workers. There were no areas of clay quarrying within the limits of excavation, but immediately west of the site a large flooded depression, traversed by a meandering watercourse, is probably the site of a partly backfilled clay-pit.

Brick was not a common building material in rural Galway in the early modern period, with mortared rubble and dressed limestone usually preferred. It is, however, often found in the internal partition walls of mansion houses and sometimes in the margins of doors and windows. The kilns at Brusk may have produced 20,000 bricks in each firing, requiring about 35 cubic metres of clay. They would have been temporary installations, probably built in a single season and for a single project—perhaps for the brick-built engine sheds and crossing-keepers cottages on the Loughrea to Attymon railway line that opened in 1890. There is no hint of brick-making at Brusk on the first edition Ordnance Survey map (1838), but the flooded clay-pit is shown on the second edition (1948), suggesting a Victorian date for the site.

3.9 Cremation burial at Curragh More[14]
by Tom Janes

Token burial is a frequent theme among the prehistoric cremations recorded along the route of the new road and is seen again on this simple excavation site in Curragh More. Two pits with cremated bone and prehistoric pottery were found by testing in pasture about 2.5 km south-west of Kiltullagh village (not illus.). The cremated bone was buried in a small, round pit, with no surviving grave marker. There was only 245 gm of bone in the pit, which is a fraction of the 1,200 to 3,000

---

14 Excavation No. E2520; Excavation Director Tom Janes; NGR 155110 224600; height 40 m OD; civil parish of Kiltullagh; barony of Athenry.

gm that a modern adult cremation would produce (McKinley 1993, 285). It was possible to identify some of the cremated bone, including two teeth. They most probably represent a single adult female, at least 21 years old. A second, smaller pit had less than 1 gm of bone. The smaller pit also contained 26 sherds of prehistoric pottery.

There was no visible evidence of burning in the pits or the adjacent soil surface but, pyre debris, made up of charcoal and fuel ash slag, was found in both pits. The presence of fuel ash slag indicates that the pyre was especially hot, perhaps reaching temperatures over 1,000 °C. The charcoal was mostly from oak with smaller amounts of various small fruiting trees (Pomoideae) and alder or hazel.

The pottery came from two vessels. Both had blackened internal accretions, indicating that they had been used in domestic contexts. One had the simple everted rim and rounded shoulder of an Early Neolithic carinated bowl. This is the earliest type of Neolithic pottery in Ireland, commonly dated to c. 4000–3700 BC. The second vessel may have been a fine beaker of Chalcolithic date (c. 2400–2200 BC).

What is the meaning of two small pits containing the incomplete cremated bone assemblage of one adult and a handful of pottery sherds from two vessels? Cooney & Grogan (1999, 136–7) would classify these as 'token burials' and suggest that 'other portions of the cremated bone and parts of the pots may have been used at different stages in an extended mortuary ritual where much of the ceremonial emphasis was placed on the cremation, funeral and burial rather than on just what was placed in the grave'. The dating evidence is harder to explain here. Token cremation burials appear in the archaeological record from the Middle Bronze Age, and this is consistent with dates for bone samples from Curragh More, at 1529–1407 BC (UB-7467) and 1628–1453 BC (UB-7488). The pottery sherds are much older than this. Was their antiquity recognised, and valued, in Middle Bronze Age times? Was the same place used for burials over many centuries? Or is it mere coincidence that the two pits were found side by side?

3.10 A multi-period landscape at Clogharevaun[15]
by Brendon Wilkins

The lands traversed by the new road in Clogharevaun seemed full of archaeological promise. Here, the new motorway crosses the Dooyertha River, about 1 km south Kiltullagh village. The river was straightened and deepened in Victorian times but its older course is still visible, meandering through low-lying boggy ground. On the higher, dry ground there are relict field banks enclosing broad, spade-dug cultivation ridges, with the biggest banks of earth and rubble forming a boundary between the tilled land and the wet ground around the river. A ruined tower house—Clogharevaun Castle—overlooks the scene from elevated ground to the east (Illus. 3.10.1). Our geophysical survey identified possible traces of ditches, field boundaries and trackways beneath the topsoil in the fields above the river. Could this be a preserved medieval landscape of tillage fields surrounding a castle?

Raising the soil in spade-dug ridges increases its temperature and improves drainage, resulting in a better crop yield. The practice dates from at least the medieval period but was most extensively seen

15 Excavation No. E2056; Excavation Director Brendon Wilkins; NGR 157692 224124; height 34 m OD; civil parish of Kiltullagh; barony of Athenry.

in Ireland between 1700 and 1850, when arable agriculture reached a historic peak (Bell & Watson 2008, 179). Against this background, our ridges at Clogharevaun are most likely to be early modern, though some of the field banks bounding them are very likely survivors of an older, medieval landscape, affording us a glimpse of farming in feudal times in east Galway.

The footprint of the road project in this area was intensively tested with hand-dug trenches on visible features and more extensive machine-cut trenches. No medieval features were found and in fact the only significant new feature discovered by testing was a Bronze Age burnt mound, in the low-lying, wet ground by the river (Area C in Illus. 3.10.2; Illus. 3.10.3). This was a horseshoe-shaped mound of heat-shattered stone and charcoal-rich sandy silt, overlying a simple earth-

Illus. 3.10.1—Clogharevaun. The castle was recorded in the ownership of the MacSweenys in the 16th century (Galway County Council).

cut pit or trough. A charcoal sample from the mound was dated to 1496–1318 BC (UB-7408) and one from the trough was dated to 1419–1268 BC (UB-7409), in the Middle Bronze Age.

In one area of testing a Neolithic polished stone axehead was found in the topsoil (Area H in Illus. 3.10.2). Numerous test-pits were dug by hand throughout this area and the topsoil from these was sieved. Overall, the returns were disappointing. A total of 248 objects was recovered from all areas combined, ranging in date from early prehistory to modern times. Apart from the Neolithic axehead, prehistoric material included an Early Bronze Age end-scraper and several other pieces of flaked or chipped chert. A few sherds of green-glazed pottery of probable 13th/14th-century date were the sole medieval finds. There were numerous sherds of early modern pottery and some clay-pipe fragments.

Sometimes what you see is what you get. The tillage fields around Clogharevaun Castle offer a striking visual record of agricultural practices in the past but invasive archaeological investigation of the soils beneath the surface added little to the story.

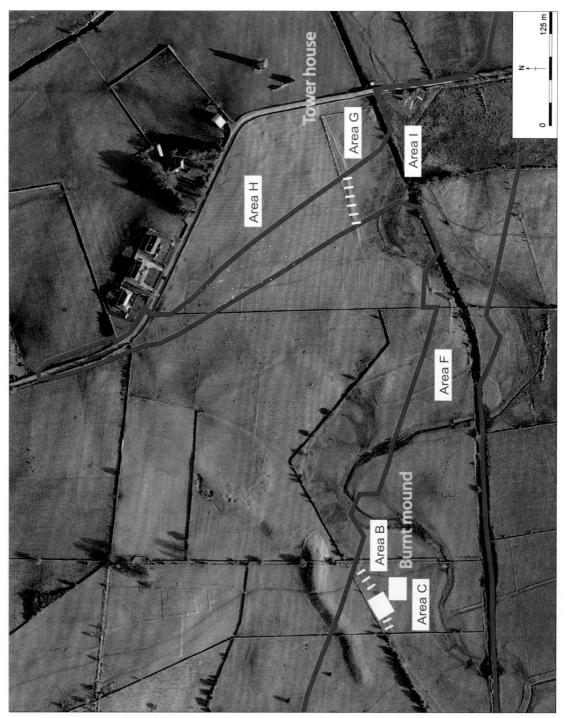

Illus. 3.10.2—Clogharevaun. In this aerial view the former, meandering course of the Dooeyertha River, extensive areas of spade-dug ridges and relict field banks are all strongly defined. The ruins of Clogharevaun Castle throw a long shadow (top) and an esker ridge snakes across the landscape (bottom) (Galway County Council).

Illus. 3.10.3—Clogharevaun. Stuart Callow and the excavation team at work on the burnt mound site (Area C), in a low-lying, wet area by the Dooyertha River (Jerry O'Sullivan).

3.11 Cemetery-settlement enclosure at Carrowkeel[16]
by Brendon Wilkins & Susan Lalonde

Ireland was converted to Christianity in the mid first millennium. After the Conversion, it was once supposed, the Christian dead were buried in the consecrated burial grounds of early monastic churches. We now know this is not entirely true or, at least, that it was only true for certain classes of persons, including pilgrims, clergy and their wealthy secular patrons. So where was everybody else buried in the centuries following the Conversion? The cemetery-settlement is a new type of archaeological site that has only been recognised within the last 20 years. It is typically a large, curvilinear, settlement enclosure—much like other cashels and ringforts of the period—but with an area reserved for burials, usually within the eastern part of the enclosure.

The townland of Carrowkeel is about 7 km north of Loughrea and 2.5 km south-east of Kiltullagh. A circular enclosure was shown on the first edition Ordnance Survey map in 1838, on the western brow of a long, rounded ridge, intervisible with several other early medieval enclosures. It had disappeared by the second edition map of 1929, giving way to improved pasture fields within

16 Excavation No. E2046; Excavation Director Brendon Wilkins; RMP No. GA097-066; NGR 159326 223949; height 38 m OD; civil parish of Kiltullagh; barony of Athenry.

rectilinear field dykes. Our geophysical survey found evidence for a levelled, backfilled enclosure ditch. This was confirmed by subsequent test excavations, which also found human skeletal remains on the site. About 60% of the enclosure lay within the lands acquired for the new road, and was excavated; the rest remains undisturbed.

Ditches and graves

The main enclosure ditch was c. 3 m wide and 1.5 m deep and enclosed an area 65 m (east–west) by 47 m. Upcast from the ditch was used to form the bank, but only a remnant of this survived where it had been 'captured' by a later field dyke in the western part of the site. Remnants of other, smaller ditches were found throughout the site and especially in the northern part. Some of these clearly pre-dated the main ditch but they were not well preserved and neither their purpose nor date could be ascertained. Inside the main enclosure, in the eastern part, a pair of shallow, curvilinear ditch segments seemed to be remnants of a smaller enclosure surrounding a group of burials within that part of the site. All of these ditches were levelled and backfilled and, at first, they formed a puzzling group of intercutting features when the topsoil was stripped from the site (Illus. 3.11.1). Modern cultivation furrows, scored into the subsoil and intercut with the earlier medieval ditches, added another layer of complexity.

A burial ground was discovered in the eastern part of the main enclosure and, as described above, was partly bounded by a smaller double ditch. Within the excavated part of the site there were 131 *in situ* burials of men, women and children, including pre- and peri-natal skeletons (Table 3.11.1). Disturbed, isolated bones represented at least another 26 individuals so that the minimum total number of burials was 157. In considering the available evidence, it should be borne in mind that the burial ground extended into the unexcavated part of the site and, therefore, neither its full extent nor the total number of burials are known.

The burials were very shallow and frequently intercutting, so that the grave pits were poorly defined at best. The skeletons were mostly supine, extended and oriented (west–east) in the manner usually associated with Christian burial. There were some variations, however, including a flexed female (i.e. legs bent with raised knees), a female with splayed limbs, and a crouched male (Illus. 3.11.2). The crouched male was one of the earliest burials on the site; he was found in the terminus of one of the little curvilinear ditches that seemed to enclose the burial ground.

Forty samples of human skeletal material were radiocarbon dated (Appendix 1). Overall, the calibrated dates span the seventh to the 15th centuries, but are concentrated between the mid seventh and mid 12th centuries. There were no clear stratigraphic boundaries between groups of earlier and later burials, but for interpretative purposes the burial ground can be divided into four phases, based partly on the dates (Table 3.11.1).

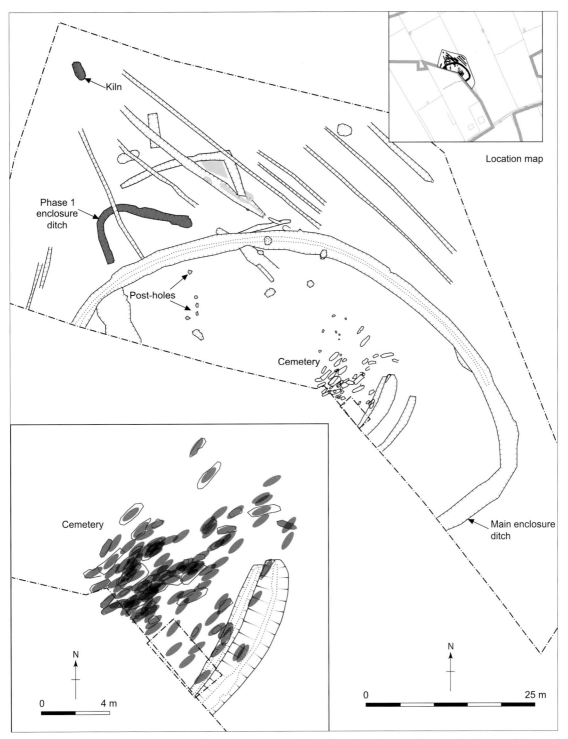

Kiln

Phase 1
enclosure
ditch

Post-holes

Cemetery

Location map

Main enclosure
ditch

Cemetery

N

0   4 m

N

0   25 m

Illus. 3.11.1—Carrowkeel. Plan of the excavated part of the ditched enclosure showing the limits of the road scheme (inset, top right) and with a schematic plan of the graves recorded in the south-east quadrant (lower left) (Rubicon Heritage Services Ltd).

Table 3.11.1—Carrowkeel. Age and sex (adult) of burials in Phases 1–4 of the cemetery

Phase	Period	Foetus	Infant < 1 yr	Juvenile 1–17 yrs	Adult male	Adult female	Total
Phase 1	AD 650–850	8	6	12	3	7	36
Phase 2	AD 850–1050	20	28	25	2	—	75
Phase 3	AD 1050–1250	3	5	6	2	2	18
Phase 4	AD 1250–1450	2	—	—	—	—	2
Total burials Phases 1–4		**33**	**39**	**43**	**7**	**9**	**131**
Disturbed bone (minimum number of individuals)		15 sub-adults			11 adults		26
Total burials (minimum)		**—**	**—**	**—**	**—**	**—**	**157**

- *Phase 1 (AD 650–850)* This earliest phase consisted of mixed adult and children's burials, mostly in shallow, oriented grave pits, in organised rows (north-west/south-east). The crouched male skeleton—one of the first burials—was dated to AD 682–872 (UB-7423). The burial ground in this phase was bounded by shallow, double ditches, enclosed in turn by the main bank-and-ditch earthwork. There were 37 individuals in Phase 1, including 10 adults.

- *Phase 2 (AD 850–1050)* The burials in this phase were also part of an organised, clearly bounded burial ground. There were 75 individuals in all but only two adults.

- *Phase 3 (AD 1050–1250)* The cemetery began to fall out of use during this phase. The graves became disorganised and no longer respected either the earlier burials in organised rows or the ditched boundaries of the burial ground. There were only 18 individuals recorded, including four adults.

Illus. 3.11.2—Carrowkeel. An adolescent in a crouched position was one of the first individuals to be buried in the cemetery (Brian Ó Domhnaill).

- *Phase 4 (AD 1250–1480)* Only foetal remains are recorded in this final phase, representing two individuals. Clearly the enclosure was all but abandoned by this time and had certainly ceased to be a formal, organised burial ground.

Illus. 3.11.3—Carrowkeel. Osteologist Susan Kidner examines the human skeletal remains in an off-site field laboratory (Brian Ó Domhnaill).

Living with the dead

Some things are clear about the big ditched enclosure at Carrowkeel. A space in the eastern half of the site was reserved for burials. For the first 200 years, from about AD 650 to AD 850, this was a mixed population of men, women and children. After that, there were fewer adult burials with children and infants (including foetal remains) especially numerous in Phase 2, between AD 850 and AD 1050. The burial ground had been more or less abandoned by AD 1250, though a couple of burials of foetal remains are recorded after this. What is less clear is who these people were and why they were buried here.

There is no evidence that Carrowkeel was an ecclesiastical enclosure. The alternative is that it was a family or kin-group burial ground, at least in Phase 1 (AD 650–850), and this is supported by the small numbers of burials from one generation to the next. The documentary sources for early Irish society hint at kindred burial grounds but they were not recognised in the archaeological record until recent years and have become the subject of lively academic discussion (Clarke & Carlin 2008; papers in Corlett & Potterton 2010; O'Brien 1992, 2003 and 2011; Ó Carragáin 2009; Stout & Stout 2008). Burial grounds in non-ecclesiastical enclosures are now known from a number of excavated sites, often occupying the south-east quadrant and sometimes within a dedicated sub-enclosure. The term 'cemetery-settlement' has been coined to describe this arrangement though some authors prefer 'secular-cemetery'. At first these cemetery-settlements seemed to be a phenomenon of the

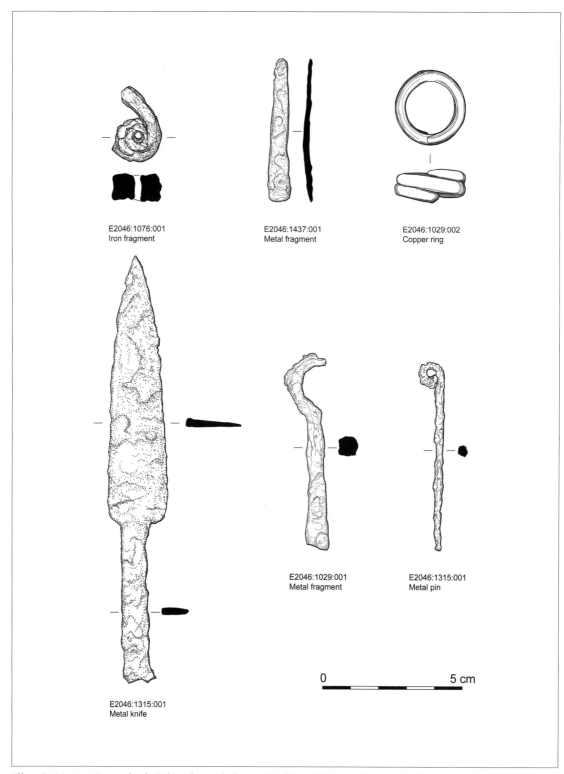

E2046:1076:001
Iron fragment

E2046:1437:001
Metal fragment

E2046:1029:002
Copper ring

E2046:1029:001
Metal fragment

E2046:1315:001
Metal pin

E2046:1315:001
Metal knife

0   5 cm

Illus. 3.11.4—Carrowkeel. Selected metal objects (Rubicon Heritage Services Ltd).

fertile, low-lying eastern parts of Ireland, but the distribution map can now be extended to include at least three newly discovered sites west of the Shannon, in County Galway (Treanbaun 2 in Chapter 4; Owenbristy in Delaney & Tierney 2011). In its later phases Carrowkeel was a cemetery for children, infants and pre- or neo-natal remains. Perhaps the adult dead in this community were now being taken elsewhere, for churchyard burial, as obedience to the Church overcame traditional loyalties to ancient family burial grounds. But rural communities have very long memories with regard to the significance of place and, in the division of old and young at Carrowkeel, we can perhaps see something of the origins of the *cillín* burial grounds, for neo-nates and very young infants, that were still common throughout rural Ireland in the early modern period.

Did the enclosure at Carrowkeel have permanent living occupants too? The artefact assemblage does not make a compelling case for this. A handful of metal objects was found, including an iron knife, a hook, a pin and a copper-alloy ring (Illus. 3.11.4). A small quantity of iron slag was recovered from the ditch fills. Three small, abraded sherds of medieval pottery were probably of local manufacture but as all of them came from disturbed contexts they are of little use in dating individual events on the site.

Animal bones provide the best evidence for occupation. In an assemblage of 13,631 bones or fragments, cattle were dominant, followed by sheep/goat, pig and horse. In smaller numbers there were bones of dog, cat, rabbit, mouse, wild birds and domestic fowl. The bones of domesticated livestock included both butchery waste and food debris. There were several bones of infant animals— again from cattle, sheep/goat and pig—and it is likely that these were raised on site.

A large oblong pit with burnt sediments and scorched sides was found outside the main enclosure. It was not radiocarbon dated and is tentatively interpreted as a cooking pit or possibly a simple grain-drying kiln—though it contained no cereal grains. Indeed, there were scarcely any plant remains at Carrowkeel and the few grains of barley and oats that were found may simply have come from stubble-burning in some much later period.

There is a well-worn saying in field archaeology that "an absence of evidence does not always amount to evidence of absence". But in this case the scanty evidence for occupation at Carrowkeel may be telling us that the people who buried their dead in the big ditched enclosure did not live there permanently, and instead only camped there occasionally, perhaps around certain religious festivals or fairs, or seasonally, when their cattle were brought to pastures in the environs. The evidence is teasing and this is compounded by the fact that all of the site was not excavated. The part of it that lies outside the lands acquired for the road remains undisturbed and available for a future investigation.

3.12 Short-cist cremation burial and ring-ditch at Ballykeeran[17]
by Brendon Wilkins

Ballykeeran had some classic features of a later prehistoric burial monument: a small ring-ditch enclosed a circle of post-holes; there was a stone-lined cist at the centre, beneath disturbed cairn

---

17 Excavation No. E2400; Excavation Director Brendon Wilkins; NGR 160421 222771; height 38 m OD; parish of Lickerrig; barony of Loughrea.

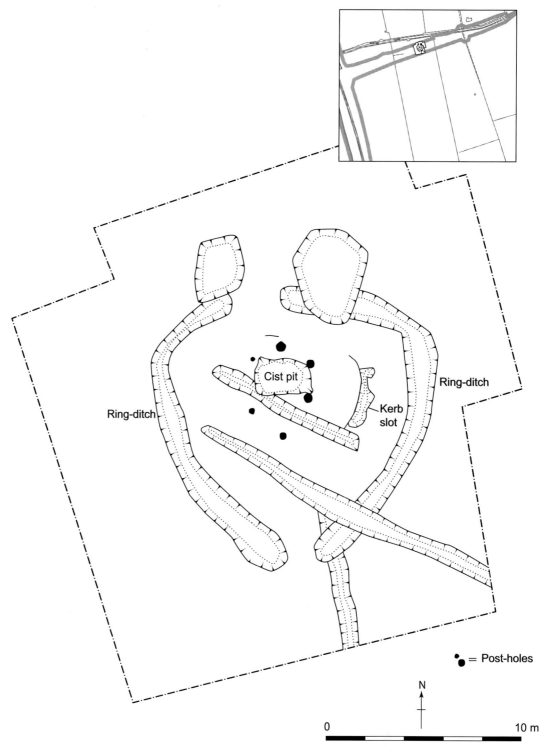

Ring-ditch

Cist pit

Kerb slot

Ring-ditch

N

0   10 m

= Post-holes

Illus. 3.12.1—Ballykeeran. General plan of the excavated cist and ring-ditch showing its location within the road scheme (inset) (Rubicon Heritage Services Ltd).

Illus. 3.12.2—Ballykeeran. View from north-east of the cist and ring-ditch in the course of excavation (Rubicon Heritage Services Ltd).

remnants (Illus. 3.12.1 and 3.12.2). The only thing missing was a burial. Was this a cenotaph or was it a looted grave?

The site was discovered by test excavations, at the foot of a slope overlooking bogland. The ring-ditch was 14 m in overall diameter and had frequent charcoal in its fills. A large oblong pit at its centre was lined with edge-set stones, forming a cist. The base was lined with flat stones, overlain by some collapsed capstones. The cist was surrounded by a group of six small post-holes in a roughly circular setting 4 m in diameter. Overlying the cist and the post-holes was a dispersed spread of small rubble or fieldstones, possibly remnants of a marker cairn. There was a shallow, curvilinear slot lying between the cist and the ring-ditch in the south-west quadrant, and this may have been the footing for a kerb, defining the edge of the cairn. Spade-dug furrows traversed the site, cutting across the ring-ditch, and there was also a small linear ditch pre-dating it.

A very small quantity (2 gm) of burnt bone was recovered from the basal fills of the cist. The bone fragments were too small for certain identification as human. A bone sample was dated to 806–550 BC (UB-7487), in the Late Bronze Age. Several charcoal samples from the site were also dated, with results ranging over the late 12th to early eighth centuries BC (Appendix 1). There was a good deal of burnt stone and charcoal in the soils that filled the cist, no doubt from an ancient cremation pyre, and also two red deer bones (phalanges; foot bones). These fills were evidently disturbed as they also contained a modern horseshoe. Seventy-four pieces of chipped stone were found on the site, including tools and waste material. There were blades, points and scrapers in chert and two 'thumbnail' scrapers in flint. Although none of the pieces could be closely dated on typological grounds, some of them are likely to be Neolithic or Early Bronze Age in date—much older certainly than the radiocarbon dates obtained from bone and charcoal samples—and they may represent an earlier episode of activity on this site.

Late Bronze Age burial practices are not as well understood as those of some other periods in prehistory. A cist like this might be expected to contain the burnt, fire-cracked bones of a cremated individual or perhaps a crouched inhumation (i.e. the skeleton of a crouched body laid on its side) and might sometimes be accompanied by grave goods. Why was there no burial deposit in the cist at Ballykeeran? Some cists dated to this period have contained only token amounts of bone, though generally in larger quantities than the 2 gm recovered at Ballykeeran. The evidence for disturbance is more convincing, with collapsed capstones, modern inclusions in the cist fills, a dispersed cairn, and cultivation furrows traversing the site. It seems likely that the cist was not only disturbed by tillage in the medieval or modern period but was also looted, with a funerary urn and its contents being removed intact.

Chapter 4

Over Kilreekill Ridge (Sector 3)
Galboley to Newcastle

Ballydonnellan Castle (Jerry O'Sullivan)

4.1 Burnt mounds and trackways at Killescragh[18]

by Ken Curran & Nóra Bermingham

The last glaciation covered Ireland in a deep blanket of ice until about 17,000 years ago. Rivers of meltwater beneath the ice scoured out sand and gravel and, as the ice retreated, the river channels were fossilised as steep-sided gravel ridges snaking across the landscape. These ridges, known as eskers, are especially characteristic of the landscape of east Galway.

The townland name Killescragh derives from an early church site on the northern flank of an esker (combining the Irish words *'cill'*, a church, and *'eiscir'*). South of the esker is a small, shallow bog, now largely reclaimed for pasture, in the catchment of the Craughwell River. Burnt mounds and wooden trackway remnants were found at the foot of the esker, in the peat bog on this southern side, at two locations (Killescragh 1 and 2) about 750 m apart (Illus. 4.1.1). An abundance of ancient wood litter and roots was also preserved by the wetland conditions of the bog (Illus. 4.1.2). The interface of esker and bog was a diverse habitat supplying its human visitors with water, wood, berries and nuts, fowl and game, and pasture or fodder for their livestock. But this was also a changing environment and our analyses at this site attempted to reconstruct these changes throughout the Bronze Age,

Illus. 4.1.1—Killescragh. This aerial view taken in 2000, several years prior to construction of the new road, shows an early church enclosure north of the esker (hence the place name elements cill *and* eiscir*) and the bog basin south of it where the burnt mounds and trackways were discovered. The esker is being still being quarried for sand and gravel today (Galway County Council).*

---

18 Killescragh 1—Excavation No. E2070; NGR 162600 224500; height 55 m OD; Killescragh 2—Excavation No. E2071; NGR 163306 225224; height 58 m OD; both in the parish of Killimordaly and barony of Athenry; Excavation Director (Killescragh 1 and 2) Ken Curran.

when it was used by the people who made the burnt mounds.

Killescragh 1: burnt mounds and platforms

The earliest phase here (Phase 1) was represented by a group of timbers beneath a burnt mound deposit. A small arrangement of closely set, split roundwood pieces was secured in position by 17 stakes, forming a flat base or platform—or possibly the base of a dismantled trough—less than 1 m long. Other stakes were randomly dispersed around the platform and eight stakes formed a cluster a few metres to the south, also sealed by the burnt mound. Cut-marks on the wood show that more than one tool was used, including an axe, adze and other flat-edged tools. The mound itself was a large, shallow spread of

Illus. 4.1.2—Killescragh 1. Masses of natural woodland debris were preserved in the peat basin (Jerry O'Sullivan).

heat-shattered stone (mainly sandstone) and charcoal flecks. Three fragments of cattle and sheep/goat bone were recovered from the mound, and other bones retrieved from the surrounding peat deposits included cattle, sheep/goat, pig and red deer bone (62 fragments in total). Charcoal (alder) from the mound was dated to 2570–2300 BC (Wk-21343), in the Late Neolithic period.

A layer of peat and silt, with tree roots, developed over the first mound before a second, smaller mound (Phase 2) was deposited on the peat, again consisting of heat-shattered stone and charcoal. There was a hearth within this second mound, filled with ash, burnt stones, charcoal and oxidised or fire-reddened clay. Charcoal samples from these deposits were dated to 2458–2144 BC (Wk-21245) and 2580–2015 BC (Wk-21246).

The latest activity on this site (Phase 3) was represented by a small platform located on the western edge of the burnt mound but separated from it by a shallow layer of peat. This second platform was made with split roundwood and brushwood consolidated with stakes. The wood was cut with a flat metal blade. A wood sample was dated to 1394–1132 BC (UB-7242) in the Middle Bronze Age, much later than the earlier mounds and timbers on this site.

Killescragh 2: burnt mounds, platforms and trackways

About 750 m east of the first site, another burnt spread was found (Phase 1), consisting of dark, friable silt with frequent charcoal and heat-shattered stone. A wood sample was dated to 2280–

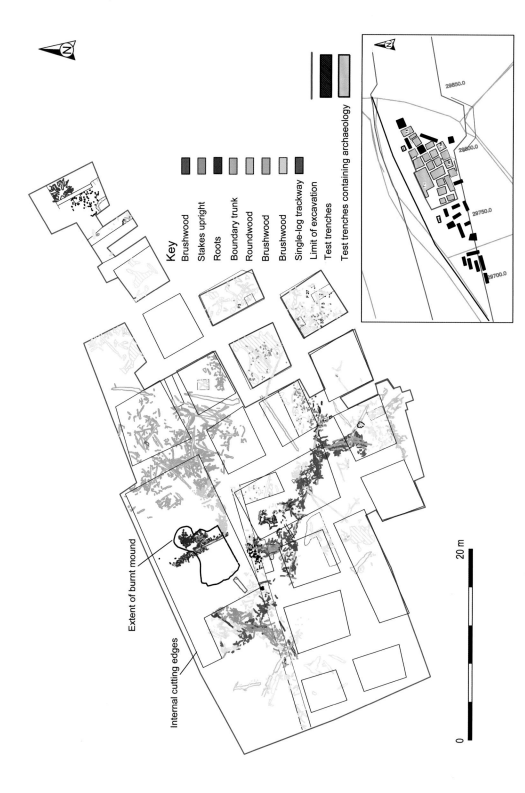

Key

Brushwood
Stakes upright
Roots
Boundary trunk
Roundwood
Brushwood
Brushwood
Single-log trackway
Limit of excavation
Test trenches
Test trenches containing archaeology

Extent of burnt mound

Internal cutting edges

0   20 m

Illus. 4.1.3—Killescragh 2. Plan of the burnt mound and principal concentrations of woodland debris. A length of split-log trackway (red) underlies the burnt mound. Trackways of brushwood and roundwood (blue) lie to the south of it. A haphazard group of worked and unworked wood (green) forms a rough platform east of the mound (CRDS Ltd).

2020 BC (Wk-21342), in the Early Bronze Age. The basal peat throughout this site contained the fallen trunks, branches, rotten tree stumps and roots of ancient woodland (Illus. 4.1.3). Two samples of this unworked, natural wood were dated to 4880–4590 BC (Beta-241472) and 2880–2570 BC (Beta-241475), attesting the presence of woodland in the peat basin over a very long period, predating the burnt mounds. East of the burnt mound, there was a mass of wood debris including some large tree trunks that lay where they had fallen and also some smaller pieces of discarded worked wood, probably associated with the burnt mound. Among this structureless mass, one group of roundwood logs formed a small platform (Illus. 4.1.4). There were toolmarks on several pieces, showing the use of a flat, metal blade.

Illus. 4.1.4—Killescragh 2. A small roundwood timber platform was found among masses of woodland debris east of the burnt mound (CRDS Ltd).

The next phase of activity at Killescragh 2 (Phase 2) was represented by another small spread of burnt mound material. This was deposited after a thin layer of silt had developed over the site and consisted of dark silt, heat-shattered stone and charcoal. A wood sample was dated to 1610–1410 BC (Wk-21341), in the Middle Bronze Age. A half-split tree trunk, 5.2 m long and 0.2 m thick, partly underlay the burnt mound and was supported by several stakes. The stakes had worked ends cut with a metal blade. This was probably a simple walkway giving dryshod access to the mound.

A more substantial trackway (Phase 3) extended south from the burnt mound. Where it was well structured, this was made with roundwood pieces laid longitudinally along the trackway but, elsewhere, seemed to incorporate earlier woodland debris in a more amorphous structure. In all, the trackway was 19 m long and up to 1.8 m wide. Wood samples from this were dated to 1190–926 BC (UB-7241) and 1260–910 BC (Beta-241474), in the Late Bronze Age. A second trackway was recorded close to the southern edge of the burnt mound. It was made with transverse pieces of brushwood and small roundwood logs. The surviving portion was 5.7 m long (east–west) and up to 2 m wide. The structure is undated, but their stratigraphic position within the peat suggests that the two trackways abutting this mound were contemporary.

There were no finds directly associated with the burnt mounds but several objects were found in the peat around the mound at Killescragh 2. These included a yew pin or peg with a bulbous head and tapering shaft, a chert end-scraper and eight other pieces of worked chert waste material.

The changing environment

The area around Killescragh is drained by the Craughwell River system. The two archaeological sites described here were located in wetlands that developed in a shallow basin between the esker and low-lying, dry ground to the south. Samples of pollen, beetles, plant macrofossils and wood, the stratigraphic profiles of peat cores and topographic survey data were all considered in the attempt to reconstruct the changing environment at this site (Illus. 4.1.5). The main episodes saw standing water give way to wooded peatlands, followed by open fenlands, before the lands were finally drained, in the modern period, for pasture.

- Within the floor of the basin there are thick deposits of the sticky blue clay or 'lake marl' commonly found beneath peatlands in central Ireland. This represents a time in earliest prehistory when standing water was present.

- Eventually, because of impeded drainage, the basin became infilled, with water giving way to peat up to 2.45 m deep. Initially, a mosaic of trees, sedges and reeds grew on the basin floor and slopes. The excavation revealed the fallen trunks and old root systems that are relics of this ancient primary woodland.

- In time, the river floodplain became too wet to support trees, and woodland gave way to a more open, fenland marsh environment. Herbaceous plants that favour wetter conditions, such as sedges, became dominant in this period.

- The silt layer recognised in the stratigraphic sequence of the excavated sites was deposited after the demise of the woodland, when the riverside fen was in place. It indicates flooding on the site, perhaps when the Craughwell River overflowed or changed its course.

- Above the alluvial silt, peat accumulation continued in much the same way as before. This open, marshy environment survived until Victorian times, when extensive drainage works allowed reclamation of most of the wetland for pasture.

The combined results of pollen, plant macrofossil, wood and beetle analyses indicate substantial woodland cover in the Neolithic period and Early Bronze Age, with a diverse understorey. This would have been an attractive environment for people, offering a variety of raw materials and food resources. Fossil pollen from the peat at Killescragh 1 suggests hazel-pine woodland was dominant with alder, birch, oak and elm also present. Other tree species, identified from plant macrofossils (fruits, nuts, cones and wood fragments), include willow, ash, bird cherry and yew. Most species probably grew on site. However, trees favouring drier conditions were also identified from archaeological contexts, including oak and ash, and this suggests that small amounts of wood were transported to the site, perhaps from the nearby esker ridge. There were hazelnut shells at Killescragh 2, representing a nutritious and easily available wild food.

The pollen record shows that wild grasses, sedges and other herbs formed the woodland understorey. Damp conditions are suggested by a combination of herbaceous plants that includes

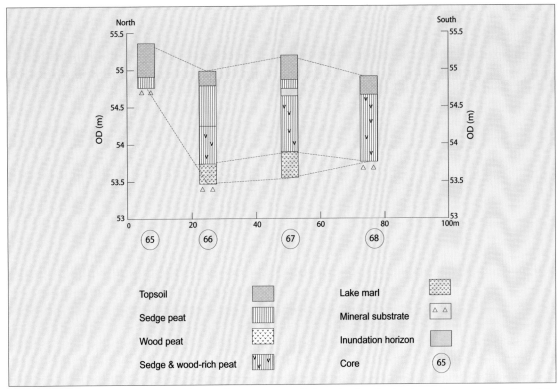

Illus. 4.1.5—Killescragh 2. One of several transects recorded in the bog basin shows the succession from lake marl, via peat, to improved topsoil with grass pasture (CRDS Ltd).

sedges and rushes, some *Ranunculaceae* (e.g. marsh-marigold and lesser spearwort) and aquatic plants, including bogbean, aquatic mint and branched burr-reed. The woodland floor was also home to bramble, raspberry, holly and mosses that thrive in damp conditions.

At Killescragh 2 there were some species of beetle specific to pine, oak, birch and willow, including some bark beetles no longer found in Ireland, and also the first recorded instance of the elm bark beetle (*Scolytus scolytus*) in an ancient Irish context. At both sites, the lower peats yielded a wide variety of ground beetles in combinations that suggest relatively open riverside woodland, but also 'hydrophilic' beetles, which show that the area was susceptible to flooding. Certain dung beetles suggest grazing by large herbivores during the earlier phases of human activity.

Higher in the peat profile, the pollen and plant macrofossil results show a decline in woodland by the Late Bronze Age. Instead, wetland herbaceous taxa, typical of open fen vegetation, became dominant. There are fewer woodland beetles and, instead, more species that suggest floodplain conditions. For example, at Killescragh 2, beetles that inhabit aquatic grasses, sedges and reeds are prevalent in these upper samples, but there are also smaller numbers of taxa representing neighbouring woodland, possibly on the esker. Taxa associated with foul vegetation or plant refuse add to the picture of wet muddy conditions.

In addition to distinguishing between early woodland and later fen, the palaeoenvironmental evidence indicates episodes of woodland clearance, rough grazing and cereal cultivation. Plant macrofossils from the lower peats include grasses, docks, buttercups and sowthistle. These are typical of disturbed ground—probably due to woodland clearance—on the nearby esker and higher dry ground.

Ribwort plantain is an indicator of open, grassland habitats and it is often seen to increase in pollen records following woodland clearance. Dung beetles are present to varying degrees and certain species can be associated with the dung of large herbivores. Domestic and wild animals are represented in the animal bones from Killescragh 1 (cattle, sheep/goat, red deer and pig) and it appears that some of these grazed the environs, as well as being slaughtered and eaten there.

There is a hint of arable farming in a single, charred grain of barley from a peat horizon close to, but earlier than, the burnt mounds at Killescragh 2. Charcoals of hazel, ash and elm were recovered from the same sample—as well as from the burnt mound—and some of these may relate to woodland clearance associated with agriculture.

Ridgeways

The interface of bog and esker created a habitat rich in potential for food, fodder and wood, but the esker itself would also have been important to the prehistoric people of Killescragh as a routeway. Geissel (2006, 99–101) suggests that this particular esker formed part of the Slí Mór—a long-distance routeway between the Atlantic and the Irish Sea that is mentioned in early medieval Irish manuscript sources. It can be assumed, because of its elevated position above flanking bogs and sluggish, meandering rivers, that the esker at Killescragh was used as a local routeway throughout prehistory too. The presence of an early church enclosure by the north flank of the esker suggests that it retained this importance in early historic times. The burnt mounds show that the esker also gave access to lower, wetter ground when it was needed. In addition, it represents the most likely location for contemporary settlement immediately to the north of the burnt mounds. Eskers were once common throughout east Galway. They are a distinctive element of our geological and human history. Unfortunately, they are also a ready source of sand and gravel for modern construction and, consequently, many of them are being quarried away.

4.2 Early medieval mill-races at Caraun More[19]
by Sheelagh Conran & Matthew Seaver

Caraun More is a large townland 4.5 km north-east of the village of New Inn and 9 km north of Loughrea. It contains much bogland but also ridges and knolls with arable soils, mostly supporting pasture grass today. The present excavation site, Caraun More 4, was located on a long, broad esker ridge. The ridge slopes gently from east to west and overlooks wetter ground. Its north side is a steep scarp-face, probably formed by fluvial action in remote antiquity, though there is only a canalised stream lying along the foot of the ridge on that side today. These features in the present landscape are important in interpreting the excavated features on this site, as will be seen.

Our discoveries on the ridge included traces of Early Bronze Age settlement (pits with burnt

---

19 Caraun More 4—Excavation No. E2073; NGR 163612 225276; height 60 m OD; civil parish of Killimordaly; Kilconnell barony; Excavation Director Sheelagh Conran.

sediment, pottery sherds and worked chert), Early Iron Age industry (a hearth and pits with iron slag—possibly bowl furnaces) and, in a much later period, some field ditches and quarry pits of post-medieval date. But the main focus of interest was in features of medieval date, including hearths, field ditches, a grain-drying kiln and an enigmatic group of stone-lined ditches, interpreted as the mill-races of an early medieval grain mill (Illus. 4.2.1). The site of the mill would have been located outside the lands acquired for the road and was not identified, but it seems that the mill-races designed to capture water on the broad, flat back of the ridge and conduct it towards an outfall on its north side. They must surely point to the site of the mill itself, even if it was not excavated.

Illus. 4.2.1—Caraun More 4. Aerial view of the excavation site from north showing early medieval mill-races on the back of a broad esker ridge and the likely location of a mill building, at the foot of the ridge (Markus Casey (†) for CRDS Ltd).

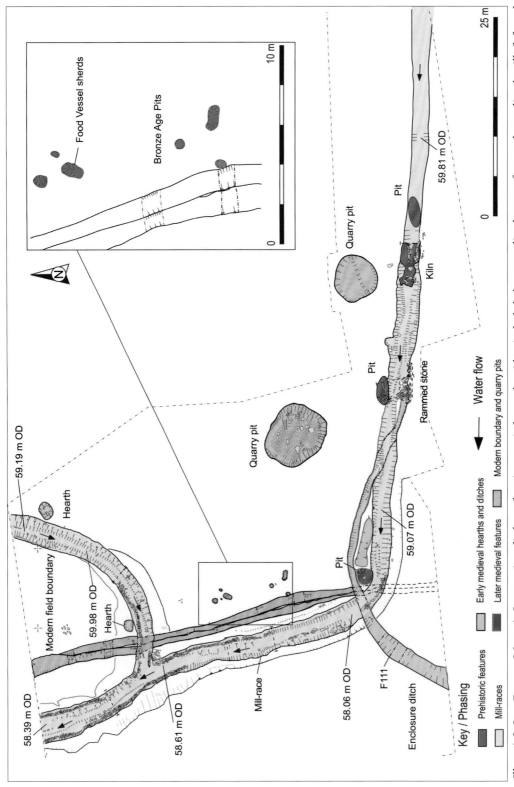

Illus. 4.2.2—Caraun More 4. Intercutting ditches of various periods on the ridge included the stone-lined races of an early medieval mill (left and bottom). A miscellany of other features includes prehistoric pits, early medieval hearths or furnace pits, post-medieval quarry pits and a modern field ditch (CRDS Ltd).

Early medieval settlement

Two hearths were recorded close to the mill channels. One contained charcoal and charred barley and weed seeds. A charcoal sample was dated to AD 430–620 (Wk-21339) in the early medieval period. The other hearth contained charcoal, charred barley, a smaller amount of oats, and fragments of burnt and unburnt bone. This second hearth was not dated but as it was partly cut by one of the watercourses described below it is also likely to be of early medieval date or earlier. An alternative interpretation for the hearths is that they are remnants of simple cereal-drying kilns.

Part of a shallow curvilinear ditch was found in the southern part of the site (Illus. 4.2.2). This was probably part of a large enclosure but, as much of it was either truncated by later features or lay outside the limits of excavation, its full form and extent were not defined. Mostly the ditch was backfilled with soil and stones but it also contained domestic waste from a settlement—a small quantity of animal bone (344 bones or bone fragments), some burnt plant remains and discarded artefacts. Among the animal bones, cattle were most common, followed by sheep/goat, pig, red deer, horse and dog. The age-at-slaughter profile suggests cattle were kept for milk, meat and haulage. The charred plant remains from the ditch were dominated by barley grains. The discarded artefacts included a bone toggle, an iron stickpin and fishhook, a chert scraper and a copper-alloy twisted wire bracelet. One animal bone from the fill (cattle) was dated to AD 593–657 (UBA-10319).

No buildings were discovered but, taken all together, the hearths, enclosure ditch and the dumped materials in the ditch fills hint at an early medieval settlement that pre-dated the stone-lined watercourses but possibly continued alongside them.

Mill-races

The biggest features on the site were two interconnecting, stone-lined ditches (Illus. 4.2.3). One ditch extended about 80 m east–west across the site before turning sharply to exit the site again in the north. It was U-shaped in profile with a scarp or ledge cut into the sides. In the north–south sector, this first ditch was conjoined with a second, curving, stone-lined ditch on its east side. This was also U-shaped with ledges cut into its sides. The two ditches were roughly 3 m wide and up to 1 m deep, widening and deepening towards the north. The upper edges of both ditches were scoured by water and the the ledges cut into the sides supported facing walls or revetments in drystone masonry. A large 'cornerstone' was set within the revetment opposite the intersection of the two ditches and there was a natural spring within the ditches at this point.

The ditches are interpreted as mill-races (i.e. the controlled water channels supplying power to a mill). The mill itself would have been located north of the road corridor, downslope from the excavation site, at the foot of the esker. The inclination of the ditches—east–west then north–south—supports this interpretation. Within the excavated area there was a fall of 1.5 m in the base of the longer ditch and a fall of 0.45 m in the base of the conjoined, curving ditch. The stone revetments would have prevented scouring and the sharply angled course of the larger ditch may also have been intended to slow the current and prevent overwhelming quantities of water from reaching the outfall too quickly. The large stone set opposite the intersection of the ditches might have been part of a sluice-gate, which is one of the eight parts of a mill listed in an early Irish law tract on mills and milling (*De Ceithri Slichtaib Athgabalá*: Mac Eoin 1982; and see also Rynne 2013).

Illus. 4.2.3—Caraun More 4. The stone-lined mill-races from north (CRDS Ltd).

During the excavation, the natural spring at their intersection caused the ditches to fill with up to 0.5 m of water. This would have supplemented whatever source, either a pond or stream, may once have existed beyond the eastern limit of the excavation.

A geophysical survey on lands adjacent to the road scheme indicates that at least one stone-lined ditch continued beyond the limits of the excavation site on the north side of the esker ridge (Elliot 2006). Any mill-house situated here would probably have been one of the tiny timber-built structures typical of the period, with a simple wheel and no gearing. (For an account of a very well preserved mill site found elsewhere on the M6 motorway see *The Mill at Kilbegly* by Jackman et al. 2013.) The mill waters could have discharged onto marginal land or been carried away by the small stream that still exists in that location, albeit now canalised within a modern drainage ditch (Illus. 4.2.1).

After the mill: dumping and crop processing

When the mill-races were abandoned and began to silt up, they became a dumping ground for domestic and agricultural waste. Layers of rotted organic matter were found interleaved with silts, slumps, and stones from the collapsing revetments. Cattle dominated the small assemblage of animal bones, followed by sheep, goat and pig. Burnt barley grains dominated the plant remains, with some weed species and cereal grains of indeterminate species also identified. Discarded objects included a fragment of a lignite bracelet, a worked flint blade and two iron knife blades. The flint is likely to be residual from prehistoric times but the other objects are typical of early medieval settlement sites. Blackthorn charcoal from one of the last episodes of dumping was dated to AD 1260–1400 (Wk-20205). The absence of medieval pottery is notable and suggests that the mill-races had fallen out of use and become infilled before the Anglo-Normans became strongly established in the area, from the mid 13th century.

A grain-drying kiln was built within the accumulating fills of the longer ditch. The kiln was badly disturbed as found, but was probably of keyhole type, with a circular bowl and single flue cut into the earth and lined with stone. Some of the stones had heat fractures and scorch marks. The kiln contained deposits of charcoal and burnt plant remains, interleaved with sands and silts. The cereal grains were mostly oats with a smaller amount of barley and some weed seeds. Carbonised grain from a compact spread of scorched clay in the kiln bowl was dated to AD 1170–1280 (Beta-241007). Further west, a sunken spread of rammed stones formed a 'hard standing' within the same ditch fills. This was possibly a winnowing stage for crop processing.

A working medieval landscape

No buildings were found at Caraun More but it is clear from the food waste and discarded objects found in ditch fills that people lived here on the high, broad expanse of the ridge, and captured its groundwaters to operate a mill. Cattle are still considered the most important economic resource in early medieval Ireland but a growing body of archaeological evidence reveals the importance of tillage also, corroborating the evidence from documentary sources that cereal cultivation formed part of a sophisticated mixed economy (Kelly 1998; Monk et al. 1998, 65–76). Porridges, gruels, breads and biscuits were important components of the early medieval diet, together with dairy products, meat (farmed and hunted), fish and gathered wild foods (Sexton 1998, 76–85). Grain was a food render paid by client farmers to lords who had loaned them animals (Charles-Edwards 2000, 75). Malted barley was an important element of these renders, to provide beer for the nobility. The cereal remains identified from Caraun More were predominantly barley, followed by oats, with a very small incidence of wheat. Social factors influenced the crops that were grown, and wheat, for instance, was considered a high-status cereal; but environmental conditions were influential too and the wetter soils in the West tend to favour barley and oats over wheat. Grain mills could either be owned outright—by nobles or monasteries—or built as joint enterprises between ordinary farmers (Kelly 1998, 245). We do not know the status of the people who built the mill at Caraun More but, despite this, the excavated archaeological features afford tantalising glimpses of the working landscape of early medieval Ireland and the economic strategy that sustained it.

4.3 Burnt mounds in Caraun More[20]

by Nóra Bermingham & Tamás Pétervári

Much of Caraun More townland is low-lying, boggy and prone to seasonal flooding. These are ideal conditions for capturing water in earth-cut pits, in order to boil it with heated stones, which results in mounds and spreads of heat-shattered stone and charcoal in the archaeological record. Three burnt mounds were discovered in Caraun More by test excavations after our geophysical survey had indicated sites of magnetic anomalies. Two mounds were within 50 m of each other—Caraun More 2 and 3—and are dated to the Bronze Age. On another site, 150 m to the west, the mound at Caraun 1 produced a date in the Iron Age. In a very rare instance of a tool being found on a burnt mound site, there was a wooden shovel in the trough at Caraun More 3. All three mounds were partly levelled by tillage and disturbed by burrowing animals.

The mound at Caraun More 1 accumulated within a hollow scarp in a hillside gully (Illus. 4.3.1). There was no underlying trough or pit so some sort of portable container was probably used to contain the heated water. A few fragments of animal bone/teeth were recovered from the mound, representing cattle, horse and dog. A charcoal sample was dated to 760–410 BC (Wk-21777), in the Late Bronze Age/Early Iron Age period. In addition to heat-shattered stone and charcoal, the mound contained lenses of silt, burnt clay and upcast subsoil. This is evidence of abandonment and reworking, suggesting more than one episode of use over a period of time.

There were several pits beneath the Caraun More 2 mound and about its edges, containing silts, burnt sediments and a few fragments of animal bone from cattle and sheep/goat. One of these was interpreted as a trough or water cistern. This was an oblong pit with steep sides and a flat base (3 m long, 1.3 m wide and 0.4 m deep), with a capacity of at least 1,500 litres. This was not the largest pit but had a silty lining, which may have been applied deliberately to the sides and base. A charcoal sample from the mound was dated to 1120–910 BC (Wk-21340) in the Late Bronze Age.

At Caraun More 3 the mound overlay a single, wattle-lined trough and a small hearth, with several small pits arranged in a wide arc north and east of the trough (Illus. 4.3.2). The mound accumulated mostly on the north side of the trough, largely within the area defined by the arc of pits. They were not obviously post-pits but may have supported some sort of screen or enclosure all

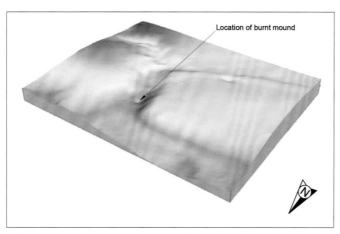

Location of burnt mound

Illus. 4.3.1—Caraun More 1. A digital terrain model of the site highlights the hillslope gully where the burnt mound was located (Cormac Bruton for CRDS Ltd).

20 Caraun More 1—Excavation No. E2074; NGR 164083 225314; height 60 m OD; Caraun More 2—Excavation No. E2055; NGR 164376 225346; height 67 m OD; Caraun More 3—Excavation No. E2072; NGR 164175 225335; height 62 m OD; all in the civil parish of Killimordaly and Kilconnell barony; Excavation Directors Nóra Bermingham (Caraun More 1 and 2) and Tamás Pétervári (Caraun More 3).

the same. The trough was an oblong pit (2.6 long by 1.6 m wide and 1.3 m deep) with a capacity of at least 5,000 litres. It consisted of alder stakes with light brushwood woven between them. The stakes had been cut and pointed with a sharp, flat metal blade. A wood sample (hazel) from the trough was dated to 1667–1393 BC (Wk-21247), in the Middle Bronze Age, making this the earliest of the three burnt mounds identified in Caraun More and—on present evidence—earlier by about three centuries than its immediate neighbour at Caraun More 2. Two animal bones (one red deer, the other unidentified), hazelnut shells and some blackberry seeds were found in the trough. There were also some insect remains, representing species associated with woodlands, with slow or stagnant waters, and two dung beetles, indicating grazing herbivores in the environs.

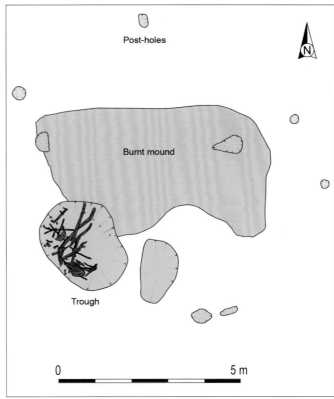

Illus. 4.3.2—Caraun More 3. Plan of the excavation site, showing the mound, pits/post-holes and trough (CRDS Ltd).

Burnt mounds very rarely produce artefacts, other than small quantities of chipped stone tools and waste flakes, so the wooden shovel that was left within the trough at Caraun More 3 is rated quite a find (Illus. 4.3.3). This was carved from a single piece of oak. An oblong blade at one end tapers to form a handle at the other. The blade is about 0.2 m wide and 0.15 m thick, tapering to 0.03 m thick at the edges. It has straight sides and a rounded blade, slightly damaged by use. The shaft is trapezoidal in section and tapers from about 0.06 m (max.) at the blade to 0.02 m at the tip. The shovel could have been used for a multitude of tasks from stirring textiles in a bath of dye to shovelling hot stones into the trough and, after use, clearing out the burnt debris.

Overall, Caraun More offers another tantalising glimpse of burnt mound sites as busy, dynamic places, where a lot of human labour was applied to capture heat energy in stone and transmit this to water. Large quantities of water were boiled in this way—up to 5,000 litres in the wattle-lined trough of Caraun More 3—but, alas, we are no wiser as to why this was done. What we can say about the burnt mounds at Caraun More—and this is a striking feature of many such sites—is that they were used and reused over extraordinarily long periods. In a world without maps or written records, suitable burnt mound sites may have had an importance in the 'remembered landscapes' of prehistory, so that generations widely separated in time retained the lore required to rediscover them when they were needed again.

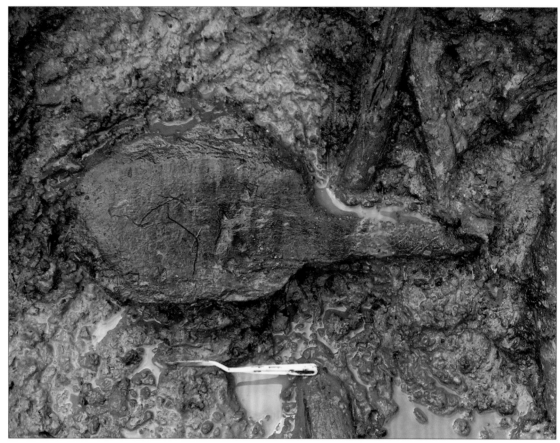

Illus. 4.3.3—Caraun More 3. The oak shovel (E2072:001) as found within the trough (CRDS Ltd).

4.4 Ring-ditches with cremations and inhumations at Cross[21]
by Gerry Mullins & Nóra Bermingham

Today we bury our dead in deep grave pits in orderly rows and mark them with inscribed headstones. Earlier Irish societies did not create large, well-ordered public cemeteries, but they did usually commit the remains of their dead to the ground in one way or another and sometimes marked them with mounds, ditches or standing stones. A hilltop at Cross was used for burials in successive periods and offers a glimpse of changing beliefs and burial practices over a very long period. Cross is 3.5 km south-west of New Inn. The hill is not especially elevated but, at 85 m OD, does command a wide view over the floodplain of the Dunkellin River system (Illus. 4.4.1). The site was identified by geophysical survey and subsequent test excavations discovered a group of ring-ditches with cremation and inhumation burials dating from the Bronze Age, Iron Age and early medieval times.

---

21 Excavation No. E2069; Excavation Director Gerry Mullins; NGR 164775 225449; height c. 85 m OD; civil parish of Grange; Kilconnell barony.

Illus. 4.4.1—Cross. Elevated view of the excavation site showing the main ring-ditch (centre) and smaller ring-ditch (left); the subsoil is striped by early modern cultivation furrows (CRDS Ltd).

Prehistoric cremation pits

The earliest feature on the site was a small cremation pit (Illus. 4.4.2). The pit contained fragments of burnt human bone mixed with ash and oak charcoal, topped up with soil. The bones represented a single adult of indeterminate gender. A range of body parts was represented with skull fragments most common. The total bone weight was 1,487 gm, suggesting that most of the bone fragments were gathered for burial, unlike some other (token) cremation burials recorded along the motorway route. A bone sample gave a date of 1380–1120 BC (Beta-241008). There was a small hearth pit close to the cremation pit but this was not dated and they may be unrelated features.

A thousand years elapsed before the next burials occurred on the hilltop—or, at any rate, within the lands that would be acquired for the new road. Again, these were cremations but, unlike the Bronze Age burial already described, these later burials contained only token amounts of bone, deposited in a group of small, intercutting pits.

One pit contained a small quantity of unburnt animal bone (cattle and sheep/goat), nine sherds of pottery and c. 300 gm of burnt bone fragments—probably human. More bone was found in a cultivation furrow that had cut into this pit. A bone sample from the pit was dated to 360–50 BC (Beta-241006). But the pottery sherds were from a single, coil-built vessel of probable Bronze Age date. Why was this found with Iron Age material? The pot sherds could simply have been disturbed, residual material, accidentally incorporated in a much later pit; but it may be that they were valued as relics of this already ancient burial ground. Other finds from the pit included fragments, variously, of a bone pin, a clay crucible fragment, two small balls or globules of copper alloy and an iron object. We do not know what significance these objects had in the mortuary rites but it seems likely that they were deliberately included in this burial.

The mortuary ritual is glimpsed also in a charcoal-flecked soil spread, which was cut by the pit, and is likely to have been the pyre site. It contained some fragments of burnt and unburnt bone (57 gm) and another small copper-alloy ball. Most of the bone was not identifiable, apart from one fragment of a cattle tibia.

About 10 m north-west of this group there was another cluster of intercutting pits with small amounts of charcoal and burnt bone in the fills. The largest pit contained c. 21 gm of burnt bone fragments. No anatomical elements could be identified, but all of the bone appears to be human. The three smaller pits in this group also contained small quantities of burnt bone. Only a single fragment was positively identified as human—a piece of a tooth crown—but some of the unidentified fragments displayed a type of warping that is characteristic of cremated human bone. None of these pits was dated.

Early medieval ring-ditch burials

Several hundred years elapsed on the hill at Cross before the ground was broken again to receive the remains of the dead. This next period is represented by a group of seven inhumation burials associated with two ring-ditches. The ring-ditches as found were simply circular gullies, but these were probably the truncated remnants of barrows—i.e. small burial mounds with an enclosing bank or ditch, or both. This way of marking graves perpetuated in early medieval times a tradition that was begun thousands of year before, in the Bronze Age. Some of the burials were in graves contained by the ring-ditches, or in the ditch fills, and others were in unenclosed graves close by (Illus. 4.4.2).

The earliest inhumation burial at Cross (Burial 5) was represented by the skeleton of a middle-aged man. A bone sample was dated to AD 252–506 (Wk-21252). This grave was cut or slighted by Ring-ditch 1 and, as the burial clearly preceded it, the ring-ditch may safely be said to date to this same period or later. There was a primary grave in the centre of this ring-ditch, with a young woman's skeleton (Burial 4), and a bone sample from this was dated to AD 337–540 (Wk-21251). An adolescent of indeterminate sex (Burial 3) was also buried within the ring-ditch, but off-centre, and was dated to AD 404–564 (Wk-21250). There were remains of the incomplete skeleton of a young man in the ditch (Burial 6), dated to AD 400–565 (Wk-21253). (The ring-ditch was truncated by cultivation furrows and it is likely that this burial was disturbed by tillage.) Close to the ring-ditch on its south side, a young woman's skeleton (Burial 2) was dated to AD 400–560 (Wk-21249). To the east, the outlying skeleton of an older woman (Burial 7) was dated to AD 382–552 (Wk-21254).

The ring-ditch itself (Ring-ditch 1) was 14.5 m in overall diameter. It was filled with soil that contained stones, charcoal, animal bone, disarticulated human bone, charred cereal grain, and a small number of artefacts—largely unidentified iron fragments. Some of the cereal grain could be identified as barley and wheat. Cattle dominated the small animal bone assemblage, with horse, pig and sheep/goat also represented.

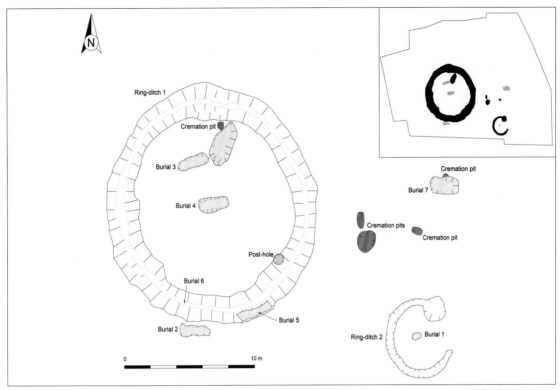

Illus. 4.4.2—Cross. Plan of the ring-ditches, inhumation burials and cremation pits (CRDS Ltd).

A nearby, smaller ring-ditch (Ring-ditch 2) measured only 4.8 m in overall diameter. There was a young child's grave in the centre of the ring-ditch (Burial 1) and a bone sample from this was dated to AD 439–648 (Wk-21248). Again, the ditch was filled with soil and this contained a small quantity of animal bones and two glass beads—yellow and turquoise (Illus. 4.4.4)—probably from an item of personal jewellery. The animal bones represented cattle, sheep/goat and pig.

Altogether, seven individuals were buried at Cross in early medieval times: five adults (three women and two men), an adolescent and a child. The bodies were treated in the traditional Christian manner: they were laid on their backs, fully extended, in oblong grave pits, with their heads in the west. The graves were either simple earth-cut pits or were roughly lined with small stones. 'Pillow-stones' supported the head of the child who was buried in the centre of Ring-ditch 2. There seems to have been no distinction made between different ages and sexes in their treatment in death, though the two individuals buried in the centre of the ring-ditches do seem to have been afforded special consideration, whatever the reason. Were these privileged people from an elite family? To the contrary, analysis of their skeletal remains indicates that they lived hard lives and often experienced want.

One of the women was a young adult and two were adults, one in her middle years or older. The older man was also middle aged and the other was a young adult. The child (Burial 1) was around 2½ years old. Dental and skeletal pathologies were observed on almost all of the skeletons. Lesions on the ribs of the child indicate a chronic disease, possibly leprosy or scurvy. The youngest woman had suffered from anaemia and a trauma to her back. 'Squatting facets' (flattening) on the leg

Illus. 4.4.3—Cross. Excavation of an early medieval skeleton in progress in mid winter conditions (CRDS Ltd).

bones of the older women suggest that they frequently squatted, perhaps while working in the fields or in homes that had no stools or benches. Disease, malnutrition or a parasitical infestation had caused lesions to develop on one woman's skull. The older man suffered from primary degenerative joint disease caused by wear and tear; also, he had suffered a severe blow to the head and recovered from this, although it damaged his skull. The range of dental problems included caries, calculus, periodontitis and enamel hypoplasia. This last is a defect in the tooth enamel that results from stress during its formation, perhaps caused by childhood malnutrition or infection.

Illus. 4.4.4—Cross. Early medieval glass beads. The turquoise bead and the larger yellow bead (Find Nos E2069:167:1 and 166:1) are from Ring-ditch 2. (The smaller yellow bead—E2006:563:1—is from an early medieval context on the hill at Rahally.) (CRDS Ltd).

Customs and beliefs

Isolated cremation pits are common in the Bronze Age and, in the Late Bronze Age especially, they often contain only a token amount of bone. The Late Bronze Age cremation pit at Cross is atypical in having a large quantity of bone, representing most of the remains of one person. He or she was certainly buried with ceremony, following the considerable effort of building a cremation pyre, but was not buried, as far as we can tell, in a designated space shared with other burials.

The Iron Age pits probably do represent a cemetery as there were several of these, some of them intercutting. They contained only token amounts of bone and also had accompanying grave goods. These included a handful of pottery sherds that would already have been very ancient at the time—perhaps recovered from a disturbed Bronze Age burial in the vicinity—and these would have imparted a sense of communion with the ancestors during the burial rites.

The early medieval burials are especially interesting because they occurred at the threshold of the Christian era in Ireland but perpetuate aspects of pre-Christian practice. The bodies were extended, oriented and supine, in oblong graves, in the Christian manner. But they were not buried in consecrated ground, in the shadow of a church, with cross-inscribed grave slabs. Instead they were buried in and around a pair of ring-ditches that echoed the barrow mounds of later prehistory in Ireland. Like the burials recorded in cemetery-settlement enclosures elsewhere on the motorway route—at Carrowkeel and Treanbaun—these graves at Cross reflect a period of transformation in burial practices, which was not completed until the end of the first millennium when consecrated churchyard cemeteries finally became the norm.

The hilltop at Cross was the scene of funerals, cremation pyres and grave-digging in three different periods, widely separated by many generations. It is hardly conceivable that the knowledge of this place survived in oral tradition alone and we can conjecture that the graves of each period were marked in some way. In addition to the features described above there were also several pits that may have held marker posts or stones, though this cannot be demonstrated from field evidence and none of the pits is dated. The site as found presented only the smooth green surface of grass pasture but excavation discovered ring-ditches representing ploughed-down barrows of early medieval date. Who knows what other stones or mounds were still visible on the hill in that period, marking the place as an ancient burial ground and an appropriate place for the early medieval dead to join the ancestors?

4.5 A hillfort, ringforts and field system at Rahally[22]
by Gerry Mullins

Some archaeological sites offer glimpses of past peoples caught in a particular moment—gathered around a fireside or a grave, for instance, or tending their cattle and sowing their crops. The Late Bronze Age hillfort at Rahally offers a much larger view of its world. We believe it was an assembly

---

22 Excavation No. E2006; Excavation Director Gerry Mullins; NGR 165990 225840; RMP No GA086:213; height 97–104 m OD; civil parish of Grange; Kilconnell barony.

Illus. 4.5.1—Rahally. The hillfort from north. It was not prominent in the landscape but yet had panoramic views over the Galway plain (Jerry O'Sullivan).

place and centre of authority within a tribal territory of the Late Bronze Age. Thus it can be said to be a window on a whole society at the threshold of the first millennium BC.

The townland of Rahally straddles a low, broad hill south of the village of New Inn. The hill is on a westerly spur of the Kilreekill Ridge—the elevated ground forming a watershed between the Suck Valley in the east and the Galway plain in the west. Although the hill is not high or steep-sided, at c. 100 m OD (Illus. 4.5.1), it has commanding views over the plain below. The Bronze Age hillfort represents only one episode in the history of this hill. Two other features were previously entered in the statutory Record of Monuments and Places: a small bivallate ringfort crowns the hill summit (RMP GA086:211) (Illus. 4.5.2), and the low earthen banks of a medieval field system (GA086:213) snake across the hill face below. The new road cuts a deep, wide swathe through the hill. It was designed to avoid the ringfort—which overlooks the motorway today—but had a direct impact on the hillfort, the field system and some other features recorded during our investigation of the site.

All in all, our investigations on the hill at Rahally recorded archaeological evidence for over 4,000 years of human activity. A scatter of flint and chert tools attests the presence of people in the Neolithic period or Early Bronze Age. The first permanent physical change to the hilltop was the construction of a large, multivallate hillfort in the Late Bronze Age. A bowl furnace and a fragment of decorative metalwork were dated to the Iron Age. In the early medieval period, in addition to the visible, upstanding ringfort on the summit, our investigations discovered remains of two other circular enclosures—an annex to the surviving ringfort and a second ringfort, on the eastern flank of the hill. There were human burials in both of these enclosures. The previously undated field

Illus. 4.5.2—Rahally. Aerial view of an early medieval ringfort on the hill summit, at the centre of the much older prehistoric hillfort (Markus Casey (†) for CRDS Ltd).

banks were dated to the later medieval period, when at least one of the ringforts may still have been occupied. Broad ridge cultivation furrows and a cereal kiln represented post-medieval or early modern agriculture on the hill.

When discovery of the hillfort was reported to the Department of the Environment, Heritage and Local Government, it was designated a National Monument by the Minister, John Gormley TD. Excavation of the part affected by the road was allowed to proceed under Ministerial Directions. The hillfort is now directly traversed by the new road, in a deep rock-cutting. About 60% of the monument survives, in farmland outside the road.

The hillfort in prehistory

The hillfort was a great circular enclosure, 450 m wide (14.4 ha in area), with four concentric ditches (Illus. 4.5.3 and 4.5.4), an outer double ditch around the hill flanks (Ditches 3 and 4), a middle ditch (Ditch 6) and an inner ditch on the summit (Ditch 5). Despite the very large scale of the enclosure, the ditches themselves were quite modest at up to 4 m wide and 1.5 m deep (max.). There is clear evidence that they were cleaned out or recut in antiquity but they eventually became infilled with silt, slumping and ploughsoil. Among these fills were inclusions of animal bone, prehistoric artefacts, charcoal and pottery.

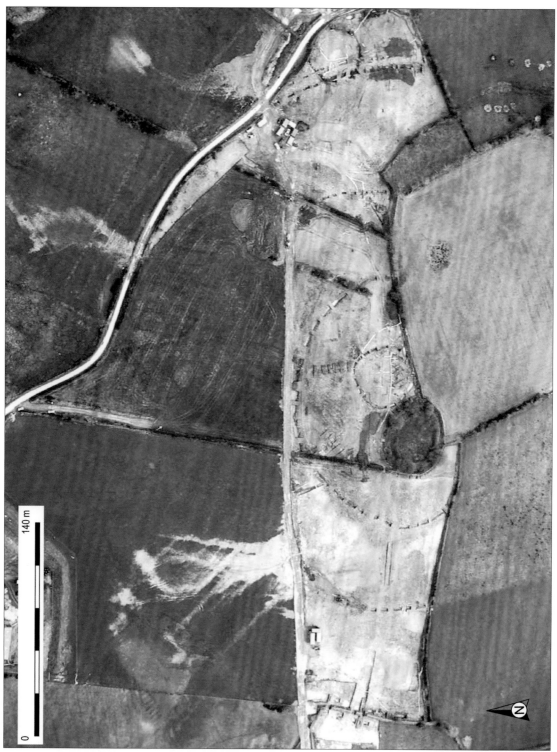

Illus. 4.5.3—Rahally. Aerial view of the partly excavated ditches of the Bronze Age hillfort and much smaller early medieval enclosures (Markus Casey (†) for CRDS Ltd).

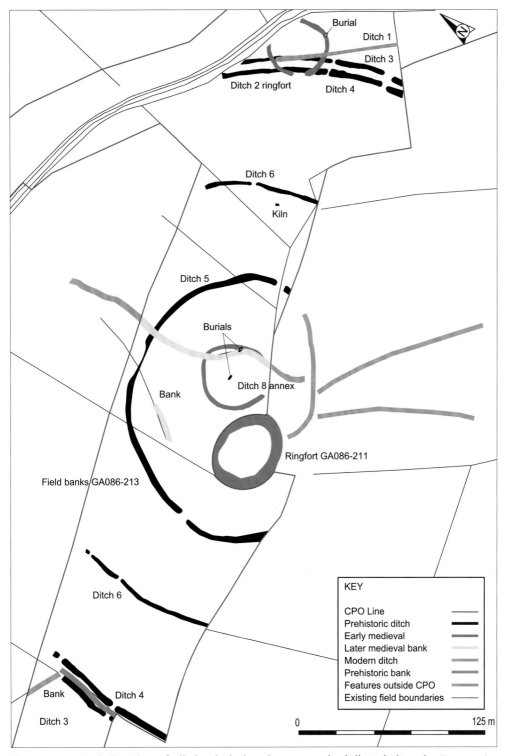

Illus. 4.5.4—Rahally. Plan of all the ditched enclosures on the hill, including the Bronze Age hillfort and early medieval ringforts (CRDS Ltd).

On the north face of the hill part of the innermost enclosure took the form of a scarp in the hillslope, rather than a proper ditch. In the west, there was a remnant of an earth bank between the outer double ditches. This survived because it had become incorporated within the base of a modern field boundary. Although this is the only upstanding evidence of any bank surviving *in situ,* it is probable that banks as well as ditches originally enclosed the whole of the hillfort. In the eastern sector, rubble in the fills of the outer, double ditches, suggests there was a stone revetment to the earthworks on that side.

The entrances to the hillfort were identified as simple breaks or gaps in the enclosing ditches, forming a series of openings aligned to the west and east. They varied in width from 1.4 m to 6.2 m. There were no structural features associated with these gaps (e.g. post-holes for gates or wooden bridges). There may have been corresponding entrances on the north and south sides, but as these would have been outside the lands acquired for the new road, in parts of the hillfort that were not excavated, we cannot be sure of this.

From the combined evidence of radiocarbon dates and artefacts the hillfort can be dated to the Late Bronze Age. Charcoals from the inner, middle and outer ditch fills were dated to 994–827 BC (UB-7244), 1090–900 BC (Wk-22637), and 790–520 BC (Wk-22636), respectively. These dates correspond with pottery fragments from all three ditches, which are also from the Late Bronze Age.

Objects recovered from the hillfort ditches include pottery sherds, a whetstone, antler picks, chipped stone tools in flint or chert, a bone pin fragment, and a polished stone axehead. There were over 450 pottery sherds, mostly from the innermost ditch (Ditch 5), representing altogether at least seven coarse, flat-bottomed, bucket-shaped vessels of Late Bronze Age type (Table 4.5.1). These were probably domestic pots and four of them were charred or scorched, which indicates that they were used for cooking. The chipped stone assemblage included several blades and scrapers of indeterminate date. The polished stone axehead was certainly Neolithic and may simply have been a stray inclusion or could have been a 'relic' found elsewhere and brought to the hillfort in Bronze Age times.

The assemblage of animal bones from Rahally is small, relative to the size of the excavation site. A total of 75 kg of bones or bone fragments was collected, representing a minimum of 5,705 individual specimens. Less than half of this material came from Bronze Age deposits. All of the hillfort ditches contained animal bones and, again, most of this came from the innermost ditch (Ditch 5). Cattle bones dominated the assemblage, followed by pig, red deer and sheep/goat (Table 4.5.2). There were bones of several dogs including one quite large individual, with a shoulder height of 62.5 cm (about the size of a modern Alsatian). Horse, hare, wildcat (probable) and some wild bird species were also represented. There was no fish bone but perhaps this simply did not survive. The red deer bone included shed antlers and some of these were used as picks or rakes, perhaps to dig out the ditches. Charred plant remains were notably absent from all of the ditches, apart from a few grain seeds in the upper fills of Ditch 3. Overall, this indicates that mixed animal husbandry was practised with no significant evidence for arable farming. Cattle were the main meat providers but hunting red deer was important too. In common with the pottery, the concentration of bone in the middle and inner ditches suggests that food was consumed in the central part of the hillfort.

The earthworks of the hillfort were probably still standing in later prehistory but there is very little evidence that it was much used in the Iron Age. A simple smelting furnace provided almost the only evidence for a human presence on the hill in this period. This was found near the summit.

Table 4.5.1—Prehistoric pottery recovered from the ditches of the Late Bronze Age hillfort at Rahally (Ditches 1, 2, 7 and 8 are assigned to other, later periods and did not form part of the hillfort)

Ditch	Location and context	Rim	Body	Base	Frags	Total
Ditch 3	Outer ditch (recut fill)	0	6	0	0	6
Ditch 4	Outer ditch (nil sherds)	0	0	0	0	0
Ditch 6	Middle ditch (basal fills)	0	3	0	0	3
Ditch 5	Inner ditch (basal fills)	24	189	9	221	443
Total	**Hillfort ditches all areas**	**24**	**198**	**9**	**221**	**452**

Table 4.5.2—Animal bones from the enclosing ditches of the Bronze Age hillfort at Rahally, showing the number and percentages of specimens of the main species represented

Ditches	Cattle		Pig		Red deer		Sheep/goat		Total
Ditches 3, 4 (outer)	27	66%	4	10%	7	17%	3	7%	41
Ditch 6 (middle)	170	61%	69	25%	22	8%	16	6%	277
Ditch 5 (inner)	226	55%	59	15%	68	17%	55	13%	408
Total	**423**	**58%**	**132**	**18%**	**97**	**13%**	**74**	**10%**	**726**

It was a simple earth-cut bowl or pit and contained a single lump of copper/copper alloy. Charcoal from the furnace was dated to 200–40 BC (Wk-22643). Small quantities of charred rye grains and weed seeds suggest a possible domestic context, though surplus grain was also an excellent fuel for any sort of hot industrial work and this may also explain its presence here.

The other evidence for Iron Age activity at Rahally is an ornate copper-alloy artefact (Illus. 4.5.5). This was found in colluvium or hillwashed soils on the north side of the hillfort, where the inner circuit of the enclosure was defined by a scarp rather than a true ditch, overlooking boggy ground. The object has no known parallels from Ireland. It was first believed to be a fragment of La Tène metalwork, perhaps part of a horse mount, but Dr Lindsay Allason-Jones of Newcastle University (pers. comm.) has since identified it as a brooch fragment of probable second-century AD date, possibly made in Ireland but with Roman influences. This is strong evidence of a high-status visitor to Rahally at this time.

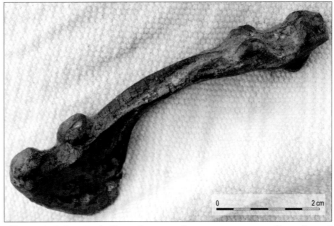

Illus. 4.5.5—Rahally. A second-century copper-alloy brooch (E2006:836:1), influenced by Roman design, was a rare Iron Age find from the site (John Sunderland for CRDS Ltd).

Medieval ringforts and burials

The ringfort that stands on the hill summit today is a small double-banked ('bivallate') enclosure with grass-clad remains of oblong buildings in the interior. It stands outside the lands acquired for the new road and was not excavated. Immediately adjacent to this, however, within the lands acquired for the road, the levelled remains of another small enclosure were discovered. This was defined by a circular ditch, 3 m wide and 1.2 m deep, forming a circular enclosure about 40 m in diameter (Ditch 8). There were vestigial remains of a low earth bank also, inside the ditch. The entrance was probably in the south. The ditch had become infilled with soil and stones. A sample of charcoal from the ditch fill was dated to AD 1020–1180 (Wk-22641), so that the ditch itself was probably dug some time late in the first millennium. (Another sample gave an earlier date, in the Iron Age, but probably represents residual charcoal accidentally incorporated in the ditch: Appendix 1.) Finds from the ditch include a penannular brooch (Illus. 4.5.6), a yellow glass bead, an iron knife blade and worked bone fragments including several bone comb pieces. Food waste from the ditch suggests a mixed farming economy with access to a wide range of resources. The animal bones were dominated by the main domesticates—cattle, sheep and pig—with smaller numbers of horse, dog, deer and (wild) goose bones. There were small quantities of rye, barley, oats and free-threshing wheat grains. This enclosure seems to have been an annex to the bivallate ringfort. Together, they would have formed a highly visible and prestigious homestead on the hilltop.

Another levelled enclosure, about 32 m in diameter, was discovered on the eastern flank of the hill, where it slighted the outermost ditches of the much earlier hillfort. This was probably a small ringfort. It was defined by a narrow ditch, about 2 m wide and 1.25 m deep (Ditch 2). There was no surviving evidence for a bank. The entrance was in the west, facing towards the bivallate ringfort and its annex on the hill summit, 180 m away. There were a few curvilinear gullies and some small pits in the interior, but no clear evidence for buildings or hearths. There was plenty of food waste, however, including animal bones and plant remains. There were charred grains of oats and barley in the ditch. Cattle again dominated the animal bones, with red deer, sheep, horse, pig and dog also present. The deer bones included both shed antlers and butchered bones. A miscellany of artefacts from the ditch contributes to the impression of a prosperous homestead of some sort. The finds were a base metal finger-ring, a glass 'melon bead', iron knife blades and bone comb fragments (Illus. 4.5.7 and 4.5.8).

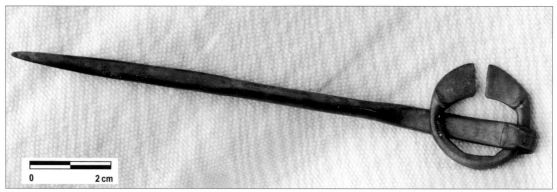

Illus. 4.5.6—Rahally. Copper-alloy brooch (E2006:630:1) from the annex to the early medieval ringfort on the hill summit (John Sunderland for CRDS Ltd).

Charcoal from the ditch was dated to AD 680–890 (Wk-22638) and this corresponds well with a date of AD 680–880 (Wk-22640) for charcoal from a pit in the interior.

There were human burials in both of these newly discovered early medieval enclosures. At the annex to the bivallate ringfort on the hill summit, the remains of a child of about 12 years were found in the ditch. A bone sample was dated to AD 1020–1200 (Beta-241480). The remains of another child, aged 4–6 years, were found near the centre of this enclosure, and dated to AD 990–1160 (Beta-241479). At the

Illus. 4.5.7—Rahally. An early medieval melon bead from a ringfort on the flank of the hill (Jerry O'Sullivan).

other ringfort, on the hill flank, a woman of 36–45 years was buried in the ditch. A bone sample was dated to AD 890–1030 (Beta-241478). In all three cases it is likely that the ditched enclosures—

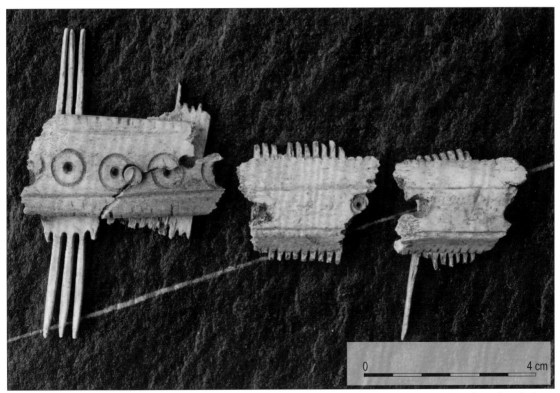

Illus. 4.5.8—Rahally. Fragments of a bone comb (E2006:148:3–16) from an early medieval ringfort ditch on the eastern flank of the hill (John Sunderland for CRDS Ltd).

already many generations old by this time—were no longer used for habitation when these bodies were brought to them for burial. We can only guess at the circumstances. By this time burial in consecrated Christian cemeteries was becoming the norm, so it may be that these were the bodies of slaves or other persons of low status, not considered worthy of burial in consecrated ground.

We may add another ringfort to the enclosures described above. This is on the west side of the hill, in neighbouring Cloonyconaun townland (i.e. outside the lands acquired for the new road). Thus, there were altogether at least four ringforts strung out across the hill. The Late Bronze Age was already a remote period by this time. Was this coincidence or did the ringfort builders value the monumental traces of antiquity they found at Rahally? It is tempting to believe that the place name derives from *Rath Uí Cheallaigh*, a pseudo-historical ancestor of the local Uí Maine kings in early medieval times. The hill may have been the home of a noble family of the Uí Maine and thus a focal place in the social and political landscape of early medieval east Galway, just as it had once been in the Late Bronze Age. At any rate, whoever built and occupied it, the bivallate ringfort on the hill summit seems to claim for itself a status borrowed from the ancient and much larger hillfort, with subordinate or dependent ringforts intervisible to east and west.

Farming the hill in later times

The levelled enclosures described above produced plenty of evidence for livestock and arable farming in early medieval times. Other excavated features, from the medieval and post-medieval periods, produced more evidence that the hill continued to be worked as valuable farmland. It was possible to date the earthen field banks that straddled the north face of the hill to the 11th or 12th century: one of them partly overlay the ringfort annex on the summit and, elsewhere, sealed a spread of charcoal that was dated to AD 1043–1218 (UB-7245). The annex itself seems to have been adapted as a yard or hard standing for farm work in the later medieval period. A dumbbell-shaped cereal-drying kiln, a stony metalled surface, some small post-holes and other minor cut features are all attributed to this phase. Charcoal from the kiln was dated to AD 1215–1285 (Wk-22646), while charcoal from one of the post-holes was dated to AD 1440–1640 (Wk-22645). Another cereal-drying kiln was found on the eastern flank of the hill. This was a keyhole-shaped kiln, built with rough fieldstones within the south-facing slope of a sheltered hollow about 30 m wide. The kiln had scorch marks but no residue of burnt grain to reveal what crop was being processed. The hollow was roughly cobbled and had remnants of a perimeter wall. A well-worn George II halfpenny (Irish issue 1740s) was recovered from the base of the topsoil that formed over the cobbles. Broad ridge cultivation furrows criss-crossed the hill slopes on all sides and are also likely to be early modern in date. Taken all together, this evidence represents a major shift in food production in later medieval and post-medieval times, when livestock—and especially cattle—became less dominant and a more mixed economy was developed, which included large-scale cereal production for the first time.

Commanding the plain

Food production is a primary concern in every society and at all times, so it is easy to understand this last strand of evidence in the archaeological record at Rahally, in the later medieval and early modern periods. But let's return to the start of this story now and ask a harder question. What was the purpose of the great earthwork enclosure built on the hill in Late Bronze Age times, c. 1000 BC?

There are over 80 prehistoric hillforts in Ireland. Only a few of these have been investigated but, despite this, ideas about their classification, date and use are well developed (e.g. Raftery 1972; Grogan 2005). On present evidence, the key period for their construction and use was around 1100–800 BC. With a diameter of 450 m, Rahally is one of the biggest examples known to date. From this gentle, rounded spur of the Kilreekill Ridge, it enjoys commanding views over the plain of east Galway—as far as the Sliabh Aughty range in the south, the Burren massif in the west and the twin hills of Knockma in the north, near the border with County Mayo. It overlooks the meeting point of three baronies—Athenry, Loughrea and Kilconnell—which may themselves preserve the boundaries of ancient tribal territories. It also overlooks the R348 road that crosses east Galway via New Inn and Kilconnell, and which some authors believe perpetuates the ancient route of the Slí Mór (e.g. Gessel 2006). All in all, the site for this hillfort was carefully chosen by people who were familiar with a very wide tract of the landscape and were concerned to have sight of it.

Although the hillfort at Rahally was strategically located, it does not seem to have been a military site. The ditches were slight compared to some other Irish hillforts—such as Haughey's Fort in County Armagh or Freestone Hill in County Kilkenny—and it would have taken a very large and disciplined force to protect the whole perimeter. Nor was it a place of permanent or long-term habitation. Food debris and domestic pottery sherds were found in the ditches but there was no evidence within the hillfort for buildings, hearths or industry of any sort. Setting aside these possibilities, the hillfort must have been built instead as a gathering place for the people who lived within the broad compass of its influence. Perhaps they came for seasonal fairs, religious festivals or the inaugurations of their chiefs—or some combination of these. In any case, it seems that the enclosing earthworks were symbolic rather than functional and intended to define a large public space rather than an exclusive, defensible one. It would have taken a large labour force and a high degree of co-ordination to clear the hill and excavate the ditches. This speaks of a central authority and there can be no doubt that the hillfort, with its panoramic view of the plain and distant hills, spoke loudly of that authority to all the people who inhabited the territory around it.

A pollen profile from Ballinphuill bog: vegetation and land-use history

by Karen Molloy, Ingo Feeser & Michael O'Connell

The raised bog at Ballinphuill is south of the new motorway, about 1 km from the hillfort at Rahally. It is a medium sized bog (1,000 m by 450 m) with deposits up to 12 m thick. Peat has been cut from the margins of the bog but the centre is intact and this is where a peat core was extracted for pollen analysis by the Palaeoenvironmental Research Unit at NUI Galway, as part of the archaeological investigations along the new road (Illus. 4.5.9). The pollen record reflects vegetation and land-use changes within a few kilometres of the basin and at a high temporal resolution. There is a full report on this work on the CD-ROM that accompanies this book. What follows is a summary.

Pre-Elm Decline woodlands: 7000–3850 BC (Zones 1 and 2)

When the record begins at c. 7000 BC (deposits below 782 cm were not investigated), there was complete woodland cover, with pine and elm the main tall-canopy trees (Z 1) (Z and SZ indicate pollen zone and pollen subzone, respectively). A peak in micro-charcoal may reflect natural fires (e.g. from lightning strikes), possibly confined to the bog surface, and is not necessarily due to fires set by Mesolithic people. There are cereal-type pollen but these derive from non-cultivated grasses as cereals had not yet been introduced to Ireland at this time. The expansion of alder (c. 4200 BC) coincides with a substantial pine decline and an increase in oak and elm.

Elm Decline and Neolithic 'Landnam': 3850–3200 BC (Zone 3)

There is a sharp decrease in elm pollen in SZ 3a, but there is no corresponding increase in ribwort plantain (*Plantago lanceolata*)—an indicator of woodland clearance for farming. This suggests that the 'Elm Decline' at Ballinphuill was caused mainly by an elm-specific disease. This was followed by substantial woodland clearance or 'Landnam', carried out by Early Neolithic farmers (c. 3700–3400 BC; SZ 3b). The tall-canopy tree populations were greatly reduced (especially elm and pine, also oak) but hazel values remain high, which suggests widespread hazel scrub. Early Neolithic farming was predominantly pastoral based (cf. Poaceae and *P. lanceolata* curves). A decline in farming at c. 3400 BC resulted in woodland regeneration, initially involving elm and oak (SZ 3c).

Middle and Late Neolithic: 3200–2400 BC (Zone 4)

Reduced farming activity, especially in SZ 4a (c. 3200–2700 BC), facilitated further woodland regeneration. Ash and yew pollen are consistently recorded for the first time, though the contribution by these trees to woodland cover in Z 4, and also later, was never large. The increased pine pollen representation in SZ 4a may reflect pine colonising peat surfaces, a widespread phenomenon during this time in western Ireland. In SZ 4b (c. 2700–2400 BC in the Late Neolithic period), pastoral farming begins to increase once again, though clearances were limited, especially if it is assumed that the decline in elm pollen was caused by disease rather than clearances.

Early and Middle Bronze Age: 2400–1050 BC (Zone 5)

This period of over 1,000 years is characterised by farming activity with fluctuating levels of intensity. The most intensive farming is recorded in SZs 5b and 5d, which span the intervals c. 2300–2050 BC and 1600–1250 BC, respectively. There are several records of cereal-type pollen, though cereal growing was still of relatively minor importance. It is likely that farming was based mainly on woodland pasture (note especially the high values for hazel) rather than open grassland.

Late Bronze Age and Iron Age: 1050 BC–AD 400 (Zones 6 and 7)

In the Late Bronze Age the local landscape assumed a semi-open character for the first time. This is indicated by higher values for non-arboreal pollen (especially Poaceae and *P. lanceolata*) at the expense of tree pollen. An increase in farming was responsible—mainly pastoral farming but with an arable component. There is evidence for disturbance extending onto the bog surface at c. 600 BC (immediately above mid SZ 6a), which may be connected with activity centred on Rahally hillfort. There was substantial woodland clearance in the Middle Iron Age (SZ 6b, c. 300 BC–0). After this (SZ 6c; c. AD 1–200), farming declined again and hazel regenerated strongly and, to a lesser extent, oak, ash and elm During the Late Iron Age (c. AD 200–400; Z7), farming was further reduced, trees regenerated (ash, elm, yew and birch) but hazel declined due, at least in part, to the expansion of tall-canopy trees. This 'Late Iron Age Lull' (LIAL) is a feature of many Irish pollen diagrams.

Historical period: AD 400–1800 (Zones 8 and 9)

Farming expanded, at first slowly, after the LIAL, and was mainly pastoral (SZ 8a). Though trees declined (especially elm and ash), an increase in hazel pollen suggests that farming was extensive rather than intensive. Farming—both pastoral and arable—increased substantially in SZ 8b (AD 600–800). This led to considerable clearance of hazel and the demise of yew and pine. Rye (*Secale*) is recorded for the first time at c. AD 1150 but rye never attained importance. During later medieval times (SZ 8d, c. AD 1250–1500), ash and elm became largely extinct and the oak- and hazel-dominated woodlands were greatly reduced as a result of intensive farming, which included a considerable cereal-growing component. In the post-medieval and early modern periods (Z 9, c. AD 1500–1800), species-rich grasslands expanded at the expense of woodland. Relative to the later medieval period, arable farming declined. The planting of exotics is recorded at the top of the profile (SZ 9b)—seen especially in the *Fagus* (beech) and *Pinus* (Scots pine) curves—reflecting the development of landed estates in east Galway. Overall, however, the uppermost samples (SZ 9b) reflect the open, more or less treeless landscape that characterised east Galway in the 19th and most of the 20th century.

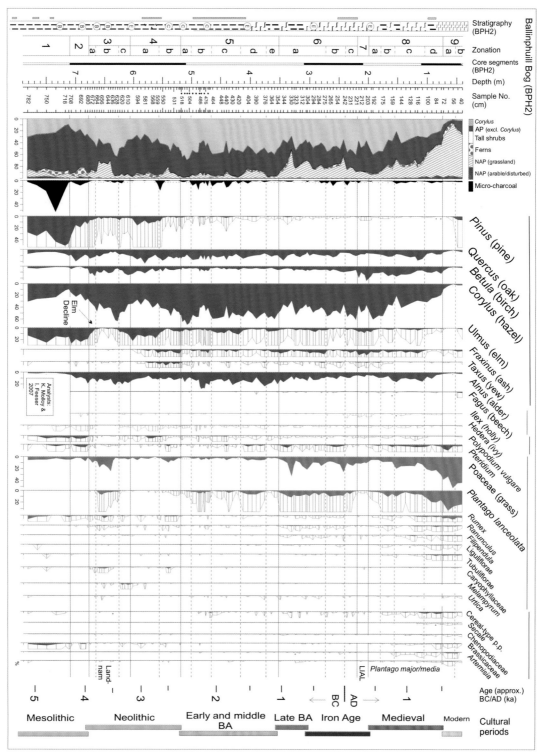

Illus. 4.5.9—Percentage pollen profile (BPH2) from Ballinphuill bog, plotted to a depth scale. For conventions used see the full report on the accompanying CD-ROM (Karen Molloy and Michael O'Connell, NUI Galway).

4.6 Bronze Age cremations and medieval light industry at Rathglass[23]

by Tamás Péterv *ry*

What is a cemetery? Our modern burial grounds are clearly defined public spaces with conspicuous monuments in carved stone over every grave. Groups of small pits with cremated bone were common in the Bronze Age but it is often unclear whether these were marked burials or, indeed, whether all of them were human burials at all. The cremation pits at Rathglass are a good case study in this conundrum. Some metalworker's furnace pits and a cereal-drying kiln of later medieval date were also recorded on this site.

The excavation site at Rathglass was on good land, in well-drained pasture, about 3 km south of the village of New Inn. The archaeological features were dispersed across gently sloping ground of north-west aspect, bounded by a stream at the foot of the slope, about 250 m away. The rising ground south-east of the excavation site is occupied by a rectangular earthwork enclosure of the Norman period and, beyond that, by two early medieval ringforts.

Bronze Age cremation pits

Clusters of small pits were found in five discrete areas (Areas 1–5; Illus. 4.6.1). Some of these contained burnt bone (Table 4.6.1) and pottery sherds. There was no evidence for a covering mound or an enclosing ditch associated with any of the pit clusters, though there were stake-holes and/or post-holes associated with some of them and especially in Areas 3 and 5. There were abraded sherds of pottery in some of the pits in Areas 1 and 3, broadly dated to the Bronze Age or perhaps earlier. A quartzite hammerstone was found in a pit in Area 3. Chipped stone was found throughout the site in small quantities and a pit in Area 5 contained 15 flakes or chunks of struck chert. In general, the quantities of bone were very small. The burnt animal bone in Area 1 is more than likely medieval and human bone was positively identified only in Area 5.

In Area 5, eight pits contained identifiable human bone, and two other pits produced

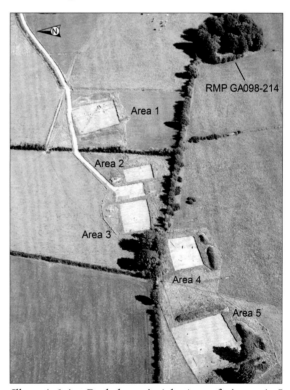

Illus. 4.6.1—Rathglass. Aerial view of Areas 1–5 from west, with the nearby Norman moated earthwork enclosure (GA086:214) at top right (Markus Casey (†) for CRDS Ltd).

---

23 Excavation No. E2121; Excavation Director Tamás Péterv* *ry; NGR 167595 226081 (Area 5); height 82 m OD; civil parish of Killaan; Kilconnell barony.

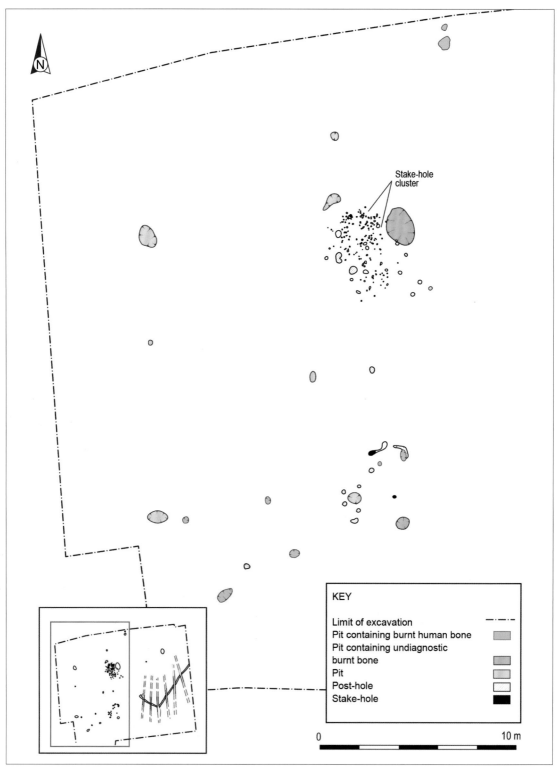

Illus. 4.6.2—Rathglass. Plan of Area 5, showing clusters of post-pits, stake-holes and cremation pits (CRDS Ltd).

unidentified burnt bone (Illus. 4.6.2). Within one small area (diameter 5 m), post-holes and pits—some with burnt bone—were grouped around a dense cluster of 125 stake-holes. A little to the south of these features was another, more dispersed group of post-holes, stake-holes and pits—again, some with burnt bone. (One of these pits contained the struck chert pieces mentioned above.) There were outlying pits to the north and west of these two main concentrations, including two cremation pits to the north.

In Area 5—the only area with identified human bone—charcoal from a deposit sealing a cremation pit was dated to 1260–841 BC (Wk-21241). Several other radiocarbon dates from suspected cremation pits, in Areas 3 and 4, range across a broad time span between the late third and early first millennium BC, with a concentration of dates in the Middle to Late Bronze Age (Appendix 1), so that the burial ground at Rathglass may have been used intermittently over a very long period.

Table 4.6.1—Rathglass. Weight of burnt bone by area and feature type. Human bone was positively identified only in Area 5. Burnt bone from Area 1 is probably medieval

Area	Feature	Weight (gm)
1	Pit (undiagnostic)	< 0.1
1	Pit (animal)	< 0.1
1	Pit (animal)	4.2
1	Furrow (undiagnostic)	0.1
2	Pit (undiagnostic)	1.0
3	Charcoal spread (undiagnostic)	0.3
3	Pit (undiagnostic bone)	3.4
4	Pit (undiagnostic)	< 0.1
4	Pit (undiagnostic)	0.4
4	Pit (undiagnostic)	0.1
5	Pit (undiagnostic)	0.2
5	Pit (undiagnostic)	< 0.1
5	Cremation pit (human bone)	47.8
5	Cremation pit (human bone)	289.9
5	Cremation pit (human bone)	16.1
5	Cremation pit (human bone)	10.5
5	Cremation pit (human bone)	51.0
5	Cremation pit (human bone)	120.7
5	Cremation pit (human bone)	72.7
5	Cremation pit (human bone)	126.5

The evidence here seems patchy but is by no means unusual for this period. The amount of burnt bone found in Bronze Age cremation pits is very often less than 1% of the skeleton (Grogan 2004, 67) and these sites usually include pits with undiagnostic bone or no bone at all. The associated post-pits and stake-holes at Rathglass are open to various interpretations. Some pits could have held marker posts. The stake-holes may have held windbreaks or indicate pyre sites—though the ground around these was not obviously scorched. But it may be a mistake to seek a mortuary explanation for all of the excavated prehistoric features at Rathglass and this returns us to the question: what is a cemetery? In the modern world we set aside dedicated, enclosed spaces for burying the dead. This separation of the living and the dead was not always the norm in antiquity. It is common in the archaeological record of the Bronze Age to find occupation evidence in burying grounds and, conversely, remains of the dead in and around the homes of the living. (For more on this see papers by Grogan 2004 and Cleary 2005.) At Rathglass, it may well be that some of the burnt bone, pottery, post-holes and pits represent transient occupation on the site rather than token burials and associated funeral rites.

Iron and bread in medieval times

Later medieval and modern activity at Rathglass was mostly recorded in Area 1. The shallow, intercutting ditches of relict field boundaries criss-crossed the site. Two small ironworker's furnace pits were recorded and a simple earth-cut cereal-drying kiln. A small assemblage of burnt grain from the kiln was dominated by bread wheat (53%), followed by oats and rye. There were no associated medieval artefacts but dates for charcoals from the furnaces—at AD 1270–1400 (Beta-241477) and AD 1300–1430 (Beta-241476)—agree closely with a date for charred grain from the kiln at AD 1280–1400 (Wk-22891).

A rectangular earthwork enclosure (RMP GA098:214) is located only 120 m from these features. It most resembles a moated earthwork of the Norman period, although it is not in the list of these sites in County Galway compiled by Holland (1994). Moated sites were built and occupied in the 13th and 14th centuries, mainly by minor Norman lords or knights and their English free tenants but also, it has been argued, by high-ranking Gaelic lords (O'Conor 1998, 68, 88). The Norman Lordship of Connacht was established after a major military incursion led by Richard de Burgo in AD 1235, but the O'Kellys were resurgent in their ancestral lands in east Galway from at least the later 14th century (Nicholls 2003, 170, 174). We do not know who built the moated enclosure and farmed the land around about it. Nonetheless, the excavated archaeological features at Rathglass remind us that good, productive land was always valued and used, by whichever ethnic group held sway at a given time.

4.7 Cremation cemetery and palisaded enclosure at Treanbaun[24]
by Marta Muñiz-Pérez & Nóra Bermingham

A small corner of the rural landscape can potentially yield a remarkable variety of archaeological discoveries. The townland of Treanbaun is the outstanding example of this on the present road scheme. Treanbaun is c. 2 km south-east of the village of New Inn. The terrain is undulating, with pasture fields draped over low, dry hillocks among lower-lying areas that are rushy and wet. Excavated features in the townland included a cremation cemetery and palisaded enclosure (Treanbaun 1), a possible lead mine pit and cist burials (Treanbaun 3)—all of prehistoric date, and also an early medieval cemetery-settlement enclosure (Treanbaun 2). None of these features was previously recorded and all of them were identified by test excavations. The cremation cemetery and palisaded enclosure are described in this first contribution on discoveries in the townland.

The site at Treanbaun 1 was located on slightly elevated ground, bounded to north and south by two streams, which converged in the west (Illus. 4.7.1). The excavated features represent a time

---

24 Treanbaun 1—Excavation No. E2064; Excavation Director Marta Muñiz-Pérez; NGR 168384 226200; height 95 m OD; civil parish of Killaan; Kilconnell barony.

Illus. 4.7.1—Treanbaun 1. Aerial view of the excavation site (from north), on elevated ground bounded by converging streams. The surrounding mounds are topsoil heaps from the excavation site (Markus Casey (†) for CRDS Ltd).

span extending from the Early Neolithic period to the Late Bronze Age and include pits, stake-holes and a palisade enclosure (Illus. 4.7.2). Over 1,000 pieces of worked chert and flint were recovered from the site, in addition to fragments of pottery representing 19 vessels. Modern plough furrows had truncated the archaeological features and, consequently, few features could be stratigraphically linked with one another. Instead, a chronological sequence was established using radiocarbon dates, artefact typology and spatial relations.

Neolithic pits (Area C)

The earliest phase of activity was represented by a group of three small pits filled with charcoal-flecked soil, located at the east end of the site in Area C (Illus. 4.7.3). There were pottery sherds and tiny pieces of chipped flint or chert in all three pits, burnt bone (unidentified) in two of them and charred hazelnut shell in one. The pottery included sherds of at least two carinated bowls and two undecorated bowls, as well as sherds from vessels of indeterminate form. Charcoal samples from two pits were dated to 3760–3630 BC (Wk-22707) and 3710–3630 BC (Wk-22706), in the Early Neolithic period. The small amount of burnt bone in the pits suggests token cremation burials, but none of it could be identified as human and—with the pottery sherds and chipped stone—it might just be refuse from a habitation site.

Also in Area C, 11 small pits contained charcoal, burnt bone, hazelnut shells, worked flint or chert and pottery sherds. The amounts of bone in each pit varied from 0.1 gm to 27.8 gm. Most of this could not be identified to species but two pits produced bone that was positively identified as human. Over 60 fragments of a Grooved Ware decorated vessel—a pottery type often associated with ritual deposits—were recovered from one pit. Other pits included flint and chert blades, three *petit tranchet* derivative arrowheads (Illus. 4.7.4), a quartzite hammerstone, a small awl, a thumbnail scraper and numerous pieces of debitage (i.e. the tiny waste pieces that inevitably result from tool-making in chipped stone). A stone axehead, made from green mudstone or shale, was found in the topsoil overlying one pit. The raw material for this was probably sourced on the west coast of Clare or in south-west Mayo. Samples of burnt bone from four of the pits were dated to 2870–2570 BC, 2860–2490 BC, 2570–2340 BC and 2860–2490 BC (Wk-22561–4), later in the Neolithic period.

Bronze Age pits and palisade

Fragments of a vase food vessel of Early Bronze Age date were recovered from a pit in Area A (Illus. 4.7.5 and 4.7.6). It was highly decorated, with incised lines forming a chevron design. There were charred residues on its interior. These vessels typically occur in funerary contexts. There was no cremated bone in the pit in this instance, though it did contain charcoal and some chipped flint and chert. Two nearby pits contained small quantities of worked chert debris and sherds of thin-walled pots.

There were also numerous pits, post-pits and stake-holes of later Bronze Age date in Area A. The pits contained, variously, charcoal, burnt stones and worked chert flakes or knapping debris. The burnt stone included significant quantities of granite—which is not native to the area—and there was also one surface spread of heat-shattered granite with several pieces of worked chert. Evidently, this group of features represents some sort of hot-stone craft or domestic activity. Charcoal

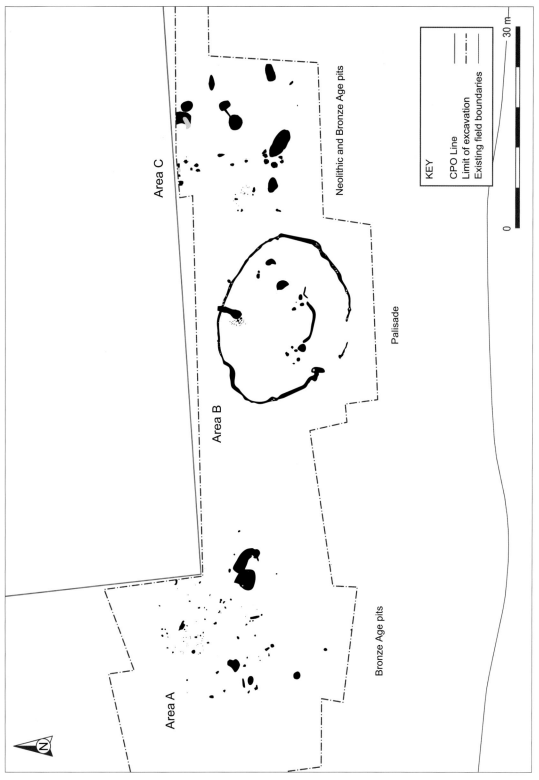

Illus. 4.7.2—Treanbaun 1. General site plan showing principal features in Areas A, B and C, including the palisaded enclosure (centre) (CRDS Ltd).

Illus. 4.7.3—Treanbaun 1. Plan of the excavated features in Area C including Neolithic and Bronze Age pits (CRDS Ltd).

Illus. 4.7.4—Treanbaun 1. Flint petit tranchet derivative arrowhead (E2064:1053:1) from a pit in Area C (CRDS Ltd).

samples from two pits were dated to 1410–1210 BC (Wk-21795) and 1370–1010 BC (Wk-21796). Some of the pits and stake-holes in Area A seemed to form a group of concentric arcs c. 14 m in diameter (Illus. 4.7.6). These pits contained, variously, charcoal flecks, burnt bone (in one pit only), and a small quantity of worked chert. There were no packing stones in any of the pits but they may have held upright timbers of small diameter (< 0.3 m). Charcoal from a pit in the innermost arc was dated to 1260–920 BC (Wk-21797). It is not at all clear that these concentric groups of timber posts formed part of a roofed building. Some sort of ritual post-ring monument is just as likely an explanation. The evidence is slight in either case.

Illus. 4.7.5—Treanbaun 1. Fragments of an Early Bronze Age food vessel (E2064:450:1) from a pit in Area A (CRDS Ltd).

The largest single feature on the site was an oval palisade enclosure measuring 20 m by 25 m (east–west). This was defined by a curvilinear slot-trench in Area B (Illus. 4.7.7 and 4.7.8). There were packing stones and post-holes throughout the trench, indicating the locations of closely set upright timbers, with diameters of about 0.15–0.2 m. Two south-facing gaps indicated entrances. The trench contained pottery sherds from a single vessel of indeterminate form, a fragment of a marble bead, and over 50 pieces of worked stone—mostly simple chert flakes, blades and debitage. Inside the entrance area was a short, curvilinear trench. This was in a likely position

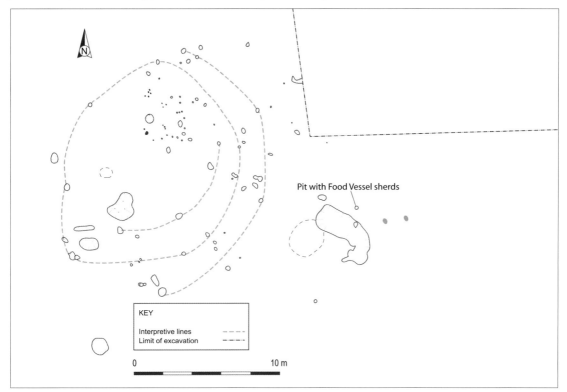

Pit with Food Vessel sherds

KEY

Interpretive lines — — —
Limit of excavation — · — · —

0   10 m

Illus. 4.7.6—Treanbaun 1. Plan of Area A highlighting Early Bronze Age pits and also curvilinear groups of later Bronze Age post-pits and stake-holes (CRDS Ltd).

Illus. 4.7.7—Treanbaun 1. Elevated view of the Middle Bronze Age palisaded enclosure in Area B, from north-west (Hawkeye for CRDS Ltd).

for a timber screen, obscuring the view from the exterior but, unlike the main palisade trench, this contained neither packing stones nor post-holes, so the case is not proven.

There were over a dozen pits of various shapes and sizes inside the palisaded area. One of these contained a few charred grains of wheat and barley. Another contained a saddle quern fragment. The cereal grain was dated to 1610–1440 BC (Wk-22710). This corresponds closely with a date for charcoal from the main palisade

Illus. 4.7.8—Treanbaun 1. Excavation Director Marta Muñiz-Pérez looks critically at the palisade trench and considers her sampling options (Jerry O'Sullivan).

trench, at 1620–1410 BC (Wk-21798). But charcoal samples from two other pits in the interior were dated to 1220–1000 BC (Wk-22709) and 1130–920 BC (Wk-22708). These radiocarbon dates span a very long period in the Middle to Late Bronze Age, perhaps representing two different episodes of activity on the site. Although there was good stratigraphic evidence for post replacement, indicating that the palisade was used and maintained over a long period, an earthfast timber post is unlikely to last more than 20 years, and so it is most unlikely that all of the Bronze Age features in Area B were related to the use of the palisaded enclosure.

The latest phase of Bronze Age activity on this site is represented by two large, shallow pits, joined by a linear cut, in Area C (Illus. 4.7.3). These pits were found in an area of natural hollows, which were largely filled with sterile silts and/or gravels. The pits contained multiple fills of silt, gravel, sand and small quantities of charcoal. There were pottery sherds from a vessel of indeterminate form in one pit, and several flint and chert blades and flakes. Charcoal from the other pit was dated to 910–800 BC (Wk-22705).

A palimpsest of prehistory

A *palimpsest* is the technical term for a parchment or vellum manuscript that has been scraped clean and used again. The original characters leave tell-tale traces that can confuse the meaning of the later script. In archaeological terms, the elevated ground between the two streams at Treanbaun was like this, being peppered with pits and post-holes of various dates, amounting to a confusing story about their purpose.

The Neolithic pits (Area C) contained pottery sherds and worked flint or chert. These could represent an occupation site, but there were also burnt bone fragments in many of the pits, and some of this was identifiably human. The pits containing burnt bone can plausibly be interpreted as a cremation cemetery—albeit with token burials only. The vase food vessel sherds from one pit (Area A) offer a more clear-cut signal of ritual activity, in the Early Bronze Age. These vessels are typically associated with burials, though no associated burnt bone was found in this instance.

At some time between 1600 and 1400 BC an oval, palisaded enclosure was erected (Area B) and was repeatedly repaired or replaced. There were south-facing entrance gaps but a screen wall inside these blocked the view to the interior. What went on here? There is no evidence that this was a roofed building and the control of sightlines from the outside strongly indicates, instead, a defined ritual space. The saddle quern fragment and burnt cereal grain should perhaps be seen in this context rather than as evidence of a simple homestead.

A neighbouring arrangement of concentric post-pits (Area A) was erected many generations later than the big palisade, perhaps some time between 1300 and 900 BC. There is no evidence that it was a roofed building and it is tempting to interpret it as a replacement ritual structure. On the other hand, in the same area and at roughly the same time, granite was collected for use in hot-stone pits, suggesting some mundane craft or domestic activity.

This favoured piece of land within the confluence of two streams was used and reused over many generations. Some of the evidence could correspond with ordinary domestic life but the big palisaded enclosure, in particular, argues that this was a holy place, for a while at least, in the Middle Bronze Age. As was often the case in Irish prehistory, it seems to have been used at various times for both the living and the dead.

4.8 Prehistoric lead mine and cists at Treanbaun[25]
by Marta Muñiz-Pérez

A unique prehistoric site was discovered at Treanbaun 3, at the western end of a low, broad ridge in pasture, about 700 m east of the palisade enclosure and pits described above at Treanbaun 1. The ridge was formed of glacial till with interbedded gravels. The underlying Carboniferous limestone bedrock contained a seam of the mineral galena. Galena in the modern period is especially associated with lead and silver mining. The principal feature on the site was a rock-cut pit interpreted as a prehistoric lead mine (Illus. 4.8.1; Area B in 4.8.2).[26] The mine pit cut through an earlier cist containing cremated bone and pottery sherds. A second cist, containing cremated bone and a chert knife, was inserted into the backfilled mine pit. Some adjacent features are interpreted as evidence of domestic activity on the site. This is unusually early evidence for lead mining and also suggests the 'other worldly' status in prehistory of metallurgy and the places where its raw materials could be extracted from the earth.

Illus. 4.8.1—Treanbaun 3. The mine pit fully excavated, revealing fissured layers of limestone bedrock, from south (CRDS Ltd).

25 Treanbaun 3—Excavation No. E2123; Excavation Director Marta Muñiz-Pérez; NGR 169610 226170 (mine pit); height c. 100 m OD; civil parish of Killaan; Kilconnell barony.

26 The palisade enclosure and pits at Treanbaun 1 are Site 28 on the location map of excavations in Sector 3 of the road scheme. The lead mine and cists at Treanbaun 3 and also an early medieval cemetery-settlement enclosure at Treanbaun 2 (below) are Site 29 on the location map and were excavated under a single Excavation Number.

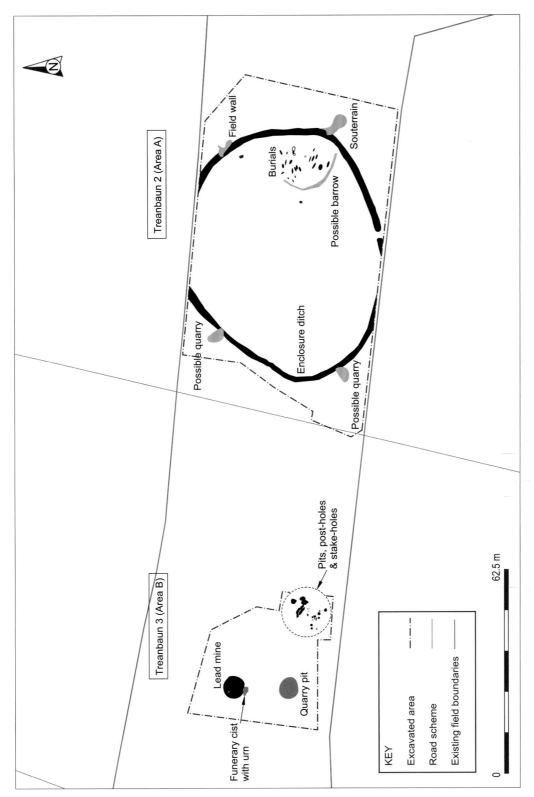

Illus. 4.8.2—Treanbaun 2 and 3. General plan of the prehistoric features at Treanbaun 3 (Area B), showing also an early medieval cemetery-settlement enclosure at Treanbaun 2 (Area A) (CRDS Ltd).

Cist with Beaker vessel

The earliest feature on the site was a cist grave, oblong in plan and 1.04 m long by 0.53 m deep, with an irregular basin-shaped profile. It was lined with stones of various shapes and sizes, all limestone. It seems there was originally a capstone but this was displaced and broken by later ploughing. The cist was also disturbed on the north side where it was cut by the later lead mine pit (Illus. 4.8.3). The cist contained the broken sherds of an inverted pot in a fill of brown soil mixed with cremated bone and some charcoal, charred barley grains and burnt hazelnut shells. The pottery was originally identified as the remains of a highly decorated, Early Bronze Age, food vessel urn but afterwards identified as a Beaker vessel (pers. comm. Mary Cahill, National Museum of Ireland) (Illus. 4.8.4). The cremated bone could not be identified to species but, in this context, is almost certainly human.

Mine pit

The Beaker cist was truncated on its north side by a large, circular pit, 7 m wide and 2.2 m deep (Illus. 4.8.1 and 4.8.3). The pit was cut through several layers of bedrock. The rock was friable and reddened, with heat-affected patches visible in places. The mineral galena was identified—from a visual inspection by geologist Dr Stephen Mandal—within the exposed bedrock in the base of the pit. This suggests that the pit was an opencast mine for the extraction of lead ore.

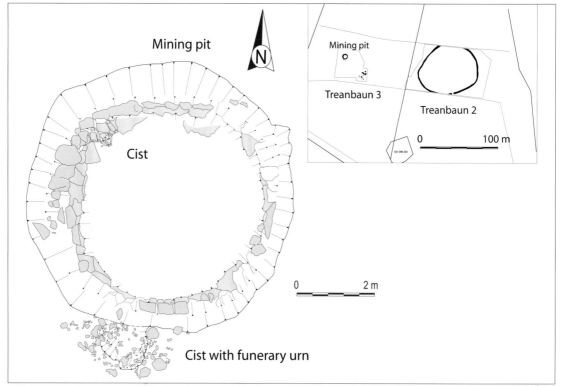

Illus. 4.8.3—Treanbaun 3. Plan of the mine pit, intercut with a cist grave containing cremated bone and Beaker pottery sherds, and with a second, later cist inserted into the soil layers filling the mine (CRDS Ltd).

Illus. 4.8.4—Treanbaun 3. Reconstructed Beaker vessel (E2123:1010:1–24) recovered from the early cist grave and (below) a detail of its decoration (CRDS Ltd).

The pit was reused several times and contained 21 fills, including natural and deliberate deposits, that appear to have accumulated over a very long period of at least 1,000 years. The basal fill was silt with charcoal flecks and small amounts of burnt bone. Charcoal from this fill was dated to 2570–2130 BC (Wk-22715), in the Late Neolithic/Early Bronze Age period. This basal fill was overlain by large stones and silt, almost 1 m deep. (The stones were quarried and probably derived from the initial digging of the pit.)

The stony deposit was covered by several layers of silt with charcoal, occasional stones, and animal bones, chiefly from cattle. These animals were probably butchered and consumed on site. There were also fragments of red deer antler. These can be trimmed to make handy picks, but these fragments were too poorly preserved to say whether they were used in that way at Treanbaun. The upper part of the mine pit was filled with several layers of dumped or redeposited soil, over 1 m deep in total. These contained abundant charcoal, small amounts of burnt bone and a chert end-scraper. They also contained two circular patches of burnt soil indicating in situ burning within the pit. Charcoal overlying one of these burnt patches was dated to 1880–1660 BC (Wk-21793) and charcoal from the uppermost fill of the pit was dated to 1020–840 (Wk-22712) BC. But another charcoal sample from this group of fills produced an anomalously late date of AD 680–870 (Wk-21792). This last sample appeared to be securely sealed within the pit and the anomalous date can possibly be explained by bioturbation resulting in intrusive material (e.g. from burrowing or root action).

Cist burial with chert knife

There was a second cist grave within the mine pit. This was inserted against its inner edge, on the north side, about 1 m from the surface (i.e. within the upper, charcoal-rich fills of the pit). The cist was a rectangular, stone-lined structure, measuring 0.6 m by 0.42 m and 0.33 m deep, with a large, flat, limestone boulder used as a capstone. The cist contained the cremated human remains of a single adult of unknown gender, a chert plano-convex knife and some charred barley grains and hazelnut shells. A sample of the cremated bone was dated to 1920–1750 BC (Wk-22560).

Domestic features?

About 30 m east of the lead mine, a miscellany of pits and stake-holes was recorded, which might represent domestic activity on the same site. There were 19 stake-holes, 21 pits and two linear features. Finds from this area included a quartzite hammerstone of Late Bronze Age type, a well-made chert end-scraper, an almost complete Late Bronze Age bucket-shaped vessel, and fragments of a second Bronze Age vessel of indeterminate form. Several of the pits contained charcoal, flakes of struck chert or pottery fragments. One of the pits was probably a fire pit or hearth: it contained fragments of animal bone and charcoal. Charcoal from this pit was dated to 1000–820 BC (Wk-21794), in the Late Bronze Age.

The sacred rock

The evidence for human activity at Treanbaun 3 spans a very long period, from the earlier cist grave to the closing up of the lead mine with a series of charcoal-rich fills, containing a second cist burial. The mine can roughly be dated to the period 2500–2100 BC, in the Early Bronze Age, on the basis of a radiocarbon date from its primary fills. The first cist, containing Beaker pottery, probably dates to this period too. It seems the mine pit was backfilled soon after it was dug. Some time in the early second millennium BC a second cist grave was inserted into it, this time with no funerary vessel—which is typical of Early Bronze Age cists. Following the insertion of the cist, the pit continued to accumulate fills, until some time in the Late Bronze Age, around the beginning of the first millennium BC. Around this time, domestic activity is implied by the nearby cluster of pits, stake-holes and artefacts found near the mine pit.

The presence of galena in a bedrock layer suggests that the pit was a small opencast mine for lead ore and possibly silver. Cist burials in Ireland and Britain have contained lead finds of jewellery and foil (Hunter & Davis 1994; Waddell 1990, 135), but the dating evidence for the present feature is problematical as the use of lead and silver is unknown in Ireland at such an early date (i.e. 2500–2100 BC). The mineral seam was identified as galena on the basis of a visual examination only (albeit a competent examination by Dr Stephen Mandal), but no detailed analysis was done to put this identification beyond doubt or to ascertain the richness of whatever metal ores it contained. Also, no hammerstones or evidence of roasting or crushing for ore extraction were found. On the other hand, the bedrock faces in the base of the pit were reddened and friable, suggesting fire-setting to weaken the rock, and quarrying could have been done with antler picks and wooden wedges. If obtaining lead ore was the objective at Treanbaun, it is a very significant discovery in terms of early Irish metallurgy. In the absence of any plausible alternative, this remains our interpretation of the pit.

Why were there two cist graves associated with the mine and why were they separated by such a long interval? We do not know who was buried at Treanbaun but the cist graves are a potent reminder that, in the prehistoric world, ritual, industrial and domestic actions were not compartmentalised into separate strands of life. A source of lead ore would have been highly valued. Transforming rock into metal tools, ornaments and weapons was no doubt a sacred and mysterious business, so that the source of the ore was itself a special place, consecrated by burials, and identified in the 'lore of place' passed from one generation to the next over many centuries.

4.9 Medieval cemetery-settlement enclosure at Treanbaun[27]

by Marta Muñiz-Pérez

One of three archaeological sites discovered in Treanbaun townland was a large ditched enclosure (Illus. 4.9.1), of early medieval date, with a group of burials in the south-east quadrant. This type of site is known as a 'cemetery-settlement' (see also Carrowkeel in Chapter 3). The close association of living space with a burial ground provides a new insight into the treatment of the dead in early medieval Ireland, indicating that life and death were not always rigidly separated in that period, and revealing that not everyone was buried in consecrated ecclesiastical burial grounds.

The site at Treanbaun 2 was located on the summit of a low, rounded hill. It was within view of a ringfort and souterrain in the same townland (RMP GA086-233), about 100 m to the south. There is also a ringfort in neighbouring Turksland townland (GA086-236), about 200 m to the east. The excavated enclosure was not a Recorded Monument and did not appear on any earlier map, but first came to light in the course of test excavations on the lands acquired for the new road (Illus. 4.9.2).

Illus. 4.9.1—Treanbaun 2. Aerial view from north of the cemetery-settlement enclosure (left) with adjacent prehistoric features (Treanbaun 3, right). Disturbed remains of another medieval earthwork can also be seen (top) (Markus Casey (†) for CRDS Ltd).

---

27 Treanbaun 2—Excavation No. E2123; Excavation Director Marta Muñiz-Pérez; NGR 169136 226170 (enclosure); height c. 100 m OD; civil parish of Killaan; Kilconnell barony.

Illus. 4.9.2—Treanbaun 2. Test excavations by machine gave way to testing by hand when a human bone was found in the topsoil overlying this previously unrecorded burial site (CRDS Ltd).

Worked chert and flint, and a polished stone axehead were found in topsoil across the site. These are stray finds, echoing the evidence for Neolithic and Bronze Age people recorded elsewhere in the same townland (Treanbaun 1 and 3, above). On the other hand, there were remnants of a later prehistoric ring-ditch inside the big ditched enclosure, and it was probably this feature that attracted further burials when the site became reused in the early medieval period.

Iron Age ring-ditch and cremation

A simple pit and part of a small, shallow ditch were recorded on the highest point of the knoll (c. 105 m OD), within the south-east quadrant of the large ditched enclosure (Illus. 4.9.3). The ditch was a curvilinear remnant only, 1 m wide by 0.3 m deep, with a projected diameter of 18 m. The pit was located at the projected centre of the ditch and contained a charcoal-rich fill with burnt bone fragments. Some of the bone was probably animal but some may also have been human, and the arrangement of these features suggests a token cremation burial at the centre of an earth-cut funerary monument of barrow type (e.g. a low mound surrounded by a shallow ditch), represented in the archaeological records by its surviving ring-ditch. Burnt bone from the pit was dated to 750–390 BC (Wk-22559). This suggests that the early medieval burials were placed within a much older, Iron Age, funerary monument, which would have been visible when the big ditched enclosure was constructed on the same hill.

Early medieval enclosure and souterrain

The early medieval enclosure was defined by a large ditch up to 2.4 m wide by 1.4 m deep, encompassing an area 80 m east–west by 70 m north–south. A narrow causeway of undisturbed natural subsoil formed a crossing point in the southern sector. Otherwise the ditch was continuous. The fills were mostly accumulated soils. There was no evidence for cleaning or recutting. Nor was there any evidence for a bank, though the site was heavily truncated by later tillage so that a bank may once have existed. Charcoal from a primary ditch fill returned a date of AD 600–690 (Wk-22713). Samples from the middle and upper ditch fills gave dates ranging across the eighth to 14th centuries (Wk-21788, Wk-21789 and Wk-21791; Appendix 1). A secondary fill returned a much

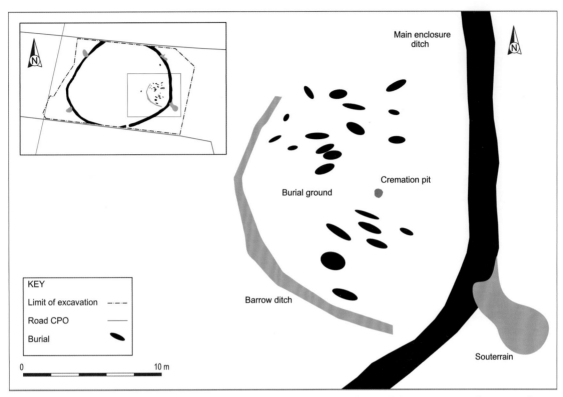

Illus. 4.9.3—Treanbaun 2. Plan of the burials in the south-east quadrant of the cemetery-settlement enclosure, showing the remnant Iron Age barrow ditch and cremation pit (CRDS Ltd).

earlier, Iron Age date of 170 BC–AD 20 (Wk-22711), but this was probably derived from disturbed, residual material incorporated incidentally in this fill.

A fire pit was recorded in the north-east quadrant of the enclosure. This was a large pit (1.25 m long by 0.19 m deep) with a succession of burnt fills, including a burnt pig mandible. Charcoal from one of the fills was dated to AD 660–870 (Wk-22714).

The disturbed remains of a drystone structure were found outside the enclosure, opening into the ditch in the south-east sector. This seemed to consist of a short passage (aligned NW–SE), 4.5 m long, 2.5 m wide and 1 m deep, ending in a circular chamber c. 4.5 m in diameter (Illus. 4.9.4). It was backfilled with mixed stones and earth, with occasional inclusions of charcoal and charred wheat, and a green glass bead. Charcoal from one of the upper fills was dated to AD 1220–1285 (Wk-21790). The structure is interpreted as a simple souterrain. It seems too large to have been a cereal-drying kiln. And even if a kiln could have been operated within the ditch, there were none of the burnt sediments in this structure that are typically associated with kilns. The construction of a souterrain in the ditch is unusual but not unknown and the radiocarbon date from the upper fills is consistent with the known date range for souterrains in Ireland, which broadly spanned the eighth to 13th centuries AD.

The earliest fills of the enclosure ditch contained small amounts of animal bone, representing cattle, sheep/goat, pig, horse, dog and red deer. Animal bones were scarcer in the upper ditch fills. The only artefact recovered from the primary fills was a broken chert flake. Three unidentified metal

Illus. 4.9.4—Treanbaun 2. Recording the fills and disturbed masonry of the souterrain adjoining the south-east part of the enclosure ditch (Ross MacLeod).

objects, several pieces of struck chert, a large loom weight and a bone spindle-whorl were found in the upper fills. Blackberry seeds also occurred in the ditch fills. As described above, a glass bead and some charred wheat grains were found in the souterrain fills.

Other recorded features on the site were unrelated to its occupation in the medieval period and represent changing land use in the post-medieval and early modern periods. These were remnant field boundaries, agricultural furrows and a miscellany of pits, including four larger pits that were probably dug for small-scale gravel extraction.

Burials and commemoration

A group of 31 burials was recorded in the south-east quadrant of the main enclosure, all within the area of the ring-ditch described above (Illus. 4.9.3). The burials were all extended inhumations in simple, shallow grave pits. Most of the burials were aligned west–east, more or less, but skeletons of two young children lay north–south. (These two were also the earliest burials.) The skeletal remains were poorly preserved (Illus. 4.9.5). They represented 15 adults and 16 sub-adults (Table 4.9.1). The majority of the younger individuals died between two and 11 years of age. Ten of the 15 adult burials could be sexed: there were four females and six males. Foetal remains were found in the abdominal region of one young adult female. Nine of the skeletons were radiocarbon dated,

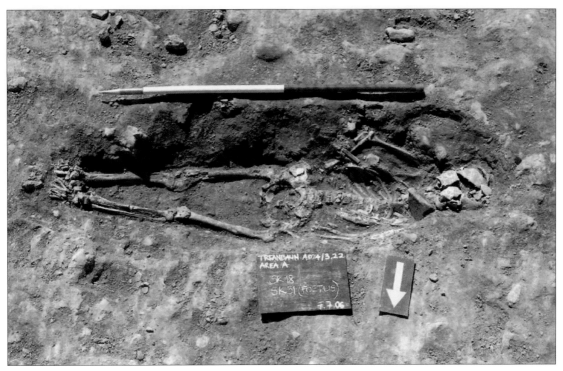

Illus. 4.9.5—Treanbaun 2. Poorly preserved skeletal remains of 31 individuals were found in shallow grave pits (CRDS Ltd).

Table 4.9.1—Treanbaun 2. Sex and age of inhumation burials within the early medieval cemetery-settlement enclosure

Age group	Male		Female		Undetermined		Total	
	No.	%	No.	%	No.	%	No.	%
Sub-adult	—	—	—	—	16	51.6	16	51.6
Adult	2	6.5	1	3.2	2	6.5	5	16.2
Young adult	1	3.2	3	9.7	1	3.2	5	16.1
Middle adult	1	3.2	—	—	2	6.5	3	9.7
Young middle adult	1	3.2	—	—	—	—	1	3.2
Old middle adult	1	3.2	—	—	—	—	1	3.2
Total	**6**	**19.3**	**4**	**12.9**	**21**	**67.8**	**31**	**—**

indicating burial between the late seventh and the early 13th centuries AD, with a concentration of date ranges in the last two centuries of the first millennium (Appendix 1).

  Like the cemetery-settlement at Carrowkeel (Chapter 3), there is teasing but insubstantial evidence that the big ditched enclosure at Treanbaun was a habitation space as well as a burial ground. A space in the south-east quadrant was reserved for oriented burials of mixed age and gender. This was defined by a small internal ditch—probably an Iron Age barrow ditch—that seemed to be focused on a token cremation burial. It follows that the remaining space was not for the dead but for the living and this assumption is supported by limited quantities of food debris and household artefacts recovered from the fire pit, ditch fills and souterrain. On the other hand, other than the souterrain, there was no evidence for buildings of any sort, and it may be that occupation of the site was temporary or seasonal rather than permanent, and involved some ancient ritual of commemoration that had its roots in the Iron Age barrow on the same site.

4.10 Cereal kilns, storage pits and metalworking at Gortnahoon[28]

by Tamás Péterváry

Good land, with well-drained arable soil, is valued and worked in all periods, even to the present day. In such settings it is common to find the footprints of many generations, with prehistoric and medieval features side by side. At Gortnahoon, about 5 km south-east of New Inn, excavations in farmland, on a gentle north-facing slope (Areas 1–4 in Illus 4.10.1), recorded a Bronze Age pottery kiln and some pits, and a series of medieval cereal kilns, metalworking features and three semi-subterranean buildings—possibly stores or workshops.

Illus. 4.10.1—Gortnahoon. Aerial view of the excavation site (Areas 1–4) from north-east, with a modern farmstead (right) (Markus Casey (†) for CRDS Ltd).

---

28 Gortnahoon—Excavation No. E2075; Excavation Director Tamás Péterváry; NGR 171950 225740; height c. 125 m OD; civil parish of Killallaghtan; Kilconnell barony.

Early Bronze Age pottery kiln and pits

The early kiln in Area 1 was a keyhole-shaped pit, with a small, circular bowl (1 m wide) and a long narrow flue (1.12 m long by 0.75 m wide) (Illus. 4.10.2). The sides of the bowl were scorched and it contained several pieces of charred wood, lying side by side, indicating that this was the firing chamber. Two sherds of Early Bronze Age pottery—base sherds of a bowl or vase—were found in the flue and suggest that the kiln may have been for pottery rather than cereal grain. A piece of charcoal from the fuel wood was dated to 2650–2200 BC (Wk-21333).

There were several small pits in Area 2 and one contained a struck chert flake. Charcoal from this pit was dated to 1880–1640 BC (Wk-21335). Four other chert flakes and a chert blade were recovered from across the site, in medieval or modern contexts, and a broken saddle quern was found in topsoil. This amounts to sketchy evidence, at best, for a domestic site, evidently much later than the pottery kiln in Area 1.

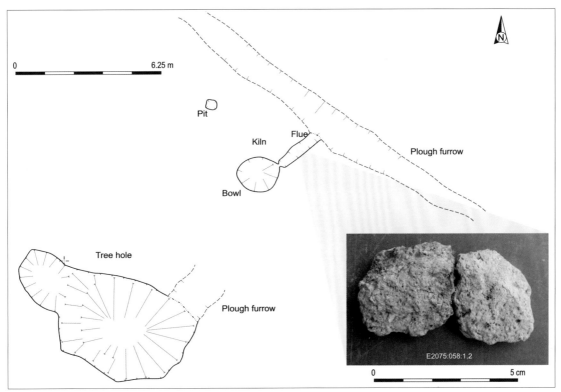

Illus. 4.10.2—Gortnahoon. Plan of the early pottery kiln and other features in Area 1 with (inset) fragments of Bronze Age pottery (E2075:58:1–2) recovered from the kiln (CRDS Ltd).

Medieval crop processing and metalworking

A simple cereal kiln in Area 2 was enclosed by a shallow, pennanular ditch, 0.45 m wide with a diameter of 7.6 m, and opening to the east (Illus. 4.10.3). On the north side, this was cut across a short trench, evidently a remnant of some earlier feature. There was evidence that the ditch itself was

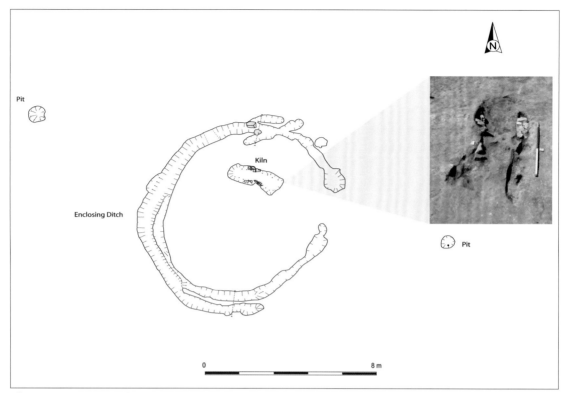

Illus. 4.10.3—Gortnahoon. Plan of the dumbbell kiln and its enclosing ditch in Area 2 (CRDS Ltd).

recut several times. The kiln was of the dumbbell type (i.e. an elongated pit with a narrow waist). It was 2.5 m long and no more than 0.23 m deep as found, with some edge-set stones lining the waist. The firing bowl, in the north-west end, had scorched sides. The kiln was filled with charcoal-rich soils and ash. Bulk soil samples from the fills of the kiln, the surrounding ditch and the earlier short trench contained small amounts of burnt cereal grain, predominantly barley but also some oats and wheat (Table 4.10.1). Grain from the base of the kiln was dated to AD 710–940 (Wk-22888).

Table 4.10.1—Gortnahoon. Cereal grains from excavated archaeological features

Context	Area	Barley	%	Oats	%	Wheat	%	Total
Kiln enclosure ditch	2	73	93.6	2	2.6	3	3.8	**78**
Dumbbell kiln	2	535	98.0	12	2.0	—	—	**547**
Trench (pre-ditch)	2	622	99.7	2	0.3	—	—	**624**
Structure A	3	276	63.0	154	35.0	9	2.0	**439**
Structure B	3	204	4.0	4817	96.0	3	—	**5024**
Structure C	3	8	15.0	26	49.0	19	36.0	**53**
L-shaped kiln	3	364	24.5	1110	74.5	15	1.0	**1489**
Kiln enclosure ditches?	3	75	17.0	348	80.5	10	2.5	**433**

Another kiln, in Area 3 (Illus. 4.10.4 and 4.10.5), was an L-shaped structure with its drying chamber at the north end and the fire pit to the south, partly cut into bedrock. It was 6.25 m in overall length, with a long, narrow flue connecting the drying chamber and fire pit. The flue was slightly off-centre to the drying chamber, which is a characteristic of this type. The sides of the kiln were lined with edge-set limestone slabs but there were no surviving lintels on the flue. Charred oats, barley and wheat were found in the fills, with oats most abundant. A grain sample was dated to AD 1150–1270 (Wk-22889). This is much later than a date (above) from the dumbbell kiln recorded in Area 2 but is corroborated by a copper-alloy stick pin of 13th-century type found in the drying chamber. A small round hammerstone or pounder was also found, among the upper fills.

Like the earlier kiln in Area 2, this L-shaped kiln in Area 3 appeared to stand off-centre within an enclosing ditch. There were only vestigial remains of this, forming short arcs to east and west of the kiln. Cereal grains from the ditch fills were again dominated by oats, which tends to support the interpretation of these ditches as remnants of a kiln enclosure.

A large, irregular pit in Area 3 was interpreted as a possible metalworking furnace (Illus. 4.10.4). It was 1.85 m long by 0.21 m deep, with a flue-like extension on its north side. The fills contained charcoal, animal bone, iron slag and vitrified clay fragments. Elsewhere in Area 3, the fills of two shallow, intercutting ditch remnants contained animal bone, iron slag and a small quantity of burnt grain. Several other small pits in Area 3 also contained slag and the total volume recovered from this miscellany of features weighed c. 28 kg. Cereal grains from one of the intercutting ditches were dated to AD 770–970 (Wk-22890).

Sunken stone-lined structures (Area 3)

Structure A was the earliest of three small, semi-subterranean or sunken buildings recorded in Area 3. They formed a radial group with their entrances in close proximity to one another (Illus. 4.10.4). Structure A was roughly oval in plan and measured 4.3 m by 3.2 m (externally), with a maximum surviving depth of 1 m. It was cut into the bedrock and lined with roughly coursed rubble. An entrance in the south-east had several broad steps descending to the interior, also cut from bedrock. A pair of small, intercutting pits at the entranceway contained cereal grain and a fragment of a rotary quern-stone. The interior was backfilled with soil with frequent charcoal flecks. The basal fill contained charcoal, animal bone, vitrified clay, pieces of iron slag and a small amount of cereal grains (Table 4.10.1). Charcoal from this fill was dated to AD 670–890 (Wk-21334).

The second of the three sunken buildings, Structure B, was oblong in plan, and measured 6.7 m by 3.32 m externally, with a maximum depth of 1.5 m (Illus. 4.10.6). Again, the base was cut into bedrock and the sides were lined with well-coursed, rubble masonry, this time with glacial till used as bonding. The entrance was in the east with several steps cut into bedrock. In the western end the walls had an inward batter, perhaps to support lintels or a corbelled roof. The structure was filled with soil, and tiplines in the fills indicated that this resulted from deliberate dumping rather than gradual accumulation. Fragments of a composite, two-sided bone comb were found lying in the entrance, on the surface of the lowest step. The fills also included small quantities of charcoal and charred grain. Charcoal samples from the basal fill were dated to AD 1020–1190 (Wk-21331) and AD 1030–1220 (Wk-21332).

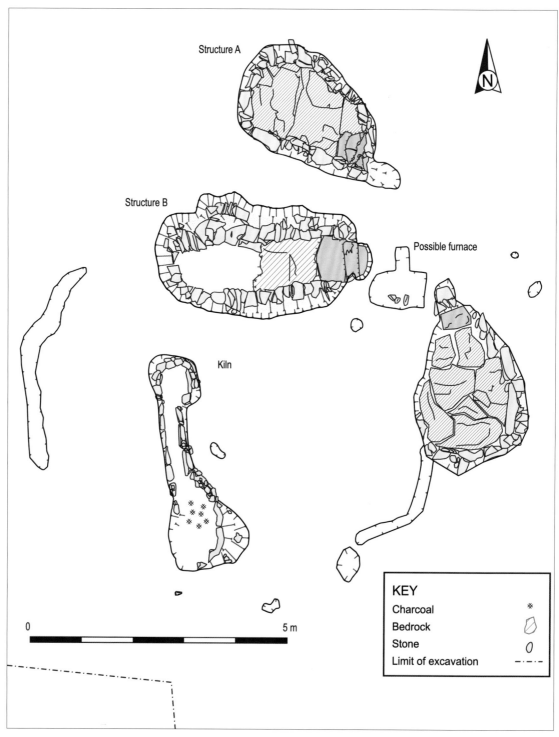

Illus. 4.10.4—Gortnahoon. Plan of Area 3 showing a group of three semi-subterranean buildings (Structures A, B and C), the L-shaped kiln, possible remnants of its enclosing ditch and a metalworking furnace (CRDS Ltd).

The third sunken building, Structure C, was located south-east of Structures A and B (Illus. 4.10.4). It was roughly oval in plan, measuring 4.85 m north–south by 3.82 m (externally) and was up to 0.85 m deep, with its entrance in the north, close to the entrances of the other two buildings. Like Structures A and B, the base and sides of Structure C were cut into bedrock. A slab in the entranceway formed a threshold step. The building was backfilled with stones and soil and, again, this appeared to represent deliberate dumping. The fills contained some animal bones, charcoal, charred grain, iron slag, patches of scorched or oxidised clay and a piece of worked chert. No radiocarbon date was obtained for Structure C.

Illus. 4.10.5—Gortnahoon. L-shaped kiln, from north, and (right) copper-alloy stick pin (E2075:67:5) recovered from the kiln's drying chamber (CRDS Ltd).

Illus. 4.10.6—Gortnahoon. Structure B: one of three semi-sunken, stone-lined buildings possibly used as grain stores (CRDS Ltd).

A centre of manufacturing and food production

We began with the commonplace observation that good land is always valued and worked. The present-day farmstead at Gortnahoon perpetuates many generations of productive work in this location. But the excavated features also offer us some more particular talking points because some of them are unusual or rare of their type.

Early Bronze Age pottery is abundant in the Irish archaeological record but the putative kiln in Area 1 offers a rare glimpse of the potter's art. The charred fuel wood lying in the base of a scorched pit invokes a larger scene of puddled clay, with stiff, wet vessels drying in the sun, and bundles of firewood stacked ready for their final firing in the kiln.

The medieval kilns were of a different sort, being grain-drying kilns but, like the Bronze Age pottery kiln, they represent a concentration of controlled, specialist work at this location, turning raw materials into consumables for the household, the market or perhaps renders to a lord. The two kilns were of different types and were not used at the the same time. The dumbbell kiln in Area 1 was early medieval and the L-shaped kiln in Area 3 was high medieval. Despite this, a passerby in either period would have seen a similar scene. Both kilns had enclosing ditches, indicating kiln yards, and at times the air may have been as thick with the golden dust of the threshing floors as it was with the smoke of the firing pits. Iron slag was also found throughout Area 3 and a small, scorched pit was interpreted as a metalworker's furnace pit, so that the noxious fumes of iron smelting would have added to the cocktail of odours and emissions at times.

The three sunken buildings are puzzling. The first problem concerns their date. A sample from the basal fill of Structure A produced a radiocarbon date spanning the late seventh to late ninth centuries, but two dates from the fills of Structure B span the early 11th to early 13th centuries. Structure C was not dated. Unlike the two cereal kilns, which were of different type and found in discrete areas, these three sunken buildings were closely grouped, with entrances in immediate proximity, and were built to a common design. There can be little doubt that they were made by the same hands and were used at the same time. But what about the discrepancy in the radiocarbon dates? The dated samples came from basal layers in the two structures but do not necessarily represent the period of their use. In fact they are more likely to have been incorporated in soil dumps shovelled in from somewhere in the immediate environs, to backfill the structures after they went out of use.

In their construction technique the three structures echo an early medieval Irish tradition of underground passages and chambers known as souterrains, but they are much simpler than most souterrains and not as deep. Also, souterrains were principally places of refuge whereas these three buildings would have been too small for effective retreat and defence, and the close proximity of their three entrances would have made them hard to conceal. There is no tradition in early medieval rural Ireland of sunken or semi-subterranean dwelling houses, so it is more likely that they had some very specific non-domestic purpose. Given their association with cereal kilns on the same site, grain storage seems a plausible explanation. They probably date to the pre-Norman period, when true souterrains were still being built and used. Like the mill-races at Gortnahoon, they offer a glimpse of organised food production on a large scale in early medieval Ireland.

4.11 Prehistoric campsite and trackway remnants at Ballynaclogh[29]
by Clare Maginness, Jean O'Dowd & Michael Tierney

The depths of a peat basin are dark, cold, wet and airless. As we saw at Killescragh, organic materials are often preserved in these conditions, which would otherwise be lost to the archaeological record. At Ballynaclogh, an alert archaeologist was monitoring peat-stripping at construction stage and called a halt to the work when a piece of ancient worked wood was spotted in a machine bucket (Illus. 4.11.1). The peat basin was about 100 m wide (east–west) and 300 m long. It was overlooked by undulating grass pastures and was transected by the motorway route (Illus. 4.11.2). The uppermost deposits had already been truncated—probably in the

Illus. 4.11.1—Ballynaclogh. This peatland site was discovered when a monitoring archaeologist spotted a piece of ancient wood with the characteristic scalloped cuts of a Bronze Age axe (The Archaeology Company).

course of drainage work or farm improvements, removing all the peat of medieval and later date. But the surviving peat deposits beneath this were rich in evidence for human life throughout the prehistoric period.

In the deepest part of the basin the peat was over 3 m thick. It overlay a layer of thick, white, sticky clay marl. This is a typical deposit in standing water of the early post-glacial period. It is evidence that the basin originally contained a small lake. Radiocarbon dated peat samples indicate that marl began

29 Ballynaclogh—Excavation No. E3874; Excavation Director Michael Tierney; NGR 174132 226476; height 100 m OD; civil parish of Killaghtan; barony of Kilconnell.

Illus. 4.11.2—Ballynaclogh. The peat basin was transected by the motorway and the excavation site spanned the full width of the road corridor. View from east (Jerry O'Sullivan).

to give way to peat from about 7000 BC (Appendix 1). Stratigraphic analysis shows that the lake became a fen, supporting reeds and sedges, with trees around the margins (Bermingham et al. 2010; CD-ROM). (A fen is fed by groundwater, unlike a true bog, which is fed by rainwater.) The peat developed very slowly and did not reach the edges of the basin until about 2000 BC. Throughout this time there were dry intervals when pine trees colonised the surface of the fen, leaving roots and stumps in the peat, which survive to the present day. For much of the time the fen was wet, however, and hence the numerous trackways that criss-crossed it in the Bronze Age (below).

People first enter the scene at Ballynaclogh in the Late Mesolithic/Early Neolithic period, after 6500 BC. These first arrivals are represented in the archaeological record by several small pits and post-holes; over a dozen hearths; faunal remains including cattle, pig, sheep/goat and red deer bones or antler; a rough wooden platform; a large chipped stone assemblage and, curiously, two human teeth (an upper canine and lower molar). Most of this material was concentrated along the margins of the basin on the west side, where it lay sealed by shallow peat, which was still expanding to fill the basin at that time. Later Mesolithic chipped stone tools are coarser and heavier than Early Mesolithic tools, though hunting and gathering would still have been the basis of subsistence. The animal bones confirm that the site was occupied during the period of transition to farming, from around 4000 BC, and some of the bones bear evidence that animals were slaughtered and butchered on the site.

The chipped stone assemblage of 2,839 pieces is the first of its kind in east Galway. In broad terms, this can be classified as Late Mesolithic/Early Neolithic in date, though there are some later pieces. The diagnostic pieces include flakes, blades and hammerstones of probable Late Mesolithic date (Illus. 4.11.3 and 4.11.4), axeheads and projectile heads of Neolithic date (Illus. 4.11.5) and some Early Bronze Age material, including scrapers and projectile heads (e.g. hollow-based arrowhead in Illus. 4.11.5; Illus. 4.11.6). Tool production on site is first indicated in the Neolithic period, by bipolar cores in particular. There is no evidence for Mesolithic tool production, reflecting Little's (2010) observation that Midlands chert assemblages in the Late Mesolithic period typically have very few cores and only a small proportion of manufacturing waste. The raw materials were mostly chert, with some flint and a few pieces in quartz/quartzite, mudstone, sandstone, chert-and-sandstone mixes, and tuff (a form of volcanic ash). Two of the hammerstones were made with a sandstone sourced in West Clare, hinting at a very broad territorial range, or at least long-distance trade, by the people who used them.

The platform was not a single, continuous structure so much as a concentration of wood lying along the western edge of the peat basin. It was built up in layers, forming a rough lattice of charred and split timbers, unworked roundwood branches and lighter branches and twigs. It extended over a total area of about 30 m long by 10 m wide and was 1.6 m thick (Illus. 4.11.7). Doubtless, much of this wood was growing at the edges of the basin and may have simply fallen into the peat, but some of it bore toolmarks made by stone axes (Moore 2010; CD-ROM). A sample from the platform was dated to 3660–3520 BC (Beta-270191), in the Early Neolithic period. (A sample from an upright timber gave a somewhat later date, but this was probably driven into the platform from a higher level, in a later period: Appendix 1.)

Three hearths or burnt spreads were also dated to the Early Neolithic period, at 3930–3660 BC (Beta-270198), 3650–3510 BC (Beta-270197), 3630–3360 BC (Beta-270196). There were altogether 17 hearths and burnt spreads (charcoals or ash) in this horizon. They were mostly discovered in areas of deeper peat and represent episodes when the surface of the fen was largely dry. Several small pits and post-holes were found on the dry western edge of the peat basin but did not form any pattern.

There were remains of up to 16 wooden trackways or *toghers* in the peat. They incorporated various elements including natural (fallen) or felled wood, roughly laid and consolidated with stakes or pegs; a single worked tree trunk or baulk; and remnants of a hurdle or panel of light, woven wattles. These would have provided access across the peat, between the areas of higher, dry ground flanking the basin, but may also have provided access into the fen. For instance, at the time of excavation there was a vigorous freshwater spring in the south-east part of the site. This may have been a major focus of interest in all periods and especially in the Bronze Age, when most of these trackways seem to have been laid down. A worked tree trunk interpreted as part of a trackway was dated to 2880–2580 BC (Beta-270193), in the Late Neolithic period, and another to 1500–1380 BC (Beta-270195), in the Middle Bronze Age. Where toolmarks could be identified they were typical of the small curved axe blades of the Bronze Age (ibid.). A dog was buried within one of the trackways. There is no way of knowing whether this was a ritual burial or simply represents the disposal of a carcass.

Fragments of a carved, decorated, wooden bowl were found within the peat near the western edge of the basin (Illus. 4.11.8). The fragments represent a large round or oval bowl, with a slightly shouldered external profile, and a simple pattern of incised lines on the outer face. It was carved from a piece of hazel wood, probably using small axes or adzes, and finished with chisels and gouges. A sample from the bowl was dated to 780–410 BC (Beta-270194), in the Late Bronze Age/Early Iron

Illus. 4.11.3—Ballynaclogh. Chipped stone flakes (Richard Hinchy).

Illus. 4.11.4—Ballynaclogh. Hammerstone (Richard Hinchy).

Illus. 4.11.5—Ballynaclogh. Chipped stone projectile heads (Richard Hinchy).

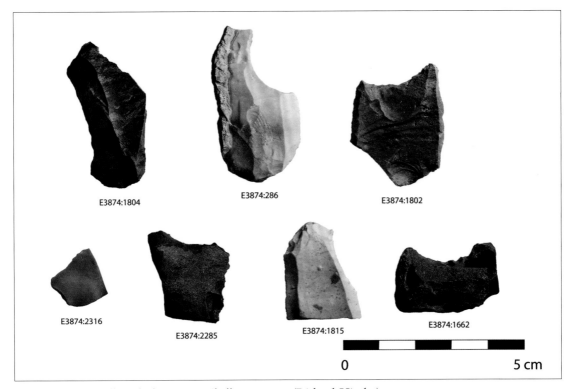

Illus. 4.11.6—Ballynaclogh. Concave/hollow scrapers (Richard Hinchy).

Illus. 4.11.7—Ballynaclogh. A platform of tree trunks and branches was laid at the edge of the peat basin in Neolithic times (The Archaeology Company).

Illus. 4.11.8—Ballynaclogh. Fragments of a Late Bronze Age/Early Iron Age decorated wooden bowl (Find No. E3878:001:010). It is the earliest known Irish example (Richard Hinchy).

Age, making it the oldest dated decorated wooden bowl in Ireland. The base of a rotary quern was also found in this part of the site but cannot be closely dated on typological grounds and could be Iron Age or much later.

A more unusual find was a large dog skull (corresponding in size with a modern Labrador), with a carved wooden stick inserted into its mouth (Illus. 4.11.9). There was a white quartz pebble lying close by, at the same level in the peat. These were found near the spring, in the south-east part of the excavation area, beneath a layer of burnt, friable stone fragments and charcoal, of the sort typically found in Bronze Age burnt mounds. The stick was found in several fragments. It was circular in section and tapered to a round, worn tip. It may originally have been a walking stick or a cattle-drover's staff. It was dated to 160 BC–AD 60 (Beta–270192), in the Iron Age. Again, there is no way of knowing for sure why it was thrust into the mouth of a large dog but, unlike the earlier dog burial (above), this one does seem to represent some sort of ritual gesture or sacrifice.

Other animal bones represent the more mundane business of day-to-day survival. They include red deer antler and a skull fragment, and small quantities of cattle, sheep/goat and pig bones. None of the bone is dated. Some of it was found in a burnt or calcined state in association with the Neolithic hearths. (From the hearths, only a cow phalange and a sheep/goat tooth could be identified.) Among the cattle bones, there were enough peripheral, non meat-bearing bones, and portions of upper meat-bearing limb bones, to indicate that complete animals were present and that slaughtering and primary butchery were carried out at the site (McCarthy 2010; CD-ROM). The bones were smashed and broken, or split, not sawn, but there was no clear evidence for the type of tools used.

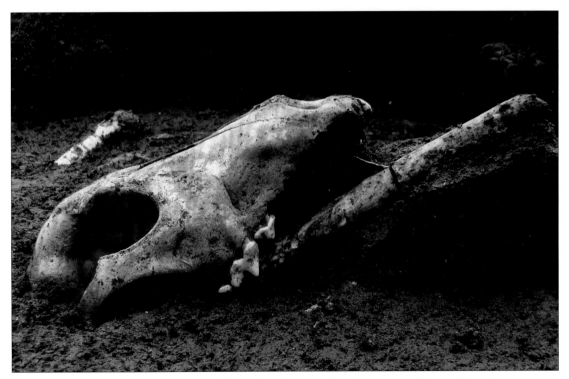

Illus. 4.11.9—Ballynaclogh. The dog skull buried with a carved stick in its mouth bears silent witness to some grim Iron Age ritual whose meaning is now lost (The Archaeology Company).

Journeys, rest and rituals

Why was a small peat basin the focus of human interest throughout long periods of prehistory? This is an unusual location for the discovery of a large early prehistoric chipped stone assemblage, as such finds more often occur on the coast or on major rivers. The Neolithic platform at the edge of the basin represents a deal of effort, even if most of it was natural wood, rearranged and consolidated. It was built up in several layers and—with the hearths and butchery evidence—represents more than a transient presence on the site. In a later period, the Bronze Age trackways represent a concentration of human interest and effort too. So what was the importance of the fen in Ballynaclogh?

We can begin with some prosaic explanations. Peatlands offer fuel (fast-growing scrubwood and pine—peat-burning is not attested in the archaeological record of Irish prehistory), food (wildfowl), building materials (thatching reeds) and clean, fresh water for people and their animals (e.g. the abundant spring in the south-east corner of our excavation site). In later prehistory, the fen at Ballynaclogh would have been part of a mosaic of resources, which included woodlands, pastures and the tillage fields of folk living in nearby settlements. For the mobile hunter-gatherers of earlier periods, Ballynaclogh may have been a well-known place of rest and refreshment in their circuit of the Suck-Shannon catchment, or on seasonal journeys from this Midlands river system westwards to the Atlantic coast (where the stone for two of the hammerstones was sourced).

The fen at Ballynaclogh may also have been part of an 'imagined' landscape of mystery and prayer. In the later prehistory of northern Europe, bog pools and such watery places seem to have been revered, and perhaps feared, and were often the sites of offerings and sacrifices. The quern-stone and the broken fragments of the Late Bronze Age bowl may have been cast into a pool at Ballynaclogh in the course of religious rituals—private or public. The Iron Age dog skull with the carved stick in its mouth was certainly buried with some sort of ritual intent and the burnt stone spread that overlay it hints that roasted or boiled meat—perhaps dog meat—had a part to play in this grim ritual.

4.12 A post-medieval farmstead at Newcastle[30]
by Donal Fallon & Richard Clutterbuck

Newcastle is a large townland c. 4 km WSW of the village of Aughrim, in a low-lying landscape of mixed tillage, pasture, bog and coniferous plantations. An earthwork enclosure stands in a clearing in one of these plantations and is recorded in the statutory Record of Monuments and Places (GA087:196). The new road was designed to avoid the monument as far as possible but did encroach on its south side and hence the excavation described here.

The excavation recorded part of the main embankment of the enclosure, remnants of a small stone building, and elements of an adjoining field system to the south. While the earthwork superficially resembles an early medieval ringfort, the finds recovered suggest that the site was occupied in the 17th and 18th centuries. Documentary sources identify two substantial settlements in the townland in the post-medieval period—the eponymous 'new castle', first noted in the 16th century, and the

---

30 Excavation No. 2076; Excavation Director Sheelagh Conran; RMP No. GA087:196; NGR 175338 226852; height 93 m OD; civil parish of Killallaghtan; barony of Kilconnell.

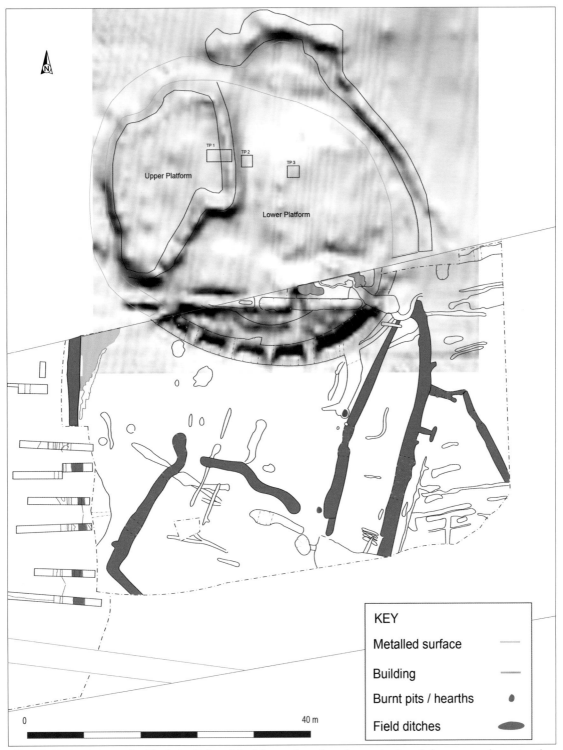

Illus. 4.12.1—Newcastle. Shaded relief model of the earthwork enclosure (top) and the excavated area in plan, showing post-medieval field ditches (brown) and walls (blue) (CRDS Ltd).

home of the Davies family, the principal landowners from the 17th century. Our settlement was probably a small tenant farmstead leased from the Davies, established on the site of a much older earthwork of medieval date.

Earthwork enclosure

The earthwork consisted of a subcircular enclosure 40 m in diameter, with a smaller, slightly elevated sub-enclosure in the interior and a rectangular annex on the north side (Illus. 4.12.1). Excavation within the footprint of the new road—at the south side of the earthwork—found that the enclosure was surrounded by a shallow ditch 1.8 m wide and 1.2 m deep. This had silted up by the late 17th century. A broad band of rubble crossing the ditch may have served as an entrance causeway. The lower fills of the ditch contained a bowl fragment from a clay tobacco pipe, an iron nail, charred grains of oats, wheat and barley, and a small number of animal bones—mostly cattle with lesser quantities of horse, sheep/goat, red deer and pig. An animal bone from the basal ditch fill was dated to AD 1440–1640 (Beta-241005). The uppermost fills included two peat deposits, suggesting the ditch was filled with standing water for some time. The same fills yielded a single sherd of 17th-century North Devon gravel-tempered ware, a clay-pipe stem, charred grains of oats and barley, and frequent animal bone, including cattle, sheep/goat, horse, pig and dog.

Building

A group of wall remnants overlay the enclosure ditch. They stood on a metalled surface of closely packed stones and sand, which in turn overlay the uppermost ditch fills. The walls consisted of larger stones forming the outer faces and a core of smaller stones and soil. They are interpreted as the remains of a single rectangular structure, 8.75 m in overall length (Illus. 4.12.2), which was evidently built after the ditch had silted up. The south side of the building was truncated by a modern field boundary. The north side lay outside the limit of the excavation, but a low bank extending beyond the excavation marked the continuing line of the building on that side. There were at least three possible hearths or 'firespots' and a stone-capped floor drain in the interior. This building was probably a small dwelling, with the floor drain suggesting that it may have been shared with livestock.

Three glass bottle fragments were found in the metalled surface. A coin weight dated 1683 (E2076:219:1) and a small glass bottle fragment were found in the floor drain. Other finds from the excavation site included buckles, horseshoes, blades, nails, glass bottles and sherds of window glass, pottery sherds (Table 4.12.1) and a badly worn copper-alloy William and Mary halfpenny, dated 1692. The coin and coin weight suggests the building was last occupied in the late 17th or early 18th century.

The purpose of a coin weight was to confirm the integrity of its equivalent reference coin—in this case a silver ducatoon valued at six shillings (Westropp 1917, 43–72; and pers. comm. Paul Duffy). The present example is a copper-alloy disc, 30 mm in diameter and 5 mm thick. On one face, the phrase 'ACCORDING TO AUTHORITY' surrounds the appropriate coin weight—XX (20) pennyweights and 16 grains; the reverse side bears a crowned harp with the phrase 'THE STANDARD OF IRELAND' (Illus. 4.12.3).

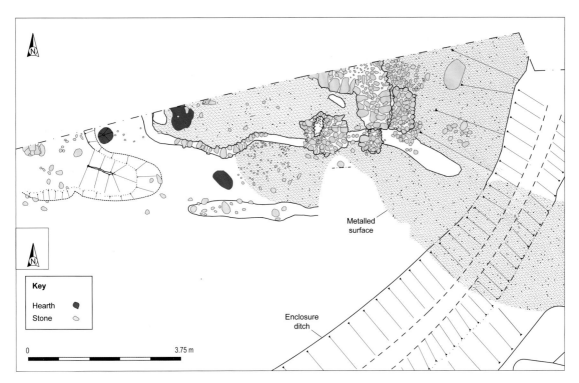

Illus. 4.12.2—Newcastle. Building remains included gable remnants (left and right), a floor drain and several hearths, all set on a metalled surface overlying the infilled enclosure ditch (CRDS Ltd).

Table 4.12.1—Newcastle. Post-medieval and modern pottery from the excavation site

Context	Pottery type	Sherd type	Date range
Topsoil	Glazed red earthenware	1 x body	17th–19th century
Topsoil	Blackware	1 x body	17th–19th century
Topsoil	Unglazed red earthenware	1 x body	17th–19th century
Upper fill of field ditch	Glazed red earthenware	1 x body	17th–19th century
Upper fill field ditch	Cream ware	2 x rim	18th–19th century
Upper fill of enclosure ditch	North Devon gravel-tempered ware	1 x basal	17th century
Metalled surface	Glazed red earthenware	1 x unident.	17th–19th century
Stray find	Glazed red earthenware	1 x body	17th–19th century

Gardens and farmstead

Immediately south of the earthwork enclosure were six narrow, shallow ditches, up to 2 m wide and 1.2 m deep, with mixed silt and clay loam fills. These ditches defined at least three small paddocks or garden enclosures, 15–25 m wide (Illus. 4.12.1). Spade-dug furrows within the enclosures indicated arable or kitchen garden cultivation. Two of the ditches flanked a trackway, 7 m wide, that led

Illus. 4.12.3—Newcastle. Coin weight of 1683 (E2076:219:1) (CRDS Ltd).

towards the building. Further west, a low, stone wall formed a boundary to these small fields. Beyond it was the metalled surface of a path or yard. The only find from among the field ditches was a single sherd of glazed red earthenware of post-medieval date. Animal bone fragments in the ditch fills were from cattle, horse, sheep/goat and birds. Four shallow burnt pits or hearths contained charred cereal grains, mostly oats with smaller quantities of free-threshing wheat and trace amounts of rye and barley. Charcoal from one hearth was dated to AD 1643–1951 (UB-7246). These hearths were possibly the truncated remains of cereal-drying kilns. The pattern of these garden enclosures was distinct from the field boundaries depicted here on the 19th-century Ordnance Survey maps, and they are almost certainly contemporary with the earthwork enclosure and stone building.

A rural tenancy in the 17th century

Who lived in this settlement at Newcastle? East Galway was O'Kelly country in the late medieval period. In 1589 and 1595 'Ffarrdorogh' O'Kelly leased the manor of Aughrim from the Earl of Ormond—including 'Nywcastell' or 'Nywcastle' (Curtis 1933, 125–6). The *Books of Survey and Distribution*, which record land transfers in the 17th-century plantations, record Laughlin Kelly holding Newcastle in 1641 (Simington 1962, 142), before the Confederacy wars of 1641–52. The O'Kellys lost most of their lands under the ensuing Cromwellian regime. In 1684 George Warburton was granted a lease of the manor of Aughrim by the Earl of Ormond and his heirs retained possession throughout the 18th century (NLI D 6, 501).

While the townland name suggests the presence of a castle or some sort of fortified structure, the location of the original 'new castle' is not known. The earliest reference to a castle is in 1574, when William O'Kelly was in possession of the 'new castle' (Nolan 1901, 120). An inquisition in 1611 refers to '*castro de Nova voc. Newcastle*' (RIA Mss 14 D, 4–7). In 1612 King James confirmed the grant of the manor of Aughrim to Thomas, Earl of Ormond, including 'the castle, towns and lands of the New Castle with the half quarter of Newcastle' (Curtis 1933, 126–7). The castle is mentioned in inquisitions detailing the Ormond properties in Aughrim in 1617, 1631 and 1633 (RIA Mss 14 D, 4–7). While the available sources do not describe the castle it was likely to have been a tower house.

A family called Davies became tenants of the Warburtons and were settled in Newcastle before 1665 (NLI Ms GO 182, 20–2). A deed of 1727 indicates their holding of 527 plantation acres included Rayhill, Moat and Knocknagappagh in addition to Newcastle (Registry: Book 86, 111, 59531). Their Newcastle residence was marked on Taylor & Skinner's map of 1777 (1783, 82), suggesting that it was the most substantial house in the townland. The family retained a home in Newcastle until at least 1825 (Kemmis 1826, 357–62). No large dwelling is recorded in the 1843 'Valuation House Books' (NAI MFGS 46), suggesting their home was demolished or abandoned before that date.

Documentary records cast some light on the site of the 'New Castle' and the lost Davies residence. Incumbered Estates Court rentals of 1851 and 1854 map seven sub-divisions of the townland (NAI M 5995 (a & b); NAI M 5402). Three of these, Curragh (or Curraghduff), Clunamore and Newcastle, are identified as separate units in a conveyance of 1666 and deeds of 1727 and 1735 (Irish Record Commission 1825, 80; Registry: Book 28, 128, 38835 and Book 86, 111, 59531). This suggests that the modern townland was an amalgamation of several pre-existing Gaelic units. The survival of Gaelic land divisions under a veneer of modern settlement is a fascinating detail. The 1851 rental names two divisions in the north of the townland as 'Newcastle' and 'Newcastle Farm'. One or both of these may have formed the original 'half quarter' of Newcastle, which contained the 'new castle' and the later Davies residence. The rental map of 1854 shows a large enclosure within Newcastle Farm, about 400 m north-west of our excavation site. A tree-lined avenue led towards this site. (This enclosure is not recorded on the rental map of 1851 or on early Ordnance Survey maps and does not survive on the ground today. The tree-lined avenue is shown on early maps and does survive.) The avenue was perhaps the approach to the Davies home and indicates a possible site for the original 'new castle', within the large enclosure.

The area of the townland containing our excavation site was marked as a separate unit, 'New Village', in the 1851 rental map. The small ditched enclosure, the later stone building and the associated field ditches which we recorded on the site, all lay within a subdivision of New Village called 'Whitehall'. There is no evidence that our settlement was directly associated with the 'new castle' or any residence of the Davies family—who were the principal landowners in the townland in the late 17th and 18th centuries. It seems instead to have been a separate farmstead, with its dwelling house, gardens or paddocks, perhaps incorporating the adjoining medieval earthwork as a stockyard. It is not recorded in any documentary sources we consulted but the material evidence suggests the occupants were small tenant farmers, probably leasing land from the Davies.

We should reconsider the 1683 coin weight in this context. In 1686 the houses of half the population were worth less than 10 shillings. William Petty, a pioneer economist among other things, estimated that 86% of the Irish population had an income of less than two pounds and six shillings in 1672. At this time the vast majority of the population were small farmers and landless labourers, engaging in only a limited number of cash transactions in a given year (Dickson 2000, 110–11). Six shillings would have been a very large sum to a small tenant farmer. It it is hard to believe that the inhabitants of the little house at Newcastle were actively engaged in the emerging cash economy and mercantilism of the early modern world. A coin weight would have been of more use to a merchant, a large landowner or one of his stewards and it remains a puzzling piece of evidence.

Chapter 5

In the Suck Valley (Sector 4)
Cloghalla Oughter to Beagh

River Suck at Pollboy (Studio Lab)

5.1 Burnt mound at Cooltymurraghy[31]
by Mick Drumm, David Fallon & John Tierney

The burnt mound at Cooltymurraghy was discovered in pasture in an area that is prone to seasonal flooding, about 1.5 km west of Aughrim village. It is typical of its kind: a mound of burnt material reduced to a blackened, stony spread by later tillage (Illus. 5.1.1). Its significance is that it now forms part of an emerging map of Bronze Age settlement in the Suck Valley.

The site presented as the classic spread of black sediment, rich in charcoal and friable, heat-shattered stone. The charcoals were from ash, alder, oak, hazel, holly and various small fruiting trees (Pomoideae). A sample of alder charcoal was dated to 2293–2042 BC (UB-7359) in the Early Bronze Age. There was no evidence for an underlying trough or even a big pit capable of holding water so that, if the burnt sediment here does represent water boiled by hot stones, then some portable container must have been used instead. A narrow, irregular channel cut into the burnt spread probably developed from natural drainage across the site. It was also slighted by several cultivation furrows.

Illus. 5.1.1—Cooltymurraghy burnt spread (Eachtra Archaeological Projects).

5.2 A spade mill and lime kiln at Coololla[32]
by Mick Drumm & John Tierney

Archaeology shows us people in the past most distinctly when we see them at work. Two of our newly discovered sites invoked echoes of early modern rural industry in the quiet pasture fields of Coololla, west of Aughrim village. The Melehan River meanders through these fields. It has been reduced in volume by successive regional and local drainage schemes, and in this sector its channel is now deepened between steep-sided banks. In former times, however, it would have had a greater potential to generate water power. One of the newly discovered sites in Coololla was a water-

---

31 Excavation No. E2448; Excavation Director John Tierney; NGR 177716 228176; height 70 m OD; civil parish of Aughrim; barony of Kilconnell.

32 Excavation No. E2477; Excavation Director John Tierney; NGR 178502 228526 (spade mill); 178569 228678 (lime kiln); height 65 m OD; civil parish of Aughrim; barony of Kilconnell.

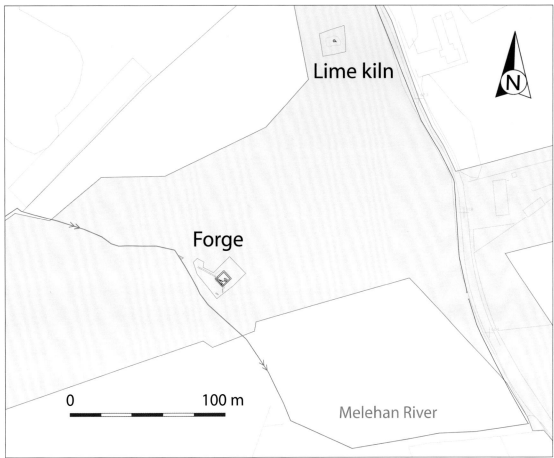

Illus. 5.2.1—Coololla. Location of the spade mill and kiln on the east side of the Melehan River (Eachtra Archaeological Projects).

powered forge, on the east bank of the river (Illus. 5.2.1), of the sort commonly known as a spade mill. A simple lime kiln and associated quarry pits were recorded on a neighbouring site.

Spade mill

The buried wall footings of a rectangular stone building were discovered on the east bank of the Melehan River (Illus. 5.2.2 and 5.2.3). The building was constructed of roughly squared limestone blocks bonded with a lime mortar. It had internal dimensions of 6.4 m (NE/SW) by 5.6 m, within walls 0.7 m thick. The floor was of plain, grey sand.

The mill-race survived over a stretch of c. 25 m. It was a narrow channel, with a single course of roughly dressed limestone blocks on each side, forming a conduit 0.42 m wide and 0.2 m deep. Within the building, the mill-race deepened to 0.9 m. Again, the sides were lined by roughly dressed blocks, but slightly splayed, so that the width of the channel tapered from 0.9 m at the top to 0.7 m at the base. The water was regulated by a sluice-gate, raised and lowered in deep, regular slots cut into two dressed limestone jambs that flanked the exit point. A curious feature of the mill-race was a

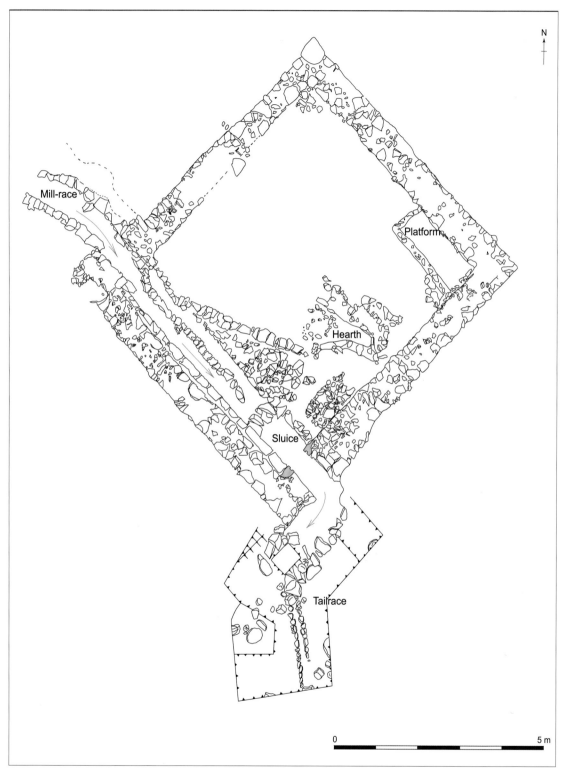

Illus. 5.2.2—Coololla. Plan of the spade mill, mill-race and tail-race (Eachtra Archaeological Projects).

Illus. 5.2.3—Coololla. The remains of the spade mill (from north) indicated a neat, square building in mortared stone (Eachtra Archaeological Projects).

single course of stones, with some red bricks, extending over about 3.5 m in the base of the channel within the building (Illus. 5.2.4). This 'idling channel' may have been intended to slow the passage

of water in the channel or to prevent scouring. Beyond the sluice-gate, the tail-race survived over a distance of 2.6 m. It was up to 0.6 m wide and 0.7 m deep. The surviving sector was stone lined with a rough capstone or lintel at its exit from the building.

Other internal features of the building included a linear stone feature extending across the sandy floor at an angle to the mill-race. It was composed of stone and brick, set in two courses, with large, flat, limestone blocks in the upper course, all bonded with lime mortar. The purpose of this feature is unknown. There was also a hearth, set upon the floor. It was built with heavily mortared small rubble and red brick,

Illus. 5.2.4—Coololla. Mill-race (within the building) and sluice gate, facing south-east (Eachtra Archaeological Projects).

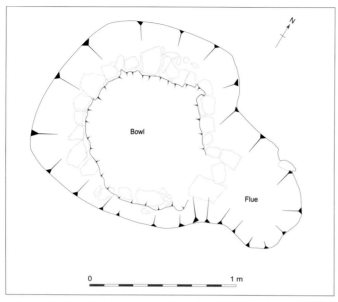

Illus. 5.2.5—Coololla. Plan of the lime-burning kiln (Eachtra Archaeological Projects).

forming side walls splaying outward from a narrow, squared recess to the rear. The walls were scorched and the bricks in particular were badly spalled. The floor of the hearth consisted of compact, scorched clay. Finally, a single course of stones and bricks, L-shaped in plan, was set within one angle of the building, and may have been the foundation for an internal working platform or bench.

Lime kiln

A simple lime kiln was found c. 150 m north-east of the mill. This was a keyhole-shaped kiln, with a round bowl and short flue, built of local fieldstones, within a large round pit, about 7.5 m long by 1 m deep, cut into the subsoil (Illus. 5.2.5). There were deposits of burnt clay with lime or mortar-like inclusions in the bowl—the residue of successive firings. Two small quarry pits were found close by that probably supplied limestone for the kiln.

Rural industry and agricultural improvements

The structural remains at Coololla are too small to represent a mill. A water-powered forge seems a more likely interpretation, and this is supported by the presence of a hearth. These forges were often called 'spade mills' because they were used for making spades, which remained the main implements of cultivation in the West of Ireland before the Famine. This preference for spade-dug tillage in the West is explained by Bell & Watson (2008, 83–96) but can be summarised here. Labour was cheap and plentiful, and the regional drainage schemes that would change the ground conditions for agriculture had not yet commenced. In these circumstances, broad ridges dug by hired labour were often preferred to the narrow ridges formed by ploughing. The soil in these broad ridges tended to be drier and warmer and therefore produced a better crop at harvest time, offsetting the expense of tilling the land by hand. The market demand for the Coololla mill products was probably from agricultural labourers who worked the land on tenanted farmsteads and also hired their labour to the larger estates.

Most recorded spade mills were small, with dimensions ranging from 20 ft to 30 ft in length and from 15 ft to 25 ft in width, so the Coololla building, at roughly 25 ft by 23 ft (7.8 m by 7 m), fits into the known size range for spade mills. The mills often consisted simply of a water-powered tilt hammer and a forge. The smaller examples consisted of the mill building alone, with the tools being finished off in separate forges at sites removed from the mill. As only one building was found at Coololla, this is probably what happened at this site. The operation of a spade mill is described by Gailey (1982, 10) as follows:

> The hydraulic tilt hammer consisted of a pivoted beam, carrying on one end an iron hammer head … Activation of the hammer was by the cams of a cam-wheel hitting against a metal plate fixed in the end of a hammer beam opposite the head. Each cam in turn came into contact with the plate which … was depressed downwards and … its own weight brought the head down to strike on an anvil fixed in the ground below.

Spade mills are known in Ireland from at least the 1750s. However, most recorded examples date to the 19th century, though there were still some in operation in the early 20th century (Rynne 2006, 268–70). A large number were built during the Napoleonic Wars, when demand for Irish grain exports was high, but the ensuing depression meant that many small mills were already out of business by the 1830s. Indeed, some spade mills were speculative business ventures that survived no longer than a decade because there had never been enough business in the locality to support them (Gailey 1982, 11–14; McCutcheon 1980, 260).

Griffith's *Primary Valuation of Ireland* (Galway was completed in 1857) records a corn mill in Coololla occupied by Robert Stanford, and a house, offices, forge and four acres of land leased by John Curley. A John Curley is also listed in Slater's *Directory* (1856) as the blacksmith of Aughrim village and, indeed, the same Curley family kept a forge in the village until the 1960s (Scannell & Cooke 2005, 4). But these records cannot account for the excavated building because it is not marked on the first or second edition Ordnance Survey maps (1838; 1928); nor is it mentioned in Lewis's *Topographical Dictionary of Ireland* (1837). This suggests it may have been among the many small spade mills that were abandoned in the depression years following the Napoleonic Wars.

The nearby lime kiln was probably used to produce agricultural lime fertiliser, which was adopted in Ireland from the mid 17th century and was widely used by the late 18th century. Simple lime kilns of this sort continued in use until the early 20th century. The common theme of these two excavated features is small-scale industrial activity supporting local tillage at a time when arable output in Ireland as a whole was especially high, relative to pastoral farming.

The development of capitalism is a major theme in post-medieval and modern archaeology and especially in the archaeology of industrial development. Small rural industrial sites, like that at Coololla, are seldom found in public lists of protected architectural or archaeological heritage (e.g. the Record of Monuments and Places or the Record of Protected Structures), but they are commonly recorded, these days, by archaeologists working on large construction sites. Thus, pre-development investigations are making contributions to the record of the rural industrial heritage that would simply not be available from other sources, and are filling gaps in the record of 'big' industry and its more monumental remains.

The spade mill at Coololla provides a glimpse of how labour, expertise and materials were marshalled to meet local market demands in a rural setting. It was an artisan operation requiring a high degree of expertise for its success. The spade-maker made a significant investment in a permanent manufactory, so that his expertise could be converted into market goods and their production maintained over a prolonged period. Perhaps the site was leased, and the landowner may have been an investor. We do not know. But the subsequent success of the Curley family, enduring in their forge at Aughrim over several generations, is a model of the sort of success that could have been achieved and was certainly sought by this investment in the excavated spade mill at Coololla.

5.3 Mesolithic tools and Bronze Age burnt mounds at Urraghry and Barnacragh[33]

by Mick Drumm, Penny Johnston & John Tierney
with a contribution by F Sternke

Two burnt mounds discovered in Urraghry and Barnacragh brought the tally of this site type to 10 along the whole of the motorway and add new elements to the map of Bronze Age settlement in the region. But the premier interest of these two sites is some much older chipped stone tools of Early Mesolithic date that were also found. A handful of chipped stone objects may not seem like a big story but, in fact, this is the first concrete evidence that has been found for the presence of the earliest hunter-gatherers in the River Suck catchment.

Illus. 5.3.1—*Urraghry. Early Mesolithic core preparation/ rejuvenation flake (E2449:3:1) (top) and single platform blade core (E2449:3:2) (Eachtra Archaeological Projects).*

Early Mesolithic tools
by Farina Sternke

Three pieces of worked chert were found at Urraghry, in an ancient stream channel underlying the burnt mound. Two of these could be identified with Early Mesolithic tool-making (c. 8000–6500 BC), based on the manufacturing technique employed. They were a core preparation/rejuvenation flake and a small single platform blade core (Illus. 5.3.1). A fragment of a blade or flake was also found. Two chipped stone objects were found on the burnt mound site at Barnacragh. One was a chert scraper

---

33 Urraghry—Excavation No. E2449; NGR 180424 228489; height 60 m OD; civil parish of Clontuskert; barony of Clonmacnowen; Barnacragh—Excavation No. E2446; NGR 181170 228507; height 70 m OD; civil parish of Kilcloony; barony of Clonmacnowen; Excavation Director (Urraghry and Barnacragh) John Tierney.

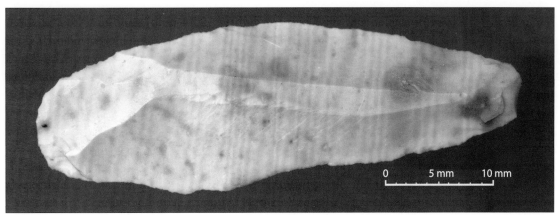

Illus. 5.3.2—Barnacragh. Early Mesolithic retouched flint blade, found in topsoil (E2446:1:1) (Eachtra Archaeological Projects).

of probable Bronze Age date—consistent with the date of the burnt mound—but the other was a retouched flint blade of Early Mesolithic type, from the the topsoil (Illus. 5.3.2). This was most likely produced using a soft hammerstone and can be classified as a slightly anomalous example of an Early Mesolithic needle point.

Bronze Age burnt mounds

The burnt mound at Urraghry was found at the edge of reclaimed peatland. The mound was a typical spread of heat-shattered stones (limestone and sandstone) and frequent charcoal, about 4 m long by 0.2 m deep (Illus. 5.3.3). Most of the charcoal was oak or ash, with some hazel and alder present. There was a large, oval pit beneath the mound—probably a water trough—1.6 m long by 0.2 m deep. There were several stake-holes in the base of the trough and these probably supported a wattlework lining. The mound sprawled across the bed of a former stream (a 'palaeochannel'). There were stake-holes in the base of this too, perhaps associated with a temporary dam. Charcoals from the mound and trough were dated to 2456–2141 (UB-7351) and 2574–2348 BC (UB-7352), in the Early Bronze Age.

About 750 m east of Urraghry, the mound at Barnacragh was also found in reclaimed peatlands. A former stream close by was canalised to form a modern drainage channel. A nearby gravel ridge or esker would have been a convenient routeway in antiquity. The mound was about 6 m long by 0.3 m deep (Illus. 5.3.4). Again it consisted of heat-shattered stone in a charcoal-rich soil matrix. Most of the charcoal at this site was hazel or ash, with alder and oak also present. A convex chert scraper of Bronze Age type was recovered from the mound and this corresponded well with a date of 2115–1831 BC (UB-7357) from a charcoal sample, also from the mound. A large pit or trough beneath the mound was 2.4 m long by 0.4 m deep (Illus. 5.3.5). There was a linear cut, probably an overflow channel, extending from one side of the trough. There was an organic peaty sediment, with splinters of wood, in the base of the trough. The rest was filled with similar material to the burnt mound. There were a dozen stake-holes around the edges of the trough and, like the trough at Urraghry, these probably once held a wattlework lining. Also underlying the mound, a concentrated swathe of 57 stake-holes extended over a span of about 5 m, south from the trough. Some of the stake-holes on the edges of

Stream bed

Trough

Stone socket

N

0   1 m

Illus. 5.3.3—Urraghry. Plan of the burnt mound site, showing the underlying trough and ancient streambed (Eachtra Archaeological Projects).

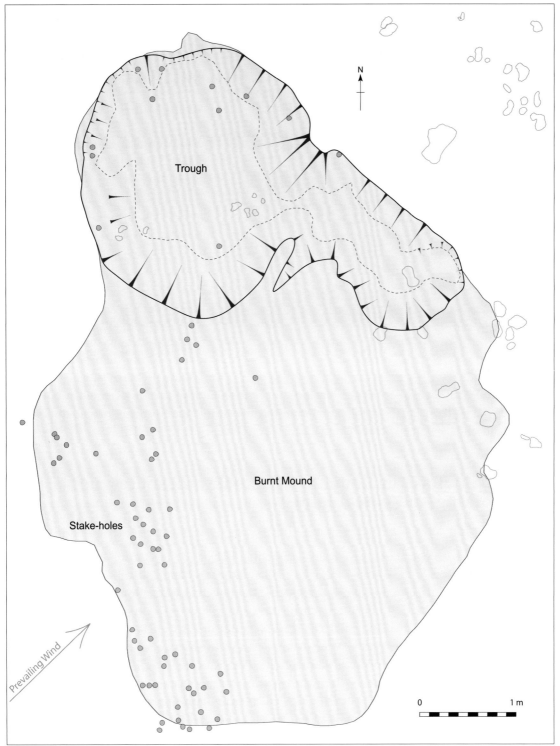

Trough

N

Burnt Mound

Stake-holes

Prevailing Wind

0   1 m

Illus. 5.3.4—Barnacragh. Plan of the burnt mound site, with a concentrated swathe of stake-holes beneath the mound and others around the edge of the underlying trough (Eachtra Archaeological Projects).

Illus. 5.3.5—Barnacragh. Excavating the trough (Galway County Council).

this group were inclined towards the centre, suggesting that they propped up some vertical element, like a wattlework windbreak.

Springs and streams

Why were the early chipped stone objects found in the same places as much later burnt mounds? Early Mesolithic hunter-gatherers would have been drawn to the sorts of watery, low-lying places where springs and streams occurred. These same springs and streams afterwards attracted the Bronze Age people whose hot-stone water-boiling work produced the burnt mounds. Peat had begun to form in the low places by then, so that all the drainage features would not have been identical with the earlier period, but in this case it seems that streams persisted at both sites, while the esker at Barnacragh was a natural routeway that would have brought people to the same points in the landscape in all periods in prehistory.

5.4 Two ringforts in Loughbown: stockyard, souterrain, metalworking and cereal kilns[34]
by Nik Bower

Thousands of archaeological sites have been excavated in Ireland in the short time since the start of the 21st century. Most of these were sites of levelled monuments, long concealed under ploughsoil and pasture, and brought into the light again by pre-development investigations. In spite of so many recent discoveries, the ringfort remains the single most commonly recorded monument type in the Irish countryside. But what is a ringfort? The term was once understood to describe a typical early medieval farmstead enclosure, but has come to embrace a wide variety of sites or, rather, similar sites that were used in different ways. This is illustrated here by two ringforts excavated in Loughbown, between Aughrim and Ballinasloe. Both ringforts are listed in the statutory Record of Monuments and Places (GA087: 178 and 177), but were levelled by farm improvements in the modern period.

---

34 Loughbown 1—Excavation No. E2442; NGR 182180 228950; RMP No GA087:178; height 65–70 m OD; civil parish of Clontuskert; barony of Clonmacnowen; Loughbown 2—Excavation No. E2054; NGR 181730 228729; RMP No GA087:177; height 83m OD; civil parish of Clontuskert; barony of Clonmacnowen; Excavation Director (Loughbown 1 and 2) Nik Bower.

Our excavations discovered that, originally, Loughbown 1 was a large, double-ditched enclosure with strong evidence for farming and settlement, food processing and metalworking; while Loughbown 2 was a simpler earthwork enclosure, lacking any evidence of human occupation, and was probably used as a stockyard. In this they very much resemble the cashels already described at Coolagh, Carnmore West and Farranablake—which were the equivalent monuments in stone on the dry, thin soils west of the Kilreekill Ridge.

A prosperous working settlement enclosure at Loughbown 1

Loughbown 1 was a large, double-ditched ringfort, on the brow of a hill with open views to north and east, across the Suck Valley (Illus. 5.4.1). It was not intervisible with Loughbown 2, further west, but was once intervisible with several other ringforts in neighbouring townlands. (Most of these are now levelled by farm improvements.) About 40% of the ringfort lay outside the footprint of the new road and was not excavated. One prehistoric feature was recorded on the site, but the ringfort itself was occupied in the early and later medieval periods.

Prehistoric ditch
The earliest feature at Loughbown 1 was a shallow ditch, 1.7 m wide by 0.7 m deep, lying NE/SW along the eastern edge of the site (not illus.). Charcoal from the ditch fills was dated to 1193–938

Illus. 5.4.1—Loughbown 1. Aerial view of the excavation site from north (Hany Marzouk for Galway County Council).

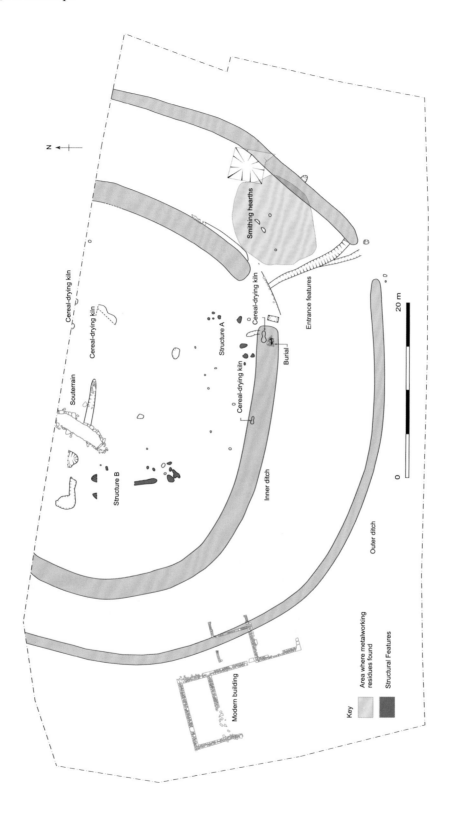

Illus. 5.4.2—Loughbown 1. Plan of the excavated features of the double-ditched ringfort (Eachtra Archaeological Projects).

BC (UB-7364), in the Middle Bronze Age. The fills also included artefacts and other occupation material from the ringfort, but as the outer ditch of the ringfort cut into the ditch, it was clearly a defunct, earlier feature.

Ringfort earthworks

Although the ringfort was largely levelled, the surviving ditches give a good idea of its size and ground plan (Illus. 5.4.2). It had a diameter of 60 m with an entrance in the south-east. The outer ditch was small (1 m wide and 0.5 m deep), and was shallowest near the entrance, where it was cut into bedrock. The inner ditch enclosed an area 42 m in diameter. It was 2.2 m wide and 1 m deep, with at least two recuts. The distance between the ditches was very variable, from 10 m in the east to 5 m in the west (upslope), which is plenty of space for an earthen bank, though none survived. There would have been an inner bank, inside the ditches, but no traces of this were recognised during the excavation. An inner bank, with an internal diameter of perhaps 25–30 m, would have reduced the size of the available habitation area considerably. Access to the interior was via a simple causeway across the ditches.

Charcoal from a trampled soil deposit in the entranceway was dated to AD 419–554 (UB-7367) and charcoal from the bottom of the outer ditch was dated to AD 563–653 (UB-7362). A human skeleton buried in the inner ditch (below) was dated to AD 782–983 (UBA-8096). Another charcoal sample, from a stony layer of collapsed bank material in the interior, gave a much later date of AD 1294–1402 (UB-7365). This layer was disturbed by modern cultivation furrows, possibly resulting in some mixing of the deposits.

Souterrain

A souterrain was discovered near the centre of the ringfort. This consisted of a single, sub-rectangular chamber, aligned NE/SW (Illus. 5.4.3). Within the limits of excavation it was 6.4 m long (internally) and up to 1.6 m wide. (A geophysical survey by Earthsound Archaeological Geophysics indicated that it extends 3 m further north, into farmland adjacent to the new road.) The souterrain was built within a broad, open trench. The side walls were built with large blocks of roughly coursed limestone rubble, with a compact fill of redeposited subsoil and smaller rubble behind. A single, edge-set slab marked the southern end of the chamber and was probably a jambstone in the entranceway. The roof consisted of irregular slabs of limestone rubble, partly corbelled in the mid section of the chamber. It was poorly constructed, however, and had largely collapsed, so that the chamber was filled with earth and rubble. These souterrain fills contained both animal bones and artefacts, including a bone comb, a perforated bone peg and quern-stone fragments.

Souterrains could have been used as sleeping places and for storage, but were also places of refuge from slave- and cattle-raiders. It is very likely that the entrance to the souterrain was concealed within a house. Unfortunately, there was no surviving evidence for this unless, perhaps, Structure B (below) was part of a large dwelling house. This teasing possibility is supported by a concentration of soil spreads immediately adjacent to the souterrain. Some of these were sterile, redeposited subsoils—no doubt upcast material from the construction of the souterrain—but these were mixed with 'anthropic' soils, enriched with occupation waste, including assorted animal bones, charcoals, marine shells and burnt cereal grains, also iron slag, an iron fish hook and a copper-alloy ringed pin of early medieval type.

Illus. 5.4.3—Loughbown 1. View of the souterrain from north, after removal of the collapsed roof and other fills, looking towards the entrance (Eachtra Archaeological Projects).

Two buildings

There was evidence for at least two buildings in the ringfort interior, recorded as Structures A and B (Illus. 5.4.2). As these were built with wood, not stone, they were not as well defined as the souterrain. Structure A was located just inside the entrance. The evidence consisted of 11 post-holes and a stake-hole suggesting a trapezoidal ground plan, measuring 6 m north–south by 7 m. There were sheep/goat and cat bones in the post-holes and also some oats and barley grains. Structure B was another possible building, located near the souterrrain entrance. It was represented by an irregular cluster of cut features: five post-holes, a stake-hole and a slot-trench. Cattle and sheep/goat bone, burnt clay fragments, charcoal and cereal grains (mostly barley) were recovered from deposits associated with the structure.

Metalworking

In the south-east quadrant of the site, a metalworking area extended over the space between the two ditches (Illus. 5.4.2). There were three small smithing hearths or furnace pits (up to 0.5 m long by 0.2 m deep). The sides were burnt and the fills contained quantities of charcoal and iron slag, including 25 'smithing hearth bottoms'. Most of the charcoal was oak. This is an ideal fuel for metalworking and was by far the commonest charcoal from all the metalworking deposits on this site. More metalworking evidence was found in the outer ditch, where the uppermost fill included a scorched soil deposit, rich in slag. Charcoal from one of the furnace pits was dated to AD 1047–1257 (UB-7363).

In all, 130 kg of slag was found on the site. Much of this was amorphous but there were also many plano-convex fragments—a result of cooling and solidifying in furnace pits. Analysis shows that the slag resulted from primary and secondary smithing (rather than iron smelting from ore). The total quantity is relatively small compared to some excavated ringforts and suggests that ironworking at Loughbown 1 was carried out on an occasional basis only, probably to meet the basic demands of its occupants. This work was concentrated between the two ditches so it can be inferred that the original bank was no longer a substantial upstanding feature here but had become reduced or perhaps entirely levelled by this time. Metalworking also spread into the outer ditch at a time when this was almost entirely backfilled. This is consistent with a late radiocarbon date (above) from one of the smithing hearths, indicating that the work was done some time in the 11th–13th centuries, several centuries after the earthwork enclosure was built.

Crops and corn-drying kilns

There were two corn-drying kilns built within the fills of the inner ditch (Illus. 5.4.2). One was an oblong pit (2.1 m long, 1.7 m wide and 0.5 m deep), with evidence for intense heat in its fire-reddened base. The fills contained oak charcoal and charred grains of wheat and oats. The second kiln was also an oblong pit (2.5 m long, 1.2 m wide and 0.3 m deep). Again, the base was intensely fire reddened. This time the fills included large amounts of cereal grain, including oats and wheat with some rye; charcoals from a range of trees, including hazel, oak and alder; and also bones of cattle, sheep/goat, horse and dog. (Evidently this kiln was ultimately used a waste pit.)

Most of the charred cereal grain in soil samples from the site came from the general area of the kilns, in the south-east quadrant of the ringfort, and probably represent dispersed kiln rakeout. The assemblage was dominated by oats (60%) and the wheat was almost entirely bread wheat. Oats became a common crop in the high medieval period and its dominance here corresponds well with the broadly 13th/14th-century date from the second kiln.

Charcoal from the bottom of the second kiln was dated to AD 1282–1395 (UB-7366). This echoes the evidence from the metalworking area (above) that the ditches of the partly levelled ringfort were used for hot, smokey, industrial work in the high medieval period.

The date of these kilns is consistent with evidence from several other sites along the road project. At Carnmore West (Sector 1), Caraun More, Rahally, Rathglass and Gortnahoon (all in Sector 3), and Mackney (in Sector 4), excavated cereal kilns produced radiocarbon dates in the high or later medieval period. (Kilns at Gortnahoon and Carnmore West also produced early medieval dates.) The ringforts and cashels of early medieval Ireland reflect a society with a mixed farming economy dominated by cattle husbandry. It was not until the high medieval period—and the floruit of the Norman Lordship in Connacht—that crops achieved something like parity with livestock in the West. This is suggested both by the pollen evidence from Ballinphuil Bog (Chapter 3) and by the archaeological evidence of the excavated kilns.

The kilns themselves were simple structures designed to induct hot air from a fire-pit into a drying chamber. The process was painstaking but worth the effort. Dried grain is less prone to fungal infection and it can be processed much faster when it is ground or milled into flour.

Plants, animals and artefacts

The charcoal assemblage from the site was dominated by oak, followed by ash, hazel, various small fruiting trees (Pomoideae) and wild cherry/blackthorn type (*Prunus* sp.). Oak is well represented in the assemblage (49% by fragment count and 37% by weight) and formed over 98% of the charcoal from deposits associated with metalworking. In contrast, charcoals from the kilns represented 'twiggy' wood, much of it derived from hazel, Pomoideae and *Prunus* species.

Almost 5,000 animal bones and 69 bird bones were recovered from excavated archaeological deposits at Loughbown 1. Most of this was from the inner ringfort ditch (Table 5.4.1). Cattle and sheep were the species of greatest economic importance. All skeletal elements of the animals were represented, including primary butchery waste and remains from the table.

Table 5.4.1—Loughbown 1. Distribution of animal bones

Period	Feature	No.	%
Bronze Age	Prehistoric linear ditch	6	0.12
Medieval	Outer ringfort ditch	88	1.80
	Ringfort entrance	1	0.02
	Inner ringfort ditch	3186	65.20
	Slumped bank material	301	6.16
	Ringfort interior (surfaces)	87	1.78
	Structure A: entranceway	4	0.08
	Structure B: interior	28	0.57
	Souterrain fills	925	18.94
	Metalworking areas	72	1.47
	Corn-drying kilns	185	3.79
	Total	**4883**	**100**

The majority of the cattle were kept to adulthood and fulfilled roles other than meat production (i.e. draught animals and dairying). One cow phalanx (part of the lower forelimb) was split axially. This might have been done by a bone-carver as the phalanx is not a meat-bearing bone and would not have been butchered for food. All age classes of sheep were represented, but mature animals were most numerous. Pigs seem to have played a minor role at the site. Horse bones were found in small numbers and some had butchery marks, which suggests they were exploited for their meat once they had outlived their usefulness. Dog bones were common and represented two broad types: a smaller breed, resembling a modern sheepdog in size, and a larger animal, resembling a modern Alsatian in size.

Bones of wild animals are rarely recovered from early medieval sites in Ireland but three species identified at Loughbown 1—deer, hare and mouse—were probably contemporary with the occupation of the site. There were bird bones too, mostly in the inner ditch. Some may have been incidental inclusions (e.g. starling, bar-tailed godwit and lapwing), but others (e.g. mallard and woodcock) may have been hunted for food.

There were several finds of coarse stone tools (Illus. 5.4.4), including a large, flat, ground limestone axehead, a slate disc, a hone stone and several quern-stone fragments (granite). The axehead is possibly Neolithic—an incidental stray find or possibly a 'trophy' object found in antiquity and brought home to the ringfort. The hone stone is a more typical early medieval find.

Other early medieval finds included fragments of a bone comb, and a copper-alloy ringed pin (Illus. 5.4.5 and 5.4.6). Lice and fleas must have been a great nuisance in early medieval Ireland because bone combs with fine, close-set teeth are very common finds on occupation sites of the

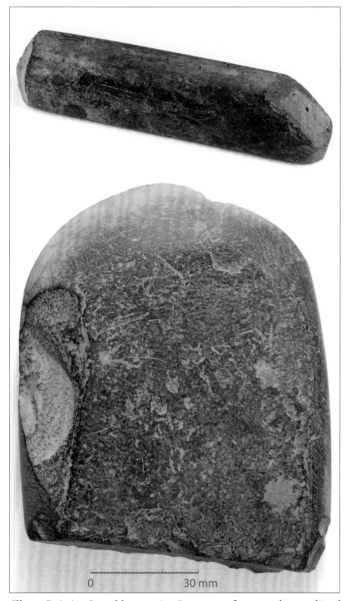

Illus. 5.4.4—Loughbown 1. Stone artefacts: early medieval hone stone (E2442:203:6) and (below) early prehistoric axehead (E2442:40:10) (John Sunderland for Eachtra Archaeological Projects).

period and are similar in design to the sort that can still be bought in chemists' shops today. Ringed pins are also common finds and were used as clothing fasteners.

Later medieval finds included fragments of a wooden comb, a bone weaving tool or 'pin beater', a fish hook, an iron knife and an iron pin (Illus. 5.4.5 and 5.4.6). A sandstone fragment from a possible metalworker's mould may also have been of this period but the identification is tentative. The only closely dated later medieval find was a silver coin from the reign of King Edward I (1272–1307)—a long-cross silver penny, probably struck in Bristol in 1280–81 (Illus. 5.4.7)—but this came from topsoil and not from any secure, early context.

A bone tuning peg and bone button may have been made in the post-medieval or modern periods. There were also numerous sherds of early modern pottery and some fragments of clay tobacco pipe, so that the finds assemblage represents all periods of occupation of the site, from early medieval times to the 19th century.

Human remains

A human skeleton was found in the base of the inner ditch, just west of the entrance. It was the remains of a child not more than 10 years old. The skeleton was laid on its left side with the head in the west and the legs flexed. The bones bore no signs of fatal disease or trauma. As already stated, a bone sample was dated to AD 782–983 (UBA-8096). There were no other human remains on the site.

Early medieval burials usually occurred within dedicated burial grounds—most often in the vicinity of a church or, alternatively, in a cemetery-settlement (like Carrowkeel and Treanbaun,

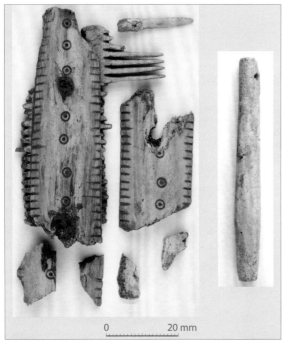

Illus. 5.4.5—Loughbown 1. Wood and bone artefacts: bone comb fragments (E2442:93:1, 2 & 4) and (right) weaving tool/pin beater (E2442:250:1) (John Sunderland for Eachtra Archaeological Projects).

in Chapters 3 and 4). The explanation in this case is probably not sinister, as the entrance to a ringfort is hardly a good hiding place for a body. More likely this was an unbaptised child who was buried 'at home' by its family after succumbing to an acute illness.

Early modern building

For completeness, we must also mention briefly some modern building remains found in the western part of the site, partly overlying the outer ringfort ditch (Illus. 5.4.2). Mortared wall remnants were overlain by a shallow layer of sandy silt, which contained iron nails, a horseshoe, and an iron hook-and-bar. The first edition Ordnance Survey map (surveyed 1838; Illus. 5.4.11, below) shows an L-plan building here, within a garden or enclosure. It was known to local people as 'The Forge', but there were no industrial residues in this part of the site and we found no evidence that the building was ever used for smithing or metalworking.

A stockyard at Loughbown 2

Loughbown 2 was a smaller ringfort, on the summit of a knoll about 500 m west of Loughbown 1. It was almost entirely levelled at the time of excavation. There are good soils in the immediate environs but the site itself was stony, with thin soils giving way to shallow bedrock. The knoll evidently attracted people in more than one period because, like its larger neighbour, there was evidence of later prehistoric activity at Loughbown 2 too. There was very little evidence, however, that the ringfort was ever inhabited, in any period.

Illus. 5.4.6—Loughbown 1. Metal artefacts: iron fish hook (E2442:203:4) and copper-alloy ringed pin (E2442:203:1) (John Sunderland for Eachtra Archaeological Projects).

Iron Age features

The earliest feature at Loughbown 2 was a remnant of a small curvilinear trench (0.4 m wide), with a post-hole at one end. This was truncated by the ringfort ditch but would originally have enclosed a circular area with a diameter of less than 2.5 m (Illus. 5.4.8). This feature is too small to represent the wall footings of a building and was interpreted in the field as remains of a ring-ditch funerary monument. No human remains were found, however, but only some burnt sheep bone fragments; and there was no evidence for *in situ* burning. Charcoal from the trench fill was dated to 396–211 BC (UBA-7758), in the Iron Age.

The 'ring-ditch' was surrounded by an irregular cluster of small pits and post-holes. These features were interpreted in the field as part of the same episode of activity in the past, but a charcoal sample from one of them produced a much later date of AD 1022–1164 (UBA-7760), in the medieval period. It seems, therefore, that the spatial relationship between the ring-ditch and at least some of the pits and post-holes was fortuitous.

Two other dated samples, from elsewhere on the site, also produced Iron Age dates. Charcoal from within the remnant ringfort bank was dated to 392–205 BC (UB-7360) and charcoal from a post-hole in the interior was dated to 361–102 BC (UB-7361).

10 mm

Illus. 5.4.7—Loughbown 1. A long-cross silver penny of the reign of King Edward I (1272–1307), probably struck in Bristol in 1280–81 (E2442:1:21) (John Sunderland for Eachtra Archaeological Projects).

Ringfort earthworks and entrance

The ringfort was a simple earthwork with a V-shaped ditch, 1.9 m wide and 1 m deep, enclosing an area 42 m in diameter (Illus. 5.4.8). The only surviving remnant of the bank was in the south-west sector, where it had been incorporated in a much later field dyke. A slot-trench in the northern part of the interior was interpreted as part of a footing trench for a wooden revetment of the bank. The entrance was indicated by a causeway across the ditch, in the south-east. It was approached by a roughly metalled stony trackway. Two large post-holes located just inside the entrance, 1.5 m apart, were probably gateposts. There was possibly a second entrance on the north side, indicated by a narrow causeway across the ditch.

Animal bone from the base of the ditch was dated to AD 778–969 (UBA-8103) but charcoal from elsewhere in the base of the ditch was dated to AD 1467–1640 (UB-7759), reminding us that the ditch was infilled over time, and with a variety of materials from the environs, which could have resulted in some mixing of the available sample material.

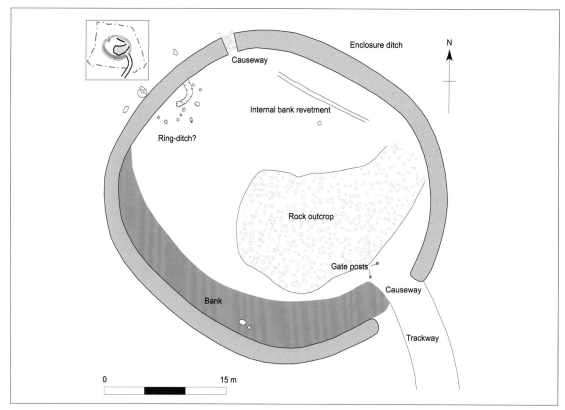

Illus. 5.4.8—Loughbown 2. Plan of the excavated features of the ringfort (Eachtra Archaeological Projects).

Plants, animals and artefacts

The soil samples collected from the site contained only a few weed seeds, some unidentified cereal grains and a hazelnut shell fragment. This is an unusually low return from an excavated ringfort. Charcoal was also very scarce and the fragment size was small. Nonetheless, various small fruiting trees (Pomoideae), oak, hazel, ash, wild cherry/blackthorn type (*Prunus* sp.), alder, elder, ivy, elm, willow/poplar and holly were all identified, with the Pomoideae most common.

There was also a small assemblage of animal bone. Much of this was scorched or burnt, resulting in greater fragmentation, and most of the bones were too small to be identified in consequence. Cattle bones were most common, followed by sheep/goat, and then pig. A high proportion of the bones that could be identified to species and body part represented meat-bearing joints, so it seems most likely that the bone assemblage as a whole represents food waste.

The few artefacts recovered from the ringfort included a shale/lignite bracelet fragment (Illus. 5.4.9), part of a rotary quern (granite), a rough hammerstone and an iron knife blade (possibly later medieval) from the ditch (Illus 5.4.10).

Homesteads and hierarchy in the early medieval landscape

There is no doubt that the ringfort at Loughbown 1 was a permanent habitation site. This is confirmed by an amount of domestic artefacts and food waste, the souterrain and other buildings

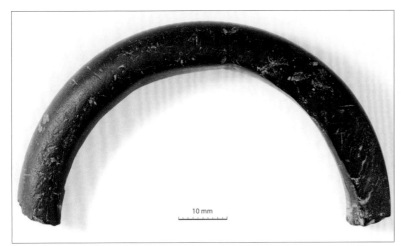

Illus. 5.4.9—Loughbown 2. A shale/lignite bracelet (E2054:45:3) was recovered from the ringfort bank (Eachtra Archaeological Projects). Producing these bracelets required skill, time and patience. They are relatively common finds on ringfort sites.

Illus. 5.4.10—Loughbown 2. Knife blade (E2054:150:1) of possible 13th-century date, recovered from the ringfort ditch (Eachtra Archaeological Projects).

remnants, and evidence for food processing and metalworking. The earthworks enclosed a prosperous homestead and the double ditch would have been understood in the early medieval world as a clear signal of the high social status of its occupants. It was also used for a very long time. The dating evidence indicates that it was probably built in the mid first millennium and was still in use in the high medieval period, until the 13th or 14th century. It may be that the ringfort was no longer a principal place of residence by then, but was merely a convenient place for dirty, smoky, noxious work like metalworking and cereal drying in kilns.

The evidence from Loughbown 2 is less clear cut. There was certainly Iron Age activity on the site but the radiocarbon dates in the early medieval period—from the ditch and interior—are more likely to represent the period of construction and use of the ringfort itself. But what was its use? Some burnt and butchered animal bones and a quern-stone hint at domestic occupation, but the evidence is meagre, at best, and there was no surviving evidence for buildings, in the form of post-holes, wall trenches or even a domestic hearth.

The two excavated ringforts at Loughbown formed part of a densely settled early medieval landscape (Illus. 5.4.11). East Galway has an unusually high density of ringforts. Locally, there were at least seven other earthwork enclosures in Loughbown townland alone, in addition to the excavated sites, and almost two dozen others within a radius of 2 km of them. (Without excavation it cannot be stated that these were all early medieval enclosures but there is a high probability that most of them were.) These were not all homesteads of equal status but represent, instead, a network of relationships and obligations between bigger landowners and their dependents including, no doubt, many near relatives.[35] More than any other form of portable wealth in this society, cattle supplied the medium of exchange in contracts for land tenure and other important transactions: a big herd was more or less identical with high status. If Loughbown 1 was one of the dominant farmsteads in this scene, then perhaps Loughbown 2, with its hard, stony interior, was a place where a freeman's cattle were corralled by one of his dependents for milking or to secure them from wolves and raiders. The herdsman's family who lived with these cattle would have spent more time on the open pastures in the hinterland than 'at home' and perhaps this is why this smaller ringfort on the stony knoll yielded so little evidence for permanent occupation.

Illus. 5.4.11—Extract from the Ordnance Survey first-edition map of 1838 showing some of the ringforts in Loughbown and neighbouring townlands. Red circles indicate the excavated ringfort sites at Loughbown 1 (right) and Loughbown 2 (Ordnance Survey of Ireland).

---

35 For a discussion of hierarchy and social networks in early Irish society, based on the spatial distribution of settlement sites and their intervisibility, see *The Irish Ringfort* by Matthew Stout (1997) and especially pages 48–109.

5.5 Bronze Age occupation sites at Mackney[36]

by David Fallon & John Tierney

Clear primary evidence for later prehistoric settlement sites—in the form of buildings, hearths or settlement enclosures—was striking by its absence on the motorway route. This cannot be interpreted as an absence of people, bearing in mind that a) their impact on the landscape is clearly flagged in the fossil pollen record, b) prehistoric burials and burnt mounds were recorded at over a dozen locations, and c) the hillfort at Rahally is clarion evidence of an organised, hierarchical society in Late Bronze Age and Early Iron Age times. It must be the case, therefore, that the lack of settlement evidence in our project results from the random nature of survival and discovery along the route. But the canvas is not entirely blank, as some possible Bronze Age settlement remains were identified at two locations in Mackney, near Ballinasloe. The two sites were about 4 km west of the River Suck and 300 m apart from one another.

Mackney 1 was discovered in an area of improved pasture with isolated pockets of peat bog. A large hearth pit, 2.5 m wide and 0.45 m deep, had scorched sides and burnt inclusions in its fills. There was also a spread of raked-out burnt sediment west of the hearth (Illus. 5.5.1). The hearth was located among a cluster of 15 small pits. Five of them were interpreted as post-holes in the field, though only three of them had packing stones for upright timbers. One of the pits contained a saddle quern (Illus. 5.5.2). (This is the simplest kind of prehistoric quern, on which grain or nutshells were ground with a smaller, hand-held rubber stone.) Another pit contained exclusively oak charcoal, suggesting an oak post had burned down while still footed in the pit. Hazel charcoal from the hearth was dated to 1117–915 BC (UB-7355). Hazel charcoal from one of the pits was dated to 1114–919 BC (UB-7356).

Bulk soil samples were examined from all of the excavated features at Mackney 1. Ten samples contained small amounts of charcoal but only one contained any sort of food debris—a nut shell of indeterminate species. The charcoal represented a variety of trees including oak, hazel, various small fruiting trees (Pomoideae), ash, wild cherry/blackthorn type (*Prunus* sp.), alder, yew and willow/aspen. The oak was from a post-hole and, as suggested above, may have burned *in situ*. The remaining charcoals may also include some structure timbers but are more likely to represent fuel wood, gathered locally. Alder and willow/aspen thrive in wet conditions.

Further east, Mackney 2 (not illus.) was located in a poorly drained natural hollow in undulating grass pasture. There was a small hearth pit, 0.6 m wide by 0.2 m deep, on the higher, dry ground at the edge of the hollow. Hazel charcoal from the hearth was dated to 1433–1270 BC (UB-7354). Four pits, of various sizes, were dispersed throughout the hollow. (The nearest one to the hearth was about 10 m away.) One of these was identified in the field as a post-hole as it had straight sides with a flat stone in the base, interpreted as a pad-stone for an upright timber. (The pit was 0.44 m wide by 0.22 m deep.) Hazel charcoal from the fill of one pit was dated to 1047–848 BC (UB-7353). There were also some modern features at Mackney 2—a field/property boundary and several shallow ditches or field drains—but these will not be considered further here. Bulk soil samples from

---

36 Mackney 1—Excavation No. E2445; NGR 183704 229507; height 50 m OD; Mackney 2—Excavation No. E2443; NGR 183703 229503; height 50 m OD; both in the civil parish of Clontuskert and barony of Clonmacnowen; Excavation Director (Mackney 1 and 2) John Tierney.

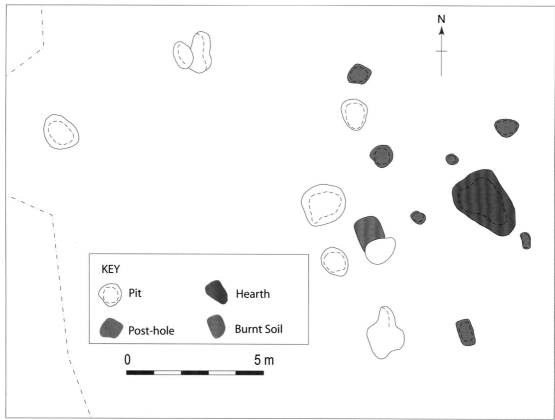

Illus. 5.5.1—Mackney 1. Plan of the Bronze Age hearth, pits and post-holes (Eachtra Archaeological Projects).

Illus. 5.5.2—Mackney 1. A saddle quern (E2445:92:1) was recovered from one of the excavated pits. Scale bar 50 mm (John Sunderland).

the excavated features contained charcoals but, again, no cereal seeds or other food debris. Hazel was dominant, with Pomoideae, *Prunus* sp., alder, oak, ash, willow/aspen, holly and birch also present.

The evidence at Mackney for settlement is very slight and begs the question: 'What is the minimum evidence that identifies a settlement site in the archaeological record?' The answer stems directly from primary human needs: water, warmth, food and shelter. Water is portable and would certainly have been available locally. Both sites had hearths but there was almost no food debris of any sort and very little evidence that the hearths were associated with buildings. Only the quern-stone hints at something more than a camp site, as this heavy stone would have been a valuable household object and an unwieldy one to carry from place to place. But a quern-stone and hearth do not make a home and, on this slight evidence, we cannot declare that Mackney 1 and 2 were permanent settlement sites.

5.6 Ringfort with round-house, souterrain and *cillín* burials at Mackney[37]
by Finn Delaney
with contributions by L Lynch, E Heckett, M Dillon & M McCarthy

The most impressive of the excavated sites in this sector of the road scheme was a large ringfort about 2 km south-west of Ballinasloe, on an elevated site with a broad view over the Suck Valley to the south and east. The ringfort was not previously recorded (i.e. it was not listed in the Record of Monuments and Places) but was identified during a walkover survey of the road corridor at EIS stage when a low curvilinear mound in pasture was recognised as the remnant bank of an earthwork enclosure. The site was recorded as Mackney 1.

At the time of excavation the site was in farmland but in an earlier period it was part of the demesne landscape of Mackney House. The house was built by a branch of the Trench family in the late 18th century. It was demolished in the 1970s. Only a farmyard and walled garden survived (Illus. 5.6.1). (The walled garden is now immediately west of Junction 15 on the motorway.) The Trenches were a very prominent Galway family, descended from French Huguenot stock. The senior Trenches were Earls Clancarty and their principal seat in Ballinasloe was at nearby Garbally House.

The ringfort itself is an outstanding example of this classic early medieval monument type, with a single, wide, deep ditch, a stone-built souterrain, at least one central round-house and several other buildings (Illus. 5.6.2). There is convincing evidence that it continued to be occupied in the later medieval period, after the Norman invasion and beyond. In the post-medieval/early modern period the ringfort became a *cillín* site (an unconsecrated rural burial ground) when the ditch was used to bury infants and juveniles. At some time in this same period the interior was exploited with spade-dug cultivation ridges. Charcoal from the site produced a series of radiocarbon dates spanning the eighth to the 17th centuries (Appendix 1) and artefacts from the site were even more broad ranging in date, from prehistoric stone tools to household refuse from Mackney House.

---

37 Excavation No. E2444; Director Finn Delaney; NGR 183745 229417; height 55 m OD; civil parish of Clontuskert; barony of Clonmacnowen.

Illus. 5.6.1—Mackney ringfort. An aerial view of the ringfort undergoing excavation with remains of the walled garden and farmyard of former Mackney House close by (Hany Marzouk for Galway County Council).

Before the ringfort

A miscellany of features was found beneath the ringfort bank (or the projected line of the bank), in the north and south-east sectors, and these are likely to have closely pre-dated its construction. They included two hearths or fire-pits, several shallow ditches or gullies, and a miscellany of pits, post-holes and stake-holes (not illus.). Charcoal from one of the fire-pits was dated to AD 728–949 (UB-7374), which amounts to a *terminus post quem* date of AD 728 for the construction of the ringfort. The pit was sealed by a layer of buried topsoil that, in turn, underlay a remnant of the ringfort bank. Thus, the dated sample comes from a securely stratified context and can be regarded as reliable.

Some worked chert and flint pieces were also found on the site, including scrapers of probable Bronze Age date (not illus.), but as they derive from a remote period unrelated to the construction and occupation of the ringfort, they will not be considered further here.

The ringfort in the medieval period

Earthworks and entrance

The ringfort was a large circular earthwork, with an internal diameter of 56 m, enclosed by a single bank and ditch. The ditch was variously 5–6 m wide and over 3 m deep (Illus. 5.6.3). The bank was not well preserved but its footprint could be traced throughout. This was possible because the

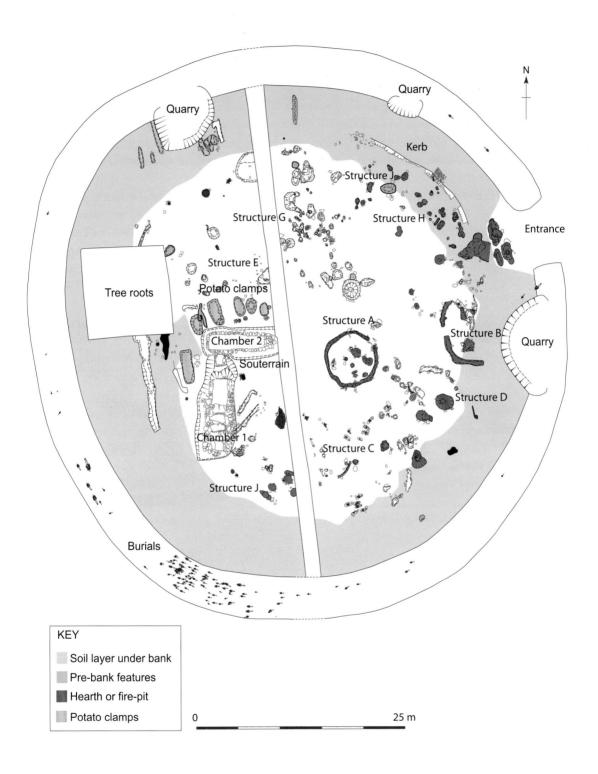

N

KEY

Soil layer under bank

Pre-bank features

Hearth or fire-pit

Potato clamps

0   25 m

Illus. 5.6.2—Mackney ringfort. Plan of the excavated features in all phases (Eachtra Archaeological Projects).

interior of the ringfort was heavily truncated whereas the area once sealed by the bank was not, so that its footprint was represented by a buried soil layer all around the edges of the interior. (The broad extent of this 'ghost bank' indicates that it represents slumped or subsided material too.) Where remnants of the bank did survive, it was constructed with layered dumps of stone, sand and gravel. If it consisted of all the upcast soil from the ditch, it would originally have been a very substantial barrier. There was a low, stone kerb or revetment along the inner face of the bank, immediately north of the entrance, and a ditch or gully in a corresponding position on the west side. This suggests that there was some sort of revetment along the inner face of the bank throughout its circuit.

The entrance itself was in the east. A break in the ditch formed a simple causeway giving access

Illus. 5.6.3—Mackney ringfort. A section through the fills of the enclosing ditch. The deposit of stones in the upper fill lay directly upon the layer containing the burials (Eachtra Archaeological Projects).

to the interior via an opening in the bank. A group of pits and post-holes in the entranceway probably represents a gate or perhaps a gate tower, but does not clearly indicate any particular structure. The picture here is muddied because there were at least two phases of construction and the replacement of the earthfast structural timbers resulted in a confusing medley of intercut features in the archaeological record.

Buildings

In the ringfort interior, remains of nine buildings, or possible buildings, were identified (Structures A–J; Illus. 5.6.2) and most of these are attributed to the early medieval phase. The ground plans of a round-house near the centre (Structure A) and a lean-to at the bank (Structure B) were both quite well defined. The evidence for the other buildings consisted of small groups of post-holes and gullies forming no clear plan and is less satisfactory.

The round-house (Structure A) was probably a dwelling house. It was a simple, one-roomed building near the centre of the ringfort. It was represented by a shallow foundation trench with a diameter of 5.4 m. There were several post-holes within the foundation trench, representing the wall line, and others dispersed across the floor, which probably held upright supports for the roof timbers (Illus. 5.6.4). The doorway was on the north-east side, towards the ringfort entrance.

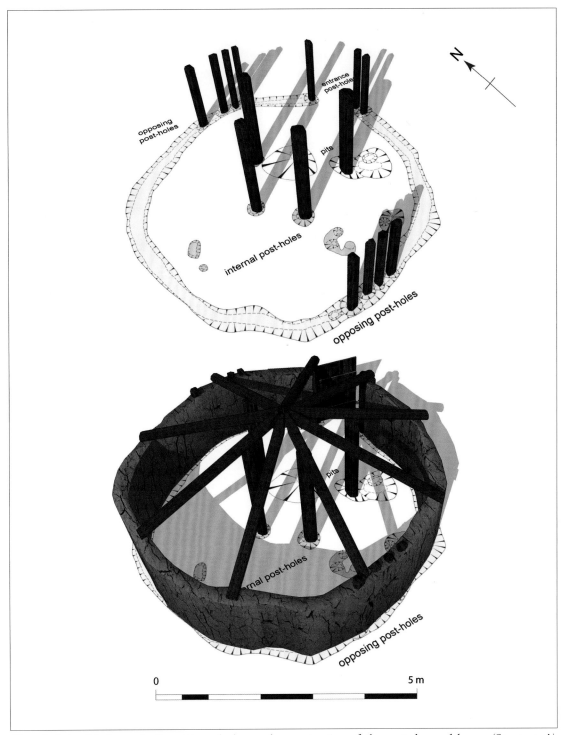

Illus. 5.6.4—Mackney ringfort. Ground-plan and reconstruction of the central round-house (Structure A). The doorway faced the ringfort entrance. There was no evidence of a hearth. (Ben Blakeman for Eachtra Archaeological Projects).

The working life of a big ringfort required stores, byres and workshops and traces of such buildings were identified at Mackney. A lean-to structure (Structure B), oblong in plan and with a hearth in the floor, stood against the face of the bank on the east side, just south of the entrance. The ground plan was defined by a footing trench for the wall timbers. There was a gap for the doorway on the west side, facing the centre of the ringfort.

Souterrain

The souterrain was located in the south-west quadrant of the ringfort, far from the entrance. It was constructed in an L-shaped trench and consisted of two chambers, set at right angles to each other (Illus. 5.6.5). A flight of five stone steps gave access from ground level to one end of the first or outer

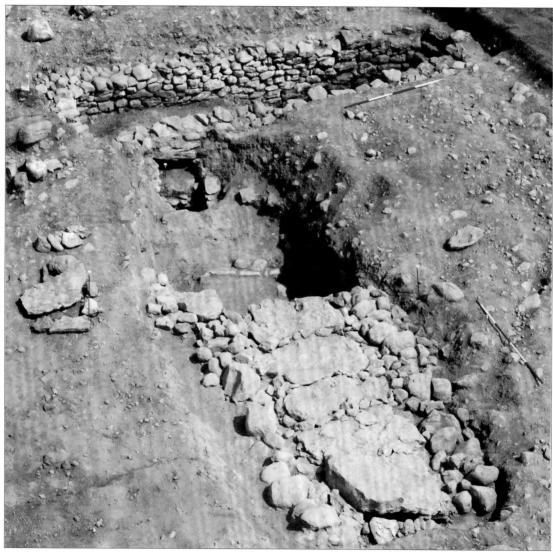

Illus. 5.6.5—Mackney ringfort. The souterrain from south with the lintel stones of the roof still in place on Chamber 1 (Eachtra Archaeological Projects).

Illus. 5.6.6—Mackney ringfort. A detail of the low doorway leading to a 'drop-creep' trapdoor between Chambers 1 and 2 of the souterrain (Eachtra Archaeological Projects).

chamber (recorded as Chamber 2). This was 7.4 m long by 1.6 m wide internally. A connecting 'drop-creep' trapdoor (Illus. 5.6.6) gave access to the second, inner chamber (Chamber 1), which was 7.6 m long by 1.6 m wide. The walls were 1.6 m high and were built with roughly coursed, drystone, limestone rubble. Both chambers had rounded ends and there was a blocked-up alcove or recess in a side wall of Chamber 1. The floors throughout were formed by a smooth, hard layer of naturally cemented sandy clay and gravel.

The souterrain roof survived over the south or rear end of Chamber 1. It was a hybrid structure of lintels and corbels. Flat slabs laid on the side walls overhung the chamber and were kept in place by counter-balancing boulders resting on their outer ends. These flat corbels in turn supported the true lintel stones, which spanned the remaining space to complete the roof structure. The five lintels that survived *in situ* were large, thick, limestone slabs. They were consolidated with a thick capping of naturally cemented sandy clay and gravel, similar to the floor layer. At its centre, Chamber 1 was up to 2 m high internally.

The souterrain was backfilled with soils, stones and refuse, some of it resulting from collapse. The basal fills were mostly sand, clay and gravel with inclusions of charcoal or animal bone. The upper fills were more mixed and included quantities of building debris and other refuse from nearby Mackney House—presumably dumped here when the house was demolished in the 1970s.

Metalworking

A miscellany of iron-smelting pits, furnace fragments (33 pieces, probably from superstructures), slag, heat-shattered stones, refuse pits and post-holes was discovered in the north-east quadrant of the ringfort, in the lee of the bank (Illus. 5.6.2). Charcoal from a furnace pit was dated to AD 775–965 (UB-7371) and charcoal from another pit, containing slag and abundant oak charcoal, was dated to AD 988–1153 (UB-7376). (The dated charcoal sample was alder. Oak charcoal was not used as old heartwood could skew the result by 200 years or more.) This pit also contained a large angular stone, with slag adhering to it, which may have been used as a rough anvil for smithing work.

The post-holes found in association with these features may represent a shelter or workshop (Structure H). Eight post-holes had packing stones for upright timbers and the post in one appeared to have been propped or secured by two smaller stakes. There was also some evidence for post replacement. This all suggests a substantial building—not just a windbreak—which may have been used and repaired over a long period. Another possible building associated with metalworking (Structure I) was identified north-west of the main focus of activity. This was represented by a group of six post-holes and five other pits.

There were three distinct kinds of iron slag. The first represents furnace bottoms that resulted from primary smelting in bowl furnaces. The second group had all the characteristics of smithing hearth bottoms, from secondary working. The third group lacked distinctive morphologies and so could not be assigned to a specific ironworking process. The total amount of slag was only 43 kg, which represents ironworking on a very small scale.

Later medieval features

The internal features of the ringfort described above are all attributed with more or less confidence to the early medieval period, but features of later medieval date were also identified in the interior. Four large hearths/ fire-pits and a series of associated pits and post-holes were located inside the line of the enclosing bank, in the south-east quadrant of the ringfort. All four hearths/pits had evidence for *in situ* burning and contained charcoal, dominated by oak, quantities of charred cereal grains and legumes. They are interpreted as simple corn-drying kilns. Charcoals from three of the features were dated to AD 1323–

Illus. 5.6.7—Mackney ringfort. Medieval artefacts from the ringfort included (a) a silver groat (obverse) from the reign of Henry VIII, minted in 1546 (E2444:78/89:13); and (b) a socketed iron bodkin-type arrowhead (E2444:302:1) (John Sunderland for Eachtra Archaeological Projects).

1442 (UB-7368), AD 1409–1448 (UB-7369) and AD 1443–1631 (UB-7370). (Again, oak was not used for dating and the samples here were from hazel/alder, birch and hazel.)

A building (Structure J) of similar date was tentatively identified nearby, south-east of the souterrain. This was represented by a group of six post-holes with packing stones, a hearth and miscellaneous associated pits. Charcoal from the hearth was dated to AD 1449–1634 (UB-7375). Other late dates came from charcoals from an isolated post-hole and from a hearth in the northern part of the ringfort, dated respectively to AD 1260–1385 (UB-7372) and AD 1446–1632 (UB-7373).

There were also artefacts from the high or later medieval period. They included two silver coins—one from the reign of Henry III (1247–72) and the other from the reign of Henry VIII (1509–47), possibly minted in 1546—and a socketed, iron arrowhead of 'bodkin' type (Illus. 5.6.7). The arrowhead is probably older than the coins as this type is usually found in 10th- to 13th-century contexts (Carroll & Quinn 2003, 284).

Plant remains and charcoal
by Mary Dillon

Oats, barley, wheat and rye were all present in the bulk soil samples collected from the ringfort at Mackney. Most of the plant remains came from hearths. Oats dominated, making up nearly 50% of the cereal assemblage, with wheat and barley at 23% and 14% respectively. Only a few grains of rye were present. In the early medieval phase, wheat was much less common than oats or barley; but in samples from later medieval features wheat replaced barley as the second most common grain. A significant number of legumes (i.e. peas, beans or related plant parts) was also present in later medieval samples. Hazelnuts were a common food, particularly in the early medieval period.

The charcoal assemblage was dominated by oak, at 62% of the total fragment count, or 70% of the total weight count. This was followed in descending order by hazel (8% and 9%), ash (7% and 4%), various small fruiting trees (Pomoideae) (6% and 4%) and wild cherry/blackthorn type (*Prunus* sp.) (4% and 4%). Willow/poplar, alder, holly, birch, spindle, yew and elder were all present in smaller amounts. Oak would have been highly valued for industrial purposes and, as a consequence, it is probably over-represented in this assemblage. Thus, it is unlikely that two-thirds of the trees around Mackney were oak. Nevertheless, oak woodlands would have been an important resource not only for wood but for oak mast too (for livestock) and their availability to the occupants of Mackney ringfort is commensurate with the evident high status of the settlement.

Animal bones
by Margaret McCarthy

Almost 7,000 animal bones were recovered during the excavation at Mackney ringfort, half of which were identified to species. Most of the bones came from the fills of the enclosing ditch and from the backfilled souterrain, and about 78% of the assemblage is attributed to occupation in the early medieval period. Domestic animals dominated the assemblage, mostly cattle and sheep. The majority of cattle bones belonged to small domestic animals of relatively low stature. The main peak of slaughter seems to have been in the second and third years. Animals over four years of age represent females kept for dairying and breeding, and males, perhaps, for traction. Sheep were second in importance to cattle. The indications are that most sheep were kept up to two years of age, at which time they were slaughtered for their meat. Pigs were less numerous than cattle and sheep, but their remains were found across the site. Predominantly young animals (1–2 years) were slaughtered for their meat. Only four goat bones were identified. Horses, dogs, cats, deer and a variety of wild bird species were also exploited, but they were not important components of the economy or the diet. Overall, there was an almost complete reliance on the three major livestock animals (cattle, sheep and pigs) for meat, complemented occasionally by horseflesh, venison, hare and wild fowl.

The ringfort in the modern period

Infant burials

Long after the ringfort was an occupied medieval homestead, it became a burial ground. Numerous human skeletons were found in the upper fills of the ringfort ditch and also in the interior. Altogether, there were 143 individual skeletons—mostly of infants under the age of six (Table 5.6.1). Most of them were located in a 15 m stretch of the ditch in the south-west arc, with some outliers to the east and west (Illus. 5.6.8). Textiles and shroud pins associated with the burials were of post-medieval and early modern types. The burials were cut into the soft silty soils that had infilled the lower part of the ditch but were sealed by a substantial layer of big stones, about 1 m deep. These stones seem to have been a deliberate attempt by the Trenches to discourage further burials by the local tenantry. They were probably dumped into the ditch in the later 18th century, at a time when this gentry family was developing a landscaped park on its demesne lands at Mackney.

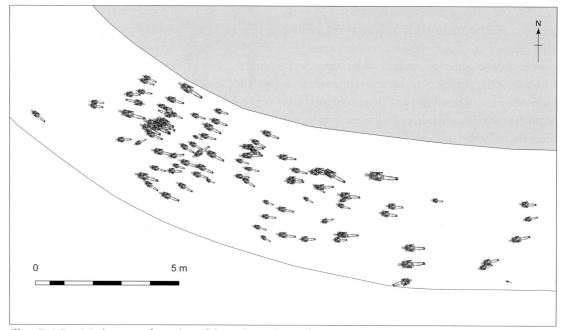

Illus. 5.6.8—Mackney ringfort. Plan of the early modern infant and juvenile burials in the south-west sector of the ditch, where most of these burials were concentrated (Eachtra Archaeological Projects).

Cultivation ridges

At some point in the post-medieval or early modern period the ringfort was disturbed by hand-dug cultivation ridges. The traces are a cross-hatch pattern of furrows in the interior, representing successive north–south and east–west ridge-and-furrow sets. Five big pits were also dug at this time (up to 3.2 m long by 0.4 m deep). They are interpreted as potato 'clamps' (storage pits). Cultivation traces like this are commonly found in ringfort interiors, when the deep humic soils resulting from human occupation in earlier centuries could be readily adapted as kitchen gardens for a rapidly growing, ever hungry rural population in the modern period.

Human skeletal remains

by Linda Lynch

Most of the individuals buried in the ringfort ditch were under the age of six years (138 individuals). There were 116 infants and 39 of these were full-term at the time of death (Tables 5.6.1 and 5.6.2). A number of probable miscarriages were also buried here, the youngest being an individual of just 24 foetal weeks. Two premature infants buried together were possibly twins, sharing a single grave. Just three adults were recovered: a young adult female, a young adult male and a middle-aged adult male.

Of the full-term foetuses, 21 were larger than the average expected size, and this is likely to have led to complications at birth. None was undersized. Conversely, the predominant factor with many of the older infants and juveniles was that they were undersized for their age-at-death, which is likely to have been due to poor health and nutrition and consequent stunted growth.

One juvenile (8–10 years) stood out from all the others—an individual with significant dental problems, a well-healed rib fracture, and a fracture to the cranial vault, received shortly before death. This individual was interred away from the main concentration of burials (literally on the opposite side of the site) and in an unusual burial position, with the limbs contorted. All the evidence suggests that this unfortunate child suffered at the hands of others during life and was buried without love or ceremony.

Table 5.6.1—Mackney 3. Demography of cillín *burials*

Age group	Number	% Total
Infant (< 1 yr)	116	81.1
Juvenile 1 (1–6 yrs)	22	15.4
Juvenile 2 (7–12 yrs)	2	1.4
Adolescent (13–17 yrs)	0	—
Young adult (18–24 yrs)	2	1.4
Middle adult (25–44 yrs)	1	0.7
Old adult (45 + yrs)	0	—
Total	**143**	**100**

Table 5.6.2—Mackney 3. Infant mortalilty profile

Age at death	Number	% Total
Perinate: < 37 foetal weeks	6	5.2
Perinate: 37–42 foetal weeks	39	33.6
Perinate: age undetermined	3	2.6
Infant: 0–3 months	10	8.6
Infant: 3–6 months	23	19.8
Infant: 6–9 months	17	14.7
Infant: 9–12 months	16	13.8
Infant: age undetermined	2	1.7
Total	**116**	**100**

Although the dead at Mackney date to the Christian era, they were not buried with the traditional west–east alignments of Christian burials. This is because they were laid within the ditch in a primarily clockwise direction with the head pointing to '12 noon' and, consequently, the orientation of individuals varied. None of them had coffins but some textile fragments from shrouds survived and could be identified ('Textiles', below).

Textiles
by Elizabeth Heckett

Textiles were found with 21 of the infant burials. They were preserved by partial mineralisation because of their contact with thin metal shroud pins. Pieces of good quality linen were found with eight of the burials and linen fibres and threads were found with a further seven. A deteriorated type of cloth was also noted. The material was coarse and dense in appearance, perhaps from wool, but it was not possible to identify the fibre definitively. It is possible that a substance such as bitumen was added to these coarse fibres. All of the textiles were used in shrouds or winding sheets.

A long time in a crowded place

The archaeology of Mackney ringfort represents several distinct episodes in the history of the Suck Valley and the lives of very different sorts of people. Telescoped by archaeology, the ghosts of medieval farmers and smiths, early modern rural tenants and their gentry landlords all crowd together in the circular arena enclosed by the great ditch.

In its primary phase the ringfort was undoubtedly a high-status early medieval farmstead, on good land, and enjoying access to a wide range of wild and domesticated resources. Fine metalwork, in the form of ornamented pins and brooches, was one indicator of prestige in the early medieval world. This is lacking at Mackney. On the other hand, the dimensions of the ringfort are certainly at the upper end of the scale for similar enclosures in Ireland and the earthworks were clearly intended for display as well as defence. But security was important too. A deep, wide ditch would have been a barrier to marauding wild pigs and wolves and would also have been a brake on assaults by human raiders. When that line of defence failed, the inhabitants would have taken refuge in the inner chamber of their souterrain, where even a boy with a pointed stick could have inflicted pain and injury on an armed man trying to negotiate the low, narrow drop-creep trapdoor in the dark.

The souterrain was also a form of domestic architecture. In peaceful times it would have been a handy cold store for dairy products and cured meat, and was perhaps where the household slaves slept at night. The most obviously domestic building was the central round-house (Structure A). This single-celled building seems small in proportion to the space enclosed by the ringfort, but much of daily life was conducted outdoors, so that the whole of the ringfort interior should be regarded as the domestic space of its inhabitants and not merely their roofed buildings. Also, the surviving evidence certainly does not represent all of the original buildings. A round-house built with posts, wattle and thatch would scarcely last a generation whereas the ringfort, as we have seen, was occupied for several hundred years. A remnant of at least one other round-house was recorded and many others may have been built, dismantled and replaced over the centuries.

Illus. 5.6.9—Mackney ringfort. Ceramic pots for luxury items were among the debris from Mackney House dumped into the souterrain. The 18th-century house was demolished in the 1970s (John Sunderland).

A ringfort was not only a homestead but, more specifically, a working farmstead, self-sufficient in terms of tool-making and food processing, among other things. This is reflected in the evidence for other buildings, admittedly poorly preserved, which was found throughout the interior. At Mackney, these ancillary buildings included workshops as well as byres and stores, including the post-built structures (Structures H and I) in the metalworking area. This was located in the north-east quadrant, where the prevailing south-west wind would have carried the smoke and noxious fumes of iron smelting away from the ringfort interior.

The ringfort is the classic settlement type of the early medieval period, but our evidence shows that Mackney ringfort was occupied in the later medieval period also. Corn-drying kilns alone do not prove this, as an abandoned earthwork enclosure would have been a convenient place to process the harvest from adjoining lands. But it seems that Mackney ringfort was not an abandoned earthwork at this time, because there are also radiocarbon dated features (hearths and a post-hole) indicating more permanent occupation. The small assemblage of later medieval artefacts makes the case compelling.

The placename Mackney can be glossed mundanely as a location where parsnips or such tap-root vegetables were grown (Joyce 1871, Vol. 2, 350) but there is a teasing echo also of Conmaicne, a pseudo-historical ancestor of the Uí Maine (latterly O'Kellys), the dominant Gaelic group in east

Galway in pre-Norman times. Richard de Burgo's invasion of 1235 inflicted crushing defeats on the Gaelic kings and sub-kings of Connacht, but the 14th century saw reversals for the Norman barons and, after the Black Death and the Bruce Wars, the O'Kellys re-emerged as an autonomous power in their heartlands of east Galway, including the hinterland of Ballinasloe (Nicholls 2003, 170, 174). It is mere speculation to suggest that Mackney ringfort was an important seat of the Uí Maine/O'Kellys, named for one of their legendary ancestors; it is a fact, however, that this impressive ringfort in their territory was occupied in the high-tide of the Norman period and beyond.

We do not know when, or in what circumstances, Mackney was finally abandoned as a settlement site. Eventually, the great silted ditch became a repository for the infant dead. *Cillín* burial grounds were used throughout rural Ireland in post-medieval/early modern times, often in marginal places like abandoned medieval earthworks. They are especially associated with unbaptised infants who were not considered fit for burial in the consecrated ground of a churchyard cemetery. Ultimately, they were considered unfit for burial in the landscaped grounds of Mackney House too, and the practice of *cillín* burial was ended when the great ditch was closed with rubble in the 18th century. In time, the Trenches came and went, like all before them, to lie beneath their own marble graveslabs. After gracing the landscape for 200 years their house was demolished and its fabric and contents were dispersed (Illus. 5.6.9). In a field nearby, the great earthwork at Mackney gradually resolved itself into a low, curvilinear bank in pasture—a tell-tale observed by a keen-eyed field archaeologist walking the proposed route of a 21st-century motorway.

Appendix 1
Radiocarbon dates from excavated sites

This table records the radiocarbon dates from excavated archaeological features on the M6 Galway to Ballinasloe road scheme. The sites are listed from west to east. They are numbered according to the site location maps in Chapter 1 (Nos 1–43) and the excavation registration numbers (E Nos) issued by the National Monuments Service. Radiocarbon ages are quoted in conventional years BP (before present: AD 1950). Calibrated date ranges are in calendrical years expressed at one-sigma and two-sigma levels of confidence (1σ = 68% probability; 2σ = 98% probability). The dates were calibrated using the IntCal04 calibration dataset (Reimer et al. 2004) and, variously, calibration programmes by Stuiver & Reimer (1993) and Stuiver et al. (2005; CALIB Rev 5.0.2) for dates with UB/UBA codes; by Bronk Ramsey (2005; OxCal v.3.10) for Waikato codes; and by Talma & Vogel (1993) for dates with Beta lab codes, except Beta-272868 to 272872, for which the IntCal13 dataset (Reimer et al. 2013) and OxCal v4.2.3 calibration programme (Bronk Ramsey 2013) were used.

Lab. code	Sample material	Years BP	dC13‰	Calibrated dates
1. Doughiska: burnt mounds (E2052)				
UB-7580	Wood (Scots pine: root or branch), Mound A	4081 ± 36	-24.0	2836–2503 BC (1σ) 2861–2491 BC (2σ)
UB-7581	Wood (oak), Mound C	2691 ± 34	-26.0	898–808 BC (1σ) 904–802 BC (2σ)
UB-7855	Charcoal (mixed species: alder, ash, elm, hazel, holly, oak, Pomoideae, *Prunus* sp.), Mound A	2825 ± 34	-31.3	1041–975 BC (1σ) 1124–846 BC (2σ)
UB-7856	Charcoal (elm), Mound C	3156 ± 23	-22.9	1450–1411 BC (1σ) 1494–1397 BC (2σ)
UB-7857	Charcoal (Mixed species: alder, ash, Pomoideae), Mound A	2803 ± 23	-24.9	993–922 BC (1σ) 1012–902 BC (2σ)
UB-7858	Charcoal (mixed species: alder, hazel), Area C	2904 ± 33	-19.0	1186–1019 BC (1σ) 1253–1001 BC (2σ)
UB-7859	Charcoal (mixed species: alder, ash, elm, hazel, holly, oak brushwood, Pomoideae, yew), Mound A	2742 ± 28	-31.3	896–836 BC (1σ) 918–814 BC (2σ)
UB-7860	Charcoal (mixed species: alder, elm, holly, oak, yew), Mound B	3944 ± 29	-26.9	2548–2405 BC (1σ) 2566–2342 BC (2σ)
UB-7861	Charcoal (mixed species: ash, hazel, *Prunus* sp.), Mound D	957 ± 25	-27.7	AD 1026–1150 (1σ) AD 1022–1155 (2σ)

Lab. code	Sample material	Years BP	dC13‰	Calibrated dates
1. Doughiska: burnt mounds (E2052)				
UB-7874	Charcoal (poss. alder buckthorn, elm) Mound D	928 ± 34	-28.5	AD 1042–1106 (1σ) AD 1024–1182 (2σ)
UB-7877	Charcoal (mixed species: alder, ash, hazel, holly, oak, *Prunus* sp.), Mound D	1054 ± 30	-21.4	AD 974–1019 (1σ) AD 897–1025 (2σ)
2. Coolagh: cashel with round-house and lime kilns (E2435)				
UB-7690	Charcoal (hazel) from a deposit beneath a drystone round-house	1322 ± 32	-26.0	AD 656–765 (1σ) AD 651–771 (2σ)
UB-7691	Charcoal (ash) from a post-hole in the cashel, near the entrance	1231 ± 32	-25.0	AD 712–864 (1σ) AD 688–882 (2σ)
UB-7692	Charcoal (hazel) from a post-hole in the cashel entranceway	2744 ± 35	-26.0	914–838 BC (1σ) 975–814 BC (2σ)
UB-7693	Charcoal (ash) from a deposit underlying a lime kiln	1152 ± 32	-26.0	AD 784–966 (1σ) AD 779–973 (2σ)
3. Carnmore West: cashel with souterrain and cereal-drying kilns (E2436)				
UB-7582	Bone sample from skeleton of small horse or donkey in blocked souterrain entrance	91 ± 30	-22.0	AD 1696–1917 (1σ) AD 1684–1954 (2σ)
UB-7684	Charcoal (oak) from post-hole at entrance to annex	1250 ± 32	-26.0	AD 688–800 (1σ) AD 676–869 (2σ)
UB-7686	Charcoal (oak, hazel) from a rock-cut hearth by the souterrain entrance	1188 ± 31	-26.0	AD 781–884 (1σ) AD 720–948 (2σ)
UB-7687	Charcoal (oak, hazel) from a rock-cut hearth by the souterrain entrance	1180 ± 31	-26.0	AD 781–888 (1σ) AD 772–965 (2σ)
UB-7688	Charcoal (oak) from a basal fill of the souterrain entrance	1268 ± 31	-25.0	AD 685–771 (1σ) AD 662–856 (2σ)
UB-7689	Charcoal (mixed species) from the fill of a truncated primary kiln	1274 ± 32	-27.0	AD 688–772 (1σ) AD 665–859 (2σ)
UBA-7864	Charcoal (oak) from around the flue of the secondary, L-shaped kiln	994 ± 27	-25.1	AD 995–1117 (1σ) AD 988–1152 (2σ)
UBA-7865	Charcoal (*Prunus* sp., hazel) from a pit underlying collapse from the cashel wall	1214 ± 26	-28.9	AD 775–868 (1σ) AD 710–889 (2σ)
UBA-7866	Charcoal (ash, *Prunus* sp.) from a post-hole in the cashel entranceway	1432 ± 28	-28.7	AD 607–646 (1σ) AD 576–655 (2σ)

Lab. code	Sample material	Years BP	dC13‰	Calibrated dates
3. Carnmore West: cashel with souterrain and cereal-drying kilns (E2436)				
UBA-7867	Charcoal (Pomoideae) from the fill of a truncated, primary kiln	1233 ± 34	–29.9	AD 709–863 (1σ) AD 687–881 (2σ)
UBA-7868	Charcoal (oak) from the firing chamber of the secondary, L-shaped kiln	1340 ± 34	–28.9	AD 650–759 (1σ) AD 641–723 (2σ)
UBA-7869	Charcoal (oak) from post-hole at entrance to annex	1230 ± 34	–29.7	AD 713–865 (1σ) AD 688–883 (2σ)
UBA-7870	Charcoal (ash, *Prunus* sp.) from the firing chamber of the secondary, L-shaped kiln	1280 ± 44	–30.7	AD 675–772 (1σ) AD 657–865 (2σ)
UBA-7871	Charcoal (alder, hazelnut) from around the flue of the secondary, L-shaped kiln	864 ± 35	–26.1	AD 1058–1221 (1σ) AD 1045–1258 (2σ)
UBA-7872	Charcoal (oak) from the flue of the secondary, L-shaped kiln	1175 ± 40	–28.8	AD 779–894 (1σ) AD 723–972 (2σ)
UBA-7873	Reeds from water-sorted sediment in the base of an infilled (livestock?) pond	110 ± 0.5	–26.3	AD 1695–1918 (1σ) AD 1694–1919 (2σ)
4. Ballygarraun West: isolated medieval burial with charcoal and antler (E2534)				
UBA-7683	Human bone	1471 ± 67	–20.1	AD 540–649 (1σ) AD 432–661 (2σ)
UBA-7863	Charcoal (hazel, alder) from a deposit of carbonised plant remains underlying skeleton	1530 ± 33	–28.1	AD 440–580 (1σ) AD 432–600 (2σ)
UBA-7862	Charcoal (hazel, alder) from a deposit of carbonised plant remains underlying skeleton	1424 ± 30	–36.2	AD 610–649 (1σ) AD 578–659 (2σ)
5. Newford: pyre, post-pits and burnt mound (E2437)				
UB-7399	Charcoal (hazel) from fill of post-hole in Area A	2863 ± 35	–25.0	1187–921 BC (1σ) 1112–979 BC (2σ)
UB-7400	Charcoal (oak) from fill of post-hole in Area A	2878 ± 33	–27.0	1193–934 BC (1σ) 1114–1009 BC (2σ)
UB-7401	Charcoal (oak) from fill of post-hole in Area A	2843 ± 33	–26.0	1114–918 BC (1σ) 1048–936 BC (2σ)
UB-7402	Charcoal (Pomoideae) from fill of post-hole in Area A	2834 ± 33	–27.0	1113–908 BC (1σ) 1026–967 BC (2σ)

Lab. code	Sample material	Years BP	dC13‰	Calibrated dates
5. Newford: pyre, post-pits and burnt mound (E2437)				
UB-7403	Charcoal (Pomoideae) from fill of post-hole in Area A	2854 ± 32	-25.0	1121–925 BC (1σ) 1108–938 BC (2σ)
UB-7404	Carbonised nut shell (hazel) from burnt mound	4746 ± 38	-27.0	3639–3380 BC (1σ) 3634–3520 BC (2σ)
UB-7406	Cremated bone (pyre)	2535 ± 35	-24.0	799–540 BC (1σ) 791–569 BC (2σ)
UB-7484	Cremated bone (pyre)	2580 ± 34	-22.0	814–559 BC (1σ) 803–674 BC (2σ)
6. Furzypark: burnt spread and pottery sherds (possible funerary vessel) (E2553)				
UB-7407	Charcoal (alder or hazel) from under the burnt spread	3248 ± 35	-26.0	1605–1455 BC (1σ) 1611–1443 BC (2σ)
7. Farranablake East: cashel (E2352)				
Nil dates				
8. Moyode: estate tenant's cottage (E2353)				
Nil dates				
9. Deerpark: cremation burial and ring-ditch (E2438)				
UB-7450	Charcoal (oak) from pit near ring-ditch fills	1017 ± 29	-24.0	AD 992–1026 (1σ) AD 905–1148 (2σ)
UB-7451	Charcoal (Pomoideae) from ring-ditch fills	2170 ± 33	-26.0	353–173 BC (1σ) 363–113 BC (2σ)
UB-7452	Charcoal (hazel) from ring-ditch fills	2570 ± 31	-26.0	800–673 BC (1σ) 808–558 BC (2σ)
UB-7485	Cremated human bone from ring-ditch	2110 ± 33	-22.0	181–60 BC (1σ) 342–45 BC (2σ)
UB-7486	Cremated human bone from ring-ditch	2167 ± 35	-25.0	353–170 BC (1σ) 362–111 BC (2σ)
10. Deerpark: kennels of Tallyho Lodge (E2057)				
Nil dates				
11. Rathgorgin: modern burnt spread (E2439)				
Nil dates				
12. Brusk: brick clamps (E2063)				
Nil dates				

Lab. code	Sample material	Years BP	dC13‰	Calibrated dates
13. Curragh More: cremation burial (E2520)				
UB-7467	Cremated human bone from cremation pit	3195 ± 36	−26.0	1529–1435 BC (1σ) 1529–1407 BC (2σ)
UB-7488	Cremated human bone from cremation pit	3270 ± 36	−23.0	1607–1501 BC (1σ) 1628–1453 BC (2σ)
14. Clogharevaun: multi-period landscape (E2056)				
UB-7408	Willow or poplar charcoal from burnt mound, Area C	3140 ± 32	−26.0	1450–1390 BC (1σ) 1496–1318 BC (2σ)
UB-7409	Oak charcoal from trough of burnt mound, Area C	3078 ± 32	−26.0	1406–1314 BC (1σ) 1419–1268 BC (2σ)
15. Carrowkeel: cemetery-settlement enclosure (E2046)				
GU-15326	Mouse bone (*Mus musculus*)	1245 ± 45	−19.5	AD 680–860 (1σ) AD 670–890 (2σ)
GU-15327	Mouse bone (*Mus musculus*)	1115 ± 35	−19.7	AD 890–975 (1σ) AD 860–1020 (2σ)
UB-7410	Foetus	499 ± 29	−19.0	AD 1415–1436 (1σ) AD 1400–1477 (2σ)
UB-7411	Child	1129 ± 31	−20.0	AD 888–970 (1σ) AD 782–989 (2σ)
UB-7412	Adult	1186 ± 32	−22.0	AD 781–885 (1σ) AD 721–960 (2σ)
UB-7413	Foetus	1148 ± 31	−20.0	AD 785–968 (1σ) AD 780–975 (2σ)
UB-7414	Child	1156 ± 31	−21.0	AD 783–960 (1σ) AD 779–971 (2σ)
UB-7416	Infant	1125 ± 31	−20.0	AD 890–970 (1σ) AD 783–991 (2σ)
UB-7417	Adult	1228 ± 31	−21.0	AD 717–865 (1σ) AD 689–884 (2σ)
UB-7418	Infant	1214 ± 31	−19.0	AD 774–871 (1σ) AD 693–890 (2σ)
UB-7419	Foetus	638 ± 30	−20.0	AD 1293–1388 (1σ) AD 1284–1396 (2σ)
UB-7420	Adult	1264 ± 31	−21.0	AD 68–773 (1σ) AD 667–861 (2σ)

Lab. code	Sample material	Years BP	dC13‰	Calibrated dates
15. Carrowkeel: cemetery-settlement enclosure (E2046)				
UB-7422	Foetus	815 ± 31	-20.0	AD 1211–1261 (1σ) AD 1169–1269 (2σ)
UB-7423	Adult	1244 ± 32	-22.0	AD 688–808 (1σ) AD 682–872 (2σ)
UB-7424	Child	1182 ± 32	-22.0	AD 781–887 (1σ) AD 726–964 (2σ)
UB-7425	Adolescent	1250 ± 34	-23.0	AD 687–802 (1σ) AD 676–870 (2σ)
UB-7426	Infant	830 ± 31	-20.0	AD 1186–1254 (1σ) AD 1159–1265 (2σ)
UB-7427	Adult	940 ± 31	-22.0	AD 1034–1153 (1σ) AD 1024–1161 (2σ)
UB-7428	Adult	906 ± 31	-21.0	AD 1045–1170 (1σ) AD 1038–1208 (2σ)
UB-7429	Child	1104 ± 31	-20.0	AD 896–981 (1σ) AD 885–1013 (2σ)
UB-7430	Child	1185 ± 31	-21.0	AD 781–886 (1σ) AD 772–951 (2σ)
UB-7431	Child	1193 ± 34	-24.0	AD 779–881 (1σ) AD 710–949 (2σ)
UB-7432	Child	1261 ± 33	-22.0	AD 688–775 (1σ) AD 668–864 (2σ)
UB-7433	Adult	954 ± 31	-21.0	AD 1026–1151 (1σ) AD 1022–1156 (2σ)
UB-7434	Infant	1215 ± 32	-22.0	AD 773–873 (1σ) AD 692–890 (2σ)
UB-7435	Child	1203 ± 32	-21.0	AD 778–870 (1σ) AD 694–936 (2σ)
UB-7436	Adult	1193 ± 31	-19.0	AD 780–880 (1σ) AD 716–943 (2σ)
UB-7437	Infant	949 ± 32	-22.0	AD 1028–1152 (1σ) AD 1023–1158 (2σ)
UB-7438	Adult	935 ± 31	-21.0	AD 1039–1153 (1σ) AD 1024–1165 (2σ)

Lab. code	Sample material	Years BP	dC13‰	Calibrated dates
15. Carrowkeel: cemetery-settlement enclosure (E2046)				
UB-7439	Child	1168 ± 32	-21.0	AD 781–934 (1σ) AD 775–968 (2σ)
UB-7440	Adult	1301 ± 31	-20.0	AD 667–766 (1σ) AD 660–772 (2σ)
UB-7441	Adult	1182 ± 31	-21.0	AD 781–887 (1σ) AD 728–962 (2σ)
UB-7442	Child	907 ± 30	-21.0	AD 1045–1168 (1σ) AD 1037–1207 (2σ)
UB-7443	Adult	1305 ± 34	-24.0	AD 665–766 (1σ) AD 658–773 (2σ)
UB-7444	Child	1113 ± 32	-21.0	AD 894–974 (1σ) AD 832–1015 (2σ)
UB-7445	Adult	1196 ± 35	-25.0	AD 779–880 (1σ) AD 694–946 (2σ)
UB-7446	Infant	1223 ± 33	-23.0	AD 723–869 (1σ) AD 689–887 (2σ)
UB-7447	Foetus	1193 ± 33	-22.0	AD 780–881 (1σ) AD 712–947 (2σ)
UB-7448	Human bone	1249 ± 31	-19.0	AD 688–801 (1σ) AD 678–869 (2σ)
UB-7449	Human bone	1113 ± 32	-20.0	AD 894–974 (1σ) AD 832–1015 (2σ)
UB-7482	Human bone	1127 ± 32	-22.0	AD 889–971 (1σ) AD 782–991 (2σ)
UB-7483	Human bone	1227 ± 31	-20.0	AD 718–866 (1σ) AD 689–884 (2σ)
16. Ballykeeran: short-cist cremation burial and ring-ditch (E2440)				
UB-7455	Charcoal (hazel) from furrow fill overlying ring-ditch	2683 ± 32	-28.3	891–805 BC (1σ) 899–801 BC (2σ)
UB-7456	Charcoal (Pomoideae) from furrow fill overlying ring-ditch	2787 ± 32	-26.0	994–988 BC (1σ) 1010–843 BC (2σ)
UB-7457	Charcoal (hazel) ring-ditch fill	2729 ± 32	-25.0	996–919 BC (1σ) 968–810 BC (2σ)
UB-7458	Charcoal (alder) from ring-ditch fill	2803 ± 31	-25.0	1001–921 BC (1σ) 1042–894 BC (2σ)

Lab. code	Sample material	Years BP	dC13‰	Calibrated dates
16. Ballykeeran: short–cist cremation burial and ring–ditch (E2440)				
UB-7461	Charcoal (hazel) from fill of cist	2809 ± 33	–25.0	1001–921 BC (1σ) 1050–850 BC (2σ)
UB-7462	Charcoal (alder/hazel) from linear feature cut by ring-ditch	2755 ± 32	–25.0	923–842 BC (1σ) 993–825 BC (2σ)
UB-7463	Charcoal (Pomoideae) from post-hole fill	2661 ± 30	–25.0	832–801 BC (1σ) 825–794 BC (2σ)
UB-7464	Charcoal (alder) from fill of cist	2778 ± 32	–20.0	977–857 BC (1σ) 1004–841 BC (2σ)
UB-7465	Charcoal (hazel) from post-hole fill	2770 ± 32	–26.0	973–847 BC (1σ) 998–837 BC (2σ)
UB-7466	Charcoal (willow) from poss. kerb slot	2838 ± 33	–26.0	1041–933 BC (1σ) 1114–913 BC (2σ)
UB-7487	Burnt bone from cist	2563 ± 34	–16.0	801–600 BC (1σ) 806–550 BC (2σ)
17. Loughrea & Attymon Light Railway: architectural heritage survey				
Nil dates				
18. Killescragh 1: burnt mounds and trackways (E2070)				
UB-7242	Wood (hazel) from platform	3023 ± 34	–26.0	1374–1216 BC (1σ) 1394–1132 BC (2σ)
Wk-21245	Charcoal (alder and ash) from upper part of burnt mound	3826 ± 41	–25.5	2344–2200 BC (1σ) 2458–2144 BC (2σ)
Wk-21246	Charcoal (alder and ash) from hearth in upper part of burnt mound	3855 ± 107	–26.0	2470–2145 BC (1σ) 2580–2015 BC (2σ)
Wk-21343	Charcoal (alder) from lower part of burnt mound	3947 ± 40	–25.4	2570–2340 BC (1σ) 2570–2300 BC (2σ)
19. Killescragh 2: burnt mounds and trackways (E2071)				
Beta-241472	Wood (pine) from peat deposit	5870 ± 60	–25.2	4800–4690 BC (1σ) 4880–4590 BC (2σ)
Beta-241473	Wood (birch) from short trackway remnant	3290 ± 40	–28.7	1620–1510 BC (1σ) 1670–1490 BC (2σ)
Beta-241474	Wood (ash) from trackway	2880 ± 60	–26.6	1130–980 BC (1σ) 1260–910 BC (2σ)
Beta-241475	Wood (elm) from wood litter horizon	4130 ± 40	–25.4	2860–2620 BC (1σ) 2880–2570 BC (2σ)

Lab. code	Sample material	Years BP	dC13‰	Calibrated dates
19. Killescragh 2: burnt mounds and trackways (E2071)				
UB-7241	Wood (alderbuckthorn) from trackway	2870 ± 35	-26.0	1115–1001 BC (1σ) 1190–926 BC (2σ)
Wk-21341	Wood (hazel) from burnt mound, secondary deposit	3211 ± 36	-27.5	1505–1435 BC (1σ) 1610–1410 BC (2σ)
Wk-21342	Wood (hazel) from burnt spread	3730 ± 37	-26.5	2200–2040 BC (1σ) 2280–2020 BC (2σ)
20. Caraun More 4: prehistoric pits and medieval watercourses (E2073)				
Beta-241007	Carbonised grain from possible corn-drying kiln; primary fill	780 ± 40	-23.7	AD 1210–1270 (1σ) AD 1170–1280 (2σ)
Beta-241471	Charcoal (alder) from pit; Area 6	3020 ± 40	-27.0	1370–1220 BC (1σ) 1400–1130 BC (2σ)
UBA-10319	Animal bone (cattle) from fill of early enclosure ditch	1423 ± 23	-20.5	AD 615–648 (1σ) AD 593–657 (2σ)
Wk-20203	Charcoal (birch) from small bowl furnace or hearth fill	2205 ± 38	-26.0	360–200 BC (1σ) 390–180 BC (2σ)
Wk-20204	Charcoal (willow) from quarry pit	314 ± 41	-25.5	AD 1510–1650 (1σ) AD 1460–1660 (2σ)
Wk-20205	Charcoal (blackthorn) upper fill of mill-race ditch	678 ± 42	-27.5	AD 1270–1390 (1σ) AD 1260–1400 (2σ)
Wk-21339	Charcoal (Pomoideae) from fill of hearth or fire pit	1516 ± 35	-25.5	AD 460–610 (1σ) AD 430–620 (2σ)
21. Caraun More 1: burnt mound (E2074)				
Wk-21777	Charcoal (Pomoideae) from burnt mound	2454 ± 30	-28.5	750–410 BC (1σ) 760–410 BC (2σ)
22. Caraun More 3: burnt mound (E2072)				
Wk-21247	Wood (hazel) from timbers in trough	3231 ± 64	-28.6	1605–1432 BC (1σ) 1667–1393 BC (2σ)
23. Caraun More 2: burnt mound (E2055)				
Wk-21340	Charcoal (Pomoideae) from burnt mound	2840 ± 36	-26.0	1050–930 BC (1σ) 1120–910 BC (2σ)
24. Cross: ring-ditches with cremations and inhumations (E2069)				
Beta-241006	Burnt human bone from pit	2080 ± 40	-21.3	340–110 BC (1σ) 360–50 BC (2σ)

Lab. code	Sample material	Years BP	dC13‰	Calibrated dates
24. Cross: ring-ditches with cremations and inhumations (E2069)				
Beta-241008	Burnt human bone from pit	2990 ± 40	-23.7	1300–1140 BC (1σ) 1380–1120 BC (2σ)
Wk-21248	Human bone: Burial 1	1489 ± 38	-20.1	AD 543–614 (1σ) AD 439–648 (2σ)
Wk-21249	Human bone: Burial 2	1587 ± 38	-21.0	AD 427–534 (1σ) AD 400–560 (2σ)
Wk-21250	Human bone: Burial 3	1581 ± 38	-20.2	AD 430–535 (1σ) AD 404–564 (2σ)
Wk-21251	Human bone: Burial 4	1628 ± 39	-20.8	AD 385–532 (1σ) AD 337–540 (2σ)
Wk-21252	Human bone: Burial 5	1674 ± 38	-21.2	AD 265–419 (1σ) AD 252–506 (2σ)
Wk-21253	Human bone: Burial 6	1538 ± 39	-20.4	AD 429–534 (1σ) AD 400–565 (2σ)
Wk-21254	Human bone: Burial 7	1604 ± 38	-21.2	AD 414–533 (1σ) AD 382–552 (2σ)
25. Rahally: hillfort, ringforts and field system (E2006)				
Beta-241478	Human bone (rib) from Burial 1 in univallate ringfort ditch	1070 ± 40	-20.4	AD 900–1010 (1σ) AD 890–1030 (2σ)
Beta-241479	Human bone (rib) from Burial 2 within the annex	980 ± 40	-21.5	AD 1020–1120 (1σ) AD 990–1160 (2σ)
Beta-241480	Human bone (rib) from Burial 3 in the annex ditch	940 ± 40	-20.6	AD 1030–1160 (1σ) AD 1020–1200 (2σ)
UB-7244	Charcoal (alder) from inner hillfort ditch (testing phase)	2756 ± 32	-26.0	924–842 BC (1σ) 994–827 BC (2σ)
UB-7245	Charcoal (oak) from burnt deposit under field system bank (first testing phase)	884 ± 29	-25.0	AD 1053–1211 (1σ) AD 1043–1218 (2σ)
Wk-22636	Charcoal (ash) from outer double hillfort ditch	2509 ± 30	-25.1	770–550 BC (1σ) 790–520 BC (2σ)
Wk-22637	Charcoal (alder) from middle hillfort ditch	2826 ± 30	-25.9	1015–925 BC (1σ) 1090–900 BC (2σ)
Wk-22638	Charcoal (Pomoideae) from univallate ringfort ditch	1225 ± 30	-26.4	AD 710–870 (1σ) AD 680–890 (2σ)

Lab. code	Sample material	Years BP	dC13‰	Calibrated dates
25. Rahally: hillfort, ringforts and field system (E2006)				
Wk-22639	Charcoal (*Prunus* sp.) from isolated pit	973 ± 30	-25.2	AD 1020–1150 (1σ) AD 1010–1160 (2σ)
Wk-22640	Charcoal (oak) from pit within univallate ringfort	1239 ± 30	-25.7	AD 690–860 (1σ) AD 680–880 (2σ)
Wk-22641	Charcoal (Pomoideae) from annex ditch	926 ± 30	-24.9	AD 1040–1160 (1σ) AD 1020–1180 (2σ)
Wk-22642	Charcoal (alder) from gully in annex	2200 ± 30	-27.3	360–200 BC (1σ) 380–180 BC (2σ)
Wk-22643	Charcoal (Pomoideae) from bowl furnace	2088 ± 30	-25.8	170–50 BC (1σ) 200–40 BC (2σ)
Wk-22644	Charcoal (oak) from annex ditch (basal fill)	1911 ± 30	-25.0	AD 65–130 (1σ) AD 20–210 (2σ)
Wk-22645	Charcoal (Pomoideae) from post-hole in annex	361 ± 30	-26.2	AD 1460–1630 (1σ) AD 1440–1640 (2σ)
Wk-22646	Charcoal (Pomoideae) from dumbbell kiln in annex	775 ± 30	-24.9	AD 1220–1275 (1σ) AD 1215–1285 (2σ)
26. Ballinphuil: peat cores				
—	See full report on CD-ROM			
27. Rathglass: Bronze Age cremations, medieval ironworking and cereal kiln (E2121)				
Beta-241476	Charcoal (alder) from furnace pit, Area 1	580 ± 40	-26.5	AD 1310–1410 (1σ) AD 1300–1430 (2σ)
Beta-241477	Charcoal (oak) from furnace pit, Area 1	660 ± 40	-25.1	AD 1280–1390 (1σ) AD 1270–1400 (2σ)
Wk-21240	Charcoal (alder) from pit with burnt bone, Area 4	3481 ± 52	-26.6	1880–1745 BC (1σ) 1941–1681 BC (2σ)
Wk-21241	Charcoal (alder) from deposit sealing a cremation pit, Area 5	2857 ± 75	-26.7	1128–915 BC (1σ) 1260–841 BC (2σ)
Wk-21242	Charcoal (ash) from cremation pit, Area 3	2931 ± 30	-29.2	1208–1055 BC (1σ) 1259–1025 BC (2σ)
Wk-21243	Charcoal (ash) from cremation pit, Area 3	2864 ± 99	-26.3	1193–912 BC (1σ) 1313–821 BC (2σ)
Wk-21244	Charcoal (ash, hazel and blackthorn) from cremation pit, Area 3	3004 ± 112	-26.5	1401–1092 BC (1σ) 1493–930 BC (2σ)

Lab. code	Sample material	Years BP	dC13‰	Calibrated dates
27. Rathglass: Bronze Age cremations, medieval ironworking and cereal kiln (E2121)				
Wk-21336	Charcoal (hazel) from cremation pit, Area 3	2990 ± 36	-26.2	1300–1130 BC (1σ) 1390–1110 BC (2σ)
Wk-21337	Charcoal (Pomoideae) from cremation pit, Area 3	2840 ± 35	-25.2	1050–930 BC (1σ) 1120–910 BC (2σ)
Wk-21338	Charcoal (hazel) from cremation pit, Area 4	3578 ± 36	-24.7	2010–1880 BC (1σ) 2030–1770 BC (2σ)
Wk-22891	Carbonised seeds from cereal-drying kiln	638 ± 30	-22.1	AD 1290–1390 (1σ) AD 1280–1400 (2σ)
28. Treanbaun 1: cremation cemetery and palisaded enclosure (E2064)				
Wk-21795	Charcoal (hazel) from pit in Area A	3052 ± 31	-26.6	1390–1290 BC (1σ) 1410–1210 BC (2σ)
Wk-21796	Charcoal (hazel) from pit in Area A	2959 ± 49	-26.8	1270–1080 BC (1σ) 1370–1010 BC (2σ)
Wk-21797	Charcoal (hazel) from post-hole in Area A	2889 ± 48	-26.0	1190–990 BC (1σ) 1260–920 BC (2σ)
Wk-21798	Charcoal (Pomoideae and hazel) from palisade trench in Area B	3231 ± 49	-24.9	1610–1430 BC (1σ) 1620–1410 BC (2σ)
Wk-22561	Burnt bone (poss. human) from pit in Area C	4111 ± 30	-26.6	2850–2580 BC (1σ) 2870–2570 BC (2σ)
Wk-22562	Burnt bone (unident.) from pit in Area C	4077 ± 30	-10.0	2840–2500 BC (1σ) 2860–2490 BC (2σ)
Wk-22563	Burnt bone (unident.) from deposit overlying poss. cremation pit in Area C	3957 ± 30	-26.3	2570–2400 BC (1σ) 2570–2340 BC (2σ)
Wk-22564	Burnt bone (poss. animal) from pit in Area C	4088 ± 30	-27.0	2840–2570 BC (1σ) 2860–2490 BC (2σ)
Wk-22705	Charcoal (alder) from pit in Area C	2703 ± 30	-26.7	895–810 BC (1σ) 910–800 BC (2σ)
Wk-22706	Charcoal (alder) from cremation pit in Area C	4870 ± 30	-25.6	3695–3635 BC (1σ) 3710–3630 BC (2σ)
Wk-22707	Charcoal (hazel and alder) from cremation pit in Area C	4896 ± 30	-24.6	3695–3650 BC (1σ) 3760–3630 BC (2σ)
Wk-22708	Charcoal (alder) from pit inside palisade in Area B	2865 ± 30	-27.8	1120–990 BC (1σ) 1130–920 BC (2σ)

Lab. code	Sample material	Years BP	dC13‰	Calibrated dates
28. Treanbaun 1: cremation cemetery and palisaded enclosure (E2064)				
Wk–22709	Charcoal (Pomoideae) from pit inside palisade in Area B	2907 ± 30	–24.4	1190–1020 BC (1σ) 1220–1000 BC (2σ)
Wk–22710	Carbonised seeds from pit in Area B	3245 ± 30	–24.5	1610–1450 BC (1σ) 1610–1440 BC (2σ)
29. (a) Treanbaun 2: early medieval cemetery–settlement enclosure (E2123)				
Wk–21778	Adult ?female bone	1085 ± 47	–20.1	AD 890–1020 (1σ) AD 820–1030 (2σ)
Wk–21779	Older child bone	1140 ± 45	–20.6	AD 890–990 (1σ) AD 810–1030 (2σ)
Wk–21780	Child bone	1187 ± 45	–20.2	AD 770–900 (1σ) AD 690–970 (2σ)
Wk–21781	Child bone	904 ± 46	–20.6	AD 1040–1190 (1σ) AD 1020–1220 (2σ)
Wk–21783	Adult male bone	1221 ± 46	–20.5	AD 720–880 (1σ) AD 670–940 (2σ)
Wk–21784	Adult (indeterminate) bone	895 ± 45	–20.7	AD 1040–1210 (1σ) AD 1020–1220 (2σ)
Wk–21785	Adult female bone	1054 ± 46	–20.3	AD 890–1030 (1σ) AD 880–1120 (2σ)
Wk–21786	Adult (indeterminate) bone	1139 ± 46	–20.3	AD 820–980 (1σ) AD 770–1010 (2σ)
Wk–21787	Adult male bone	1142 ± 46	–20.3	AD 780–980 (1σ) AD 770–1000 (2σ)
Wk–21788	Charcoal (Pomoideae) from tertiary ditch fill	1168 ± 27	–25.4	AD 780–940 (1σ) AD 770–970 (2σ)
Wk–21789	Charcoal (*Prunus* sp.) from upper ditch fill	950 ± 26	–24.8	AD 1020–1160 (1σ) AD 1020–1160 (2σ)
Wk–21790	Charcoal (*Prunus* sp.) from souterrain fill	749 ± 26	–27.0	AD 1255–1285 (1σ) AD 1220–1285 (2σ)
Wk–21791	Charcoal (Pomoideae) from upper ditch fill	634 ± 26	–25.4	AD 1295–1390 (1σ) AD 1280–1400 (2σ)
Wk–22559	Burnt bone (human/animal) from 'cremation pit' in the ditched enclosure	2418 ± 30	–28.0	540–400 BC (1σ) 750–390 BC (2σ)

Lab. code	Sample material	Years BP	dC13‰	Calibrated dates
29. (a) Treanbaun 2: early medieval cemetery-settlement enclosure (E2123)				
Wk-22711	Charcoal (alder/hazel) from primary ditch fill	2052 ± 30	-27.0	110 BC–0 (1σ) 170 BC–AD 20 (2σ)
Wk-22713	Charcoal (unspecified) from primary ditch fill	1369 ± 30	-22.6	AD 640–675 (1σ) AD 600–690 (2σ)
Wk-22714	Charcoal (unspecified) from 'fire pit' in the ditched enclosure	1263 ± 30	-26.0	AD 685–775 (1σ) AD 660–870 (2σ)
29. (b) Treanbaun 3: Bronze Age cists and lead mine (E2123)				
Wk-21792	Charcoal (hazel, Pomoideae, alder) from mine pit, secondary fill	1245 ± 27	-26.6	AD 680–810 (1σ) AD 680–870 (2σ)
Wk-21793	Charcoal (Pomoideae and hazel) from mine pit, secondary fill	3436 ± 32	-23.0	1870–1680 BC (1σ) 1880–1660 BC (2σ)
Wk-21794	Charcoal (hazel) from fire pit or hearth near the mine pit	2758 ± 31	-24.9	930–840 BC (1σ) 1000–820 BC (2σ)
Wk-22560	Cremated human bone from cist burial in the mine pit	3515 ± 30	-23.7	1890–1770 BC (1σ) 1920–1750 BC (2σ)
Wk-22712	Charcoal (birch) from uppermost fill of the mine pit	2795 ± 30	-27.6	995–905 BC (1σ) 1020–840 BC (2σ)
Wk-22715	Charcoal (unspecified) from primary fill of the mine pit	3883 ± 75	-24.9	2470–2210 BC (1σ) 2570–2130 BC (2σ)
30. Gortnahoon: cereal kilns, storage pits and metalworking (E2075)				
Wk-21331	Charcoal (hazel) from fills of Structure B, Area 3	933 ± 36	-26.7	AD 1030–1160 (1σ) AD 1020–1190 (2σ)
Wk-21332	Charcoal (hazel) from fills of Structure B, Area 3	902 ± 44	-27.1	AD 1040–1190 (1σ) AD 1030–1220 (2σ)
Wk-21333	Charcoal (alder) from *in situ* burnt timbers in possible pottery kiln, Area 2	3953 ± 63	-25.2	2570–2340 BC (1σ) 2650–2200 BC (2σ)
Wk-21334	Charcoal (hazel) from basal fill of Structure A, Area 3	1238 ± 43	-26.8	AD 690–860 (1σ) AD 670–890 (2σ)
Wk-21335	Charcoal (diffuse porous) from pit fill with chert flake, Area 2	3438 ± 36	-25.6	1870–1680 BC (1σ) 1880–1640 BC (2σ)
Wk-22888	Carbonised seed from basal fill of dumbbell kiln, Area 2	1195 ± 30	-23.2	AD 775–880 (1σ) AD 710–940 (2σ)
Wk-22889	Carbonised seed from basal fill of L-shaped kiln, Area 3	823 ± 33	-23.1	AD 1185–1260 (1σ) AD 1150–1270 (2σ)

Lab. code	Sample material	Years BP	dC13‰	Calibrated dates
30. Gortnahoon: cereal kilns, storage pits and metalworking (E2075)				
Wk-22890	Carbonised seed from ditch fill in Area 3	1166 ± 32	-21.9	AD 780–940 (1σ) AD 770–970 (2σ)
31. Ballynaclogh: chipped stone assemblage, hearths, trackway remnants (E3874)				
Beta-270190	Wood: upright timber driven into wooden platform at edge of peat basin	4020 ± 40	-28.9	2580–2480 BC (1σ) 2630–2470 BC (2σ)
Beta-270191	Wood: timber from platform at edge of peat basin	4820 ± 40	-28.4	3650–3540 BC (1σ) 3660–3520 BC (2σ)
Beta-270192	Wood: carved rod found inserted into dog skull	2030 ± 40	-27.4	60 BC–AD 10 (1σ) 160 BC–AD 60 (2σ)
Beta-270193	Wood: single-plank trackway	4150 ± 40	-24.8	2870–2630 BC (1σ) 2880–2580 BC (2σ)
Beta-270194	Wood: decorated wooden bowl fragment	2470 ± 40	-31.7	760–510 BC (1σ) 780–410 BC (2σ)
Beta-270195	Wood: trackway remnant	3160 ± 40	-28.4	1460–1410 BC (1σ) 1500–1380 BC (2σ)
Beta-270196	Charcoal from hearth	4680 ± 40	-27.2	3520–3370 BC (1σ) 3630–3360 BC (2σ)
Beta-270197	Charcoal from hearth	4790 ± 40	-26.7	3640–3530 BC (1σ) 3650–3510 BC (2σ)
Beta-270198	Charcoal spread	4980 ± 40	-24.6	3790–3700 BC (1σ) 3930–3660 BC (2σ)
Beta-272868	Basal peat: centre of basin	8030 ± 50	-32.3	7063–6830 BC (1σ) 7082–6709 BC (2σ)
Beta-272869	Basal peat: at western edge of basin	3590 ± 40	-28.6	2014–1892 BC (1σ) 2116–1779 BC (2σ)
Beta-272870	Basal peat: 10 m from western edge of basin	6920 ± 50	-26.0	5969–5716 BC (1σ) 5844–5736 BC (2σ)
Beta-272871	Pollen monolith (0.94–1.04 m)	5070 ± 50	-27.6	3948–3800 BC (1σ) 3970–3731 BC (2σ)
Beta-272872	Pollen monolith (0.28–0.43 m)	3790 ± 40	-28.9	2286–2146 BC (1σ) 2401–2046 BC (2σ)
32. Newcastle: post-medieval settlement (E2076)				
Beta-241005	Animal bone from enclosure ditch, primary fill	330 ± 40	-22.0	AD 1450–1620 (1σ) AD 1440–1640 (2σ)

Lab. code	Sample material	Years BP	dC13‰	Calibrated dates
32. Newcastle: post-medieval settlement (E2076)				
UB-7246	Charcoal (oak) from hearth	218 ± 29	-23.0	AD 1648–1951 (1σ) AD 1643–1951 (2σ)
33. Cooltymurraghy: burnt mound (E2448)				
UB-7359	Charcoal (alder) from burnt mound	3768 ± 35	-26.0	2278–2137 BC (1σ) 2293–2042 BC (2σ)
34. Coololla: spade mill and lime kiln (E2477)				
Nil dates				
35. Coololla: Metal detecting on Aughrim battlefield (1691) (R002)				
Nil dates				
36. Urraghry: Mesolithic tools and Bronze Age burnt mound (E2449)				
UB-7351	Charcoal (hazel) from burnt mound	3817 ± 34	-27.0	2334–2155 BC (1σ) 2456–2141 BC (2σ)
UB-7352	Charcoal (diffuse porous) from fill of trough	3966 ± 34	-24.0	2566–2462 BC (1σ) 2574–2348 BC (2σ)
37. Barnacragh: burnt mounds (E2446)				
UB-7357	Charcoal (hazel) from burnt mound	3597 ± 35	-27.0	2015–1905 BC (1σ) 2115–1831 BC (2σ)
38. Loughbown 2: ringfort and earlier ring-ditch (E2054)				
UBA-8103	Animal bone (cattle vertebra) from ringfort ditch	1159 ± 29	-24.1	AD 782–945 (1σ) AD 778–969 (2σ)
UB-7360	Charcoal (Pomoideae) from remnant of ringfort bank	2245 ± 33	-26.0	384–215 BC (1σ) 392–205 BC (2σ)
UB-7361	Charcoal (diffuse porous) from post-hole in ringfort interior	2162 ± 34	-29.0	353–167 BC (1σ) 361–102 BC (2σ)
UBA-7759	Charcoal (*Prunus* sp. and Pomoideae) from ringfort ditch	342 ± 32	-28.8	AD 1488–1632 (1σ) AD 1467–1640 (2σ)
UBA-7760	Charcoal (hazel) from post-hole near poss. ring-ditch	941 ± 33	-21.0	AD 1033–1153 (1σ) AD 1022–1164 (2σ)
UBA-7758	Charcoal (hazel) from poss. Ring-ditch trench	2266 ± 24	-22.9	391–258 BC (1σ) 396–211 BC (2σ)

Lab. code	Sample material	Years BP	dC13‰	Calibrated dates
39. Loughbown 1: ringfort with souterrain, ironworking, cereal kilns and modern building remains (E2442)				
UB-7362	Charcoal (hazel/alder) from basal fill of outer ditch	1444 ± 32	-27.0	AD 597–645 (1σ) AD 563–653 (2σ)
UB-7363	Charcoal (hazel/alder) from fill of bowl furnace	863 ± 31	-26.0	AD 1156–1219 (1σ) AD 1047–1257 (2σ)
UB-7364	Charcoal (hazel) from fill of Bronze Age linear ditch	2881 ± 32	-24.0	1114–1012 BC (1σ) 1193–938 BC (2σ)
UB-7365	Charcoal (Pomoideae) from stony layer in the interior	614 ± 30	-26.0	AD 1300–1394 (1σ) AD 1294–1402 (2σ)
UB-7366	Charcoal (hazel) from fill of corn-drying kiln	644 ± 29	-26.0	AD 1291–1387 (1σ) AD 1282–1395 (2σ)
UB-7367	Charcoal (Pomoideae) from fill of gully in entrance	1572 ± 30	-24.0	AD 434–536 (1σ) AD 419–554 (2σ)
UBA-8096	Bone sample (fibula) from a human skeleton in the inner ditch	1138 ± 29	-25.4	AD 882–970 (1σ) AD 782–983 (2σ)
40. Mackney 1: Bronze Age hearth, pits and saddle quern (E2445)				
UB-7355	Charcoal (hazel) from hearth	2842 ± 35	-27.0	1048–934 BC (1σ) 1117–915 BC (2σ)
UB-7356	Charcoal (hazel) from pit	2844 ± 32	-25.0	1048–937 BC (1σ) 1114–919 BC (2σ)
41. Mackney 2: Bronze Age hearth and pits (E2443)				
UB-7353	Charcoal (hazel) from pit	2804 ± 33	-25.0	998–918 BC (1σ) 1047–848 BC (2σ)
UB-7354	Charcoal (hazel) from hearth	3093 ± 34	-26.0	1416–1316 BC (1σ) 1433–1270 BC (2σ)
42. Mackney 3: ringfort with souterrain, round-houses and *cillín* burials (E2444)				
UB-7368	Charcoal (hazel/alder) from fill of hearth/cereal kiln	524 ± 30	-26.0	AD 1403–1433 (1σ) AD 1323–1442 (2σ)
UB-7369	Charcoal (birch) from fill of hearth/cereal kiln	484 ± 28	-23.0	AD 1421–1441 (1σ) AD 1409–1448 (2σ)
UB-7370	Charcoal (hazel) from fill of hearth/cereal kiln	524 ± 30	-26.0	AD 1449–1616 (1σ) AD 1443–1631 (2σ)
UB-7371	Charcoal (hazel/alder) from furnace pit	1173 ± 30	-26.0	AD 781–892 (1σ) AD 775–965 (2σ)

Lab. code	Sample material	Years BP	dC13‰	Calibrated dates
42. Mackney 3: ringfort with souterrain, round-houses and *cillín* burials (E2444)				
UB-7372	Charcoal (hazel/alder) from isolated post-hole	702 ± 30	–25.0	AD 1270–1376 (1σ) AD 1260–1385 (2σ)
UB-7373	Charcoal (alder) from layer overlying hearth	377 ± 30	–27.0	AD 1452–1617 (1σ) AD 1446–1632 (2σ)
UB-7374	Charcoal (hazel/alder) from fill of fire pit	1183 ± 29	–27.0	AD 782–886 (1σ) AD 728–949 (2σ)
UB-7375	Charcoal (hazel/alder) from hearth associated with Structure J	365 ± 30	–27.0	AD 1457–1620 (1σ) AD 1449–1634 (2σ)
UB-7376	Charcoal (alder) from fill of metalworking feature	991 ± 31	–28.0	AD 997–1147 (1σ) AD 988–1153 (2σ)
43. Pollboy: Grand Canal survey				
Nil dates				

Bibliography

Alcock, O, de hÓra, K & Gosling, P 1999 *The Archaeological Inventory of County Galway Volume II: North Galway*. Dúchas the Heritage Service/The Stationery Office, Dublin.

ArchaeoPhysica 2004 M Roseveare & A Roseveare *Geophysical Survey of the Route of the Galway to East Ballinasloe National Road Scheme,* 2 Vols. Unpublished technical report to Galway County Council.

Bell, J & Watson, M 2008 *A History of Irish Farming 1750—1950.* Four Courts Press, Dublin.

Bermingham, N, Gearey, B R & Hopla, E 2010 *Stratigraphic and Topographic Investigations at Ballynaclogh, Co. Galway, including an Assessment of a Pollen Sequence from the Site.* Unpublished report to The Archaeology Company.

Bronk Ramsey, C 2005 *OxCal Program v.3.10* (http://c14.arch.ox.ac.uk/oxcal).

Carroll, M & Quinn, A 2003 'Ferrous and non-ferrous artefacts', *in* R M Cleary & M F Hurley, *Cork City Excavations,* 1984–2000, 257–98. Cork City Council, Cork.

Cawley, T 2004 'Soils, geology and hydrogeology', *in* RPS-MCOS Ltd *Environmental Impact Statement for the N6 Galway to East Ballinasloe Road Scheme. Glennascaul to East Ballinasloe,* Vol. 3B (Part 2), 346–55. Galway County Council.

Charles-Edwards, T 2000 *Early Christian Ireland.* Cambridge University Press, Cambridge.

Clarke, L & Carlin, N 2008 'Living with the dead at Johnstown 1: an enclosed burial, settlement and industrial site', *in* N Carlin, L Clarke & F Walsh, *The Archaeology of Life and Death in the Boyne Floodplain. The linear landscape of the M4 Kinnegad—Enfield—Kilcock motorway,* 55–85. NRA Scheme Monograph 2, National Roads Authority, Dublin.

Cleary, K 2005 'Skeletons in the closet: the dead among the living on Irish Bronze Age settlements', *Journal of Irish Archaeology,* Vol. 14 (2005), 23–7.

Cooney, G & Grogan, E 1999 (second edition) *Irish Prehistory. A social perspective.* Wordwell Ltd, Dublin.

Corlett, C & Potterton, M (eds) 2010 *Death and Burial in Early Medieval Ireland in the Light of Recent Archaeological Excavations.* Wordwell Press, Dublin.

Cunningham, B 1996 'From warlords to landlords. Political and social change in Galway 1540–1640', *in* G Moran & R Gillespie (eds), *Galway History and Society. Interdisciplinary essays on the history of an Irish county,* 97–130. Irish County History Series No. 9, Geography Publications, Dublin.

Curtis, E (ed.) 1933 'Original documents relating to the Butler lordship of Achill, Burrishoole and Aughrim 1236–1640', *Journal of the Galway Archaeological and Historical Society,* Vol. 15 (1930–31), 121–8.

DAHGI & NRA 2000 *Code of Practice between the National Roads Authority and the Minister for Arts, Heritage, Gaeltacht and Islands.* Dublin.

Delaney, F & Tierney, J 2011 *In the Lowlands of South Galway. Archaeological investigations on the N18 Oranmore to Gort national road scheme.* NRA Scheme Monographs 7. Dublin.

Dickson, D 2000 *New Foundations: Ireland 1660–1800.* Irish Academic Press, Dublin.

Doyle, N 2007 *Pottery Report, Deerpark, Co. Galway.* Unpublished technical report for Rubicon Heritage Ltd on behalf of Galway County Council.

Elliot, I 2006 *Report on Archaeogeophysical Survey (Licence No 06R173) at Caraun More, Co. Galway.* Unpublished technical report for CRDS Ltd on behalf of Galway County Council.

Farrelly, P 2004 'Material assets: agriculture', *in* RPS-MCOS Ltd *Environmental Impact Statement for the N6 Galway to East Ballinasloe Road Scheme. Glennascaul to East Ballinasloe,* Vol. 3B (Part 2), 395–484. Galway County Council.

Fitzpatrick, M & Crumlish, R 2000 'The excavation of three burnt mounds on the outskirts of Galway City', *Journal of the Galway Archaeological and Historical Society,* Vol. 52 (2000), 135–43.

Gailey, A 1982 *Spade Making in Ireland.* Ulster Folk and Transport Museum, Holywood.

Geissel, H 2006 *A Road on the Long Ridge. In search of the ancient highway on the Esker Riada.* CRS Publications, Newbridge.

Gosling, P 1993 *The Archaeological Inventory of County Galway Volume I: West Galway.* Office of Public Works/The Stationery Office. Dublin.

Griffith, R 1847–1964 *The Primary Valuation of Ireland.* Valuation Office (facsimile) and National Library of Ireland (manuscript), Dublin.

Grogan, E 2004 'Middle Bronze Age burial traditions in Ireland', *in* H Roche, J Bradley, J Coles, E Grogan & B Raftery (eds), *From Megaliths to Metals. Essays in honour of George Eogan,* 61–71. Oxbow Books, Oxford.

Grogan, E 2005 *The North Munster Project. Volume 2: the later prehistory of North Munster.* Discovery Programme Monographs 6. Dublin.

Holland, P 1994 'Anglo-Norman Galway: rectangular earthworks and moated sites', *Journal of the Galway Archaeological and Historical Society,* Vol. 46 (1994), 203–11.

Hunter, F & Davis, M 1994 'Early Bronze Age lead–a unique necklace from southeast Scotland', *Antiquity,* Vol. 68, 824–30.

Irish Record Commission 1825 *Public Records of Ireland: Volume III.* Dublin.

Jackman, N, Moore, C, Rynne, C 2013 *The Mill at Kilbegly. An archaeological investigation on the M6 Ballinasloe to Athlone national road scheme.* NRA Scheme Monographs 12, Dublin.

Jones, C 2004 *The Burren and the Aran Islands, Exploring the Archaeology.* Collins Press, Cork.

Joyce, P W 1869, 1871 & 1913 *Names of Irish Places,* 3 Vols. Phoenix Publishing Co. Ltd, Dublin, Cork and Belfast.

Kelly, F 1988 *A Guide to Early Irish Law.* Institute for Advanced Studies, Dublin.

Kelly, F 1998 *Early Irish Farming. A study based mainly on texts of the 7th and 8th centuries AD.* Institute for Advanced Studies, Dublin.

Kemmis, H 1826 *The Fourteenth Report of the Commissioners on Courts of Justice, Ireland. Judge or Commissary of the Courts of Prerogative and Faculties.* HC 1826 (68). House of Commons, London.

Lane, P G 1996 'The encumbered estates court and Galway land ownership 1849–1858', *in* G Moran & R Gillespie, *Galway History and Society. Interdisciplinary essays on the history of an Irish county, 395–420. Irish County* History Series No. 9, Geography Publications, Dublin.

Lewis, S 1837 *A Topographical Dictionary of Ireland.* Lewis & Co., London.

Little, A 2010 *Tasks, Temporalities and Textures: reconstructing the social topography of an Irish Mesolithic landscape.* Unpublished PhD thesis, University College Dublin.

Mac Eoin, G 1982 'The early Irish vocabulary of mills and milling', *in* B G Scott (ed.) *Studies on Early Ireland. Essays in honour of M V Duignan, 13–19.* Association of Young Irish Archaeologists, Belfast.

MacNeill, E 1923 'Ancient Irish Law: law of status and franchise', *Proceedings of the Royal Irish Academy,* Vol. 36 C, 265–316.

McCabe, M 2008 *Glacial Geology and Geomorphology. The Landscapes of Ireland.* Dunedin Academic Press, Edinburgh.

McCarthy, M 2010 *Ballynaclogh, Co. Galway (E3874). Osteoarchaeological Analysis of Animal Bones.* Unpublished report to The Archaeology Company.

McCutcheon, W A 1980 *The Industrial Archaeology of Northern Ireland.* Fairleigh Dickinson University Press, New Jersey.

McKinley, J I 1993 'Bone fragment size and weight of bone from modern British cremations and the implications for the interpretation of archaeological cremations', *International Journal of Osteoarchaeology,* Vol. 3, 283–7.

Melville, P 1996 'The Galway tribes as landowners and gentry', *in* G Moran & R Gillespie (eds), *Galway History and Society. Interdisciplinary essays on the history of an Irish county.* Irish County History Series No. 9, 319–70. Geography Publications, Dublin.

Mitchell, F & Ryan, M 2001 *Reading the Irish Landscape.* Town House, Dublin.

Monk, M, Tierney, J & Hannon, M 1998 'Archaeobotanical studies and early medieval Munster', *in* M Monk & J Sheehan (eds), *Early Medieval Munster, Archaeology, History and Society, 65–75.* Cork University Press, Cork.

Moore, C 2010 *Ballynaclogh, Co. Galway (E3874). Wood Technology Report.* Unpublished report to The Archaeology Company.

Müller's Pinakotek 7, 57, IIb. 4to. Copy of a Dutch print depicting the Battle of Aughrim (1691). Danish Royal Library, Copenhagen.

NAI M 5402 *Incumbered Estates Court Rental of the Lands of Newcastle, etc., Kilconnell Barony, Co. Galway, the Property of William Bevan to be Sold Oct. 7, 1854.* National Archives of Ireland, Dublin.

NAI M 5995 (a) *Incumbered Estates Court Rental of Newcastle, etc., Co. Galway and Caltra, Co. Westmeath, the Property of Sophia Mary Ireland and Another, for Sale March 21, 1851.* National Archives of Ireland, Dublin.

NAI M 5995 (b) *In the Court of the Commissioners for Sale of Incumbered Estates in Ireland: in the matter of the estate of Sophia Maria Ireland and another (owners) ex parte George Nelson Wheeler (petitioner). Rental of the Lands of Newcastle, Curraghduff, Clunamore, Knocknakappa, Rehill and Moate situate in the County of Galway.* National Archives of Ireland, Dublin.

NAI MFGS 46 [microfilm] *Valuation Office House Books,* National Archives of Ireland, Dublin.

Nicholls, K 2003 *Gaelic and Gaelicised Ireland in the Middle Ages,* Gill History of Ireland 4, Dublin (first edn 1972); revised and reprinted by Lilliput Press, Dublin.

NLI D 6, 501 *Photostat copy of an Indenture of George Warburton 1684.* National Library of Ireland, Dublin.

NLI Ms GO 182 *Genealogy of the Davies family of Newcastle, County Galway.* National Library of Ireland, Dublin.

Nolan, J P 1901 'Galway castles and owners in 1574', *Journal of the Galway Archaeological and Historical Society,* Vol. 1 (1900–1901), 109–23.

O'Brien, E 1992 'Pagan and Christian burial in Ireland during the first millennium AD: continuity and change', *in* N Edwards & A Lane (eds), *The Early Church in Wales and the West,* 130–7. Oxbow Monograph 16, Oxford.

O'Brien, E 2003 'Burial practices in Ireland: first to seventh centuries AD', *in* J Downes & A Ritchie (eds), *Sea Change. Orkney and northern Europe in the later Iron Age, AD 300–800,* 62–72. Pinkfoot Press, Balgavies, Scotland.

O'Brien, E 2010 'Burnt magic', *in* G Cooney & U MacConville (eds), *A Glorious Gallimaufry,* 195–98 Wordwell, Dublin.

O'Brien, E 2011 'The context and content of the cemetery at Owenbristy', *in* F Delaney & J Tierney, *In the Lowlands of South Galway. Archaeological excavations on the N18 Oranmore to Gort national road scheme,* 94–8. NRA Scheme Monographs 7. Dublin.

O'Brien, W 1994 *Mount Gabriel. Bronze Age mining in Ireland.* Bronze Age Studies 3, Galway University Press. Galway.

O'Brien, W 2004 *Ross Island. Mining, metal and society in early Ireland.* Bronze Age Studies 6, Galway University Press, Galway.

Ó Carragáin, T 2009 'Cemetery settlements and local churches in pre-Viking Ireland in light of comparisons with England and Wales ', *in* J Graham-Campbell & M Ryan (eds), *Anglo-Saxon/Irish Relations before the Vikings,* 329–66. Oxford University Press, Oxford.

O'Conor, K D 1998 *The Archaeology of Medieval Rural Settlement in Ireland.* Discovery Programme Monograph No. 3, Royal Irish Academy, Dublin.

O'Donovan, J 1843 *The Tribes and Customs of the Hy-Many Commonly Called O'Kelly's Country.* Irish Archaeological Society, Dublin.

Ó Drisceóil, D A 1990 '*Fulachta fiadh:* the value of early Irish literature', *in* V Buckley (ed.), *Burnt Offerings. International contributions to burnt mound archaeology,* 157–64. Wordwell Press, Bray.

Ó Floinn, R 1988 'Lehinch, Co. Offaly', *in* 'Excavations Bulletin 1977–79: summary accounts of archaeological excavations in Ireland', *Journal of Irish Archaeology,* Vol. 4 (1987–88), 77.

O'Hara, R 2009 'Collierstown 1: a Late Iron Age–early medieval enclosed cemetery', *in* M B Deevy & D Murphy (eds), *Places Along the Way. First findings on the M3.* NRA Scheme Monographs 5, 83–100. Dublin.

Quinn, B & Moore, D 2009 '*Fulachta fiadh* and the beer experiment', *in* M Stanley, E Danaher & J Eogan (eds), *Dining and Dwelling. Proceedings of a public seminar on archaeological discoveries on national road schemes, August 2008,* 43–53. Archaeology and the National Roads Authority Monograph Series No. 6, National Roads Authority. Dublin.

Raftery, B 1972 'Irish hillforts', *in* C Thomas (ed.), *The Iron Age in the Irish Sea Province,* 37–58. CBA Research Report 9, Council for British Archaeology, London.

Randolph-Quinney, P 2007 'An unusual burial at Ballygarraun West', *Seanda,* 2, 30–1.

Registry: Book 28, Memorial No. 38835. *A Leasehold Agreement between Thomas Davies of Newcastle and Frederick Trench of Garbally of 1727.* Registry of Deeds, Dublin.

Registry: Book 86, Memorial No. 59531 (1735) [untitled]. Registry of Deeds, Dublin.

Reimer, P J, Baillie, M G L, Bard, E, Bayliss, A, Beck, J W, Bertrand, C J H, Blackwell, P G, Buck, C E, Burr, G S, Cutler, K B, Damon, P E, Edwards, R L, Fairbanks, R G, Friedrich, M, Guilderson, T P, Hogg, A G, Hughen, K A, Kromer, B, McCormac, G, Manning, S, Ramsey, C B, Reimer, R W, Remmele, S, Southon, J R, Stuiver, M, Talamo, S, Taylor, F W, van der Plicht, J & Weyhenmeyer, C E 2004 'IntCal04 terrestrial radiocarbon age calibration, 0–26 cal kyr BP', *Radiocarbon* Vol. 46, 1029–58.

RIA Mss 14 D Royal Irish Academy [NLI Microfilm reference 5354] *Copies of Inquisitions Held in the County of Galway at Various Dates in the 16th and 17th centuries Made by the Ordnance Survey Office with an Index of Place-names,* 4 Vols. Dublin.

Roy, J C 1997 'Triumphal gateway, Moyode Castle, County Galway', *Journal of the Galway Archaeological and Historical Society,* Vol. 49 (1997), 194–201.

Roy, J C 2001 *The Fields of Athenry. A journey through Irish history.* Westview Press; Boulder, Colorado and Oxford, UK.

Rynne, C 2006 *Industrial Ireland 1750–1930. An archaeology.* The Collins Press, Cork.

Rynne, C 2013 'Mills and milling in early medieval Ireland', *in* N Jackman, C Moore & C Rynne, *The Mill at Kilbegly. An archaeological investigation on the M6 Ballinasloe to Athlone national road scheme,* 115–47. NRA Scheme Monographs 12. Dublin.

Sabin, D & Donaldson, K 2004 *Archaeological Surveys Metal Detection Report: N6 Galway to Ballinasloe National Road Scheme Lutrell's Pass A024/5.1.* Unpublished technical report for ArchaeoPhysica Ltd on behalf of Galway County Council.

Scannell, J & Cooke, C 2005 *A Social History of Aughrim since 1691.* Aughrim Development Company, Aughrim.

Sexton, R 1998 'Porridges, gruels and breads: the cereal foodstuffs of early medieval Ireland', *in* M Monk & J Sheehan (eds), *Early Medieval Munster, Archaeology, History and Society,* 76–86. Cork University Press, Cork.

Shiels, D forthcoming 'Military artefacts from Lutrell's Pass on the 1691 Aughrim battlefield', *Journal of the Galway Archaeological and Historical Society.*

Shine, D 2008 *Landscape and Archaeology of the M6 Route Corridor in East Galway.* Unpublished study on landscape and archaeological background of the M6 Galway to Ballinasloe motorway corridor. CRDS Ltd for Galway County County Council.

Simington, R C 1962 *Books of Survey and Distribution. Vol. III: County of Galway.* Irish Manuscripts Commission, Dublin.

Slater, I 1856 *Royal National Commercial Directory of Ireland.* Manchester.

Stout, G & Stout, M 2008 *Excavation of an Early Medieval Secular Settlement at Knowth, Site M, County Meath.* Wordwell Ltd, Dublin.

Stout, M 1997 *The Irish Ringfort.* Four Courts Press, Dublin.

Stuiver, M & Reimer, P J 1993 'Extended ^{14}C database and revised CALIB radiocarbon calibration program', *Radiocarbon* Vol. 35, No. 1, 215–30.

Stuiver, M, Reimer, P J & Reimer, R W 2005 *CALIB Rev 5.0.2* (http://calib.qub.ac.uk/calib).

Talma, A S & Vogel, J C 1993 'A simplified approach to calibrating ^{14}C dates', *Radiocarbon* Vol. 35, No. 2, 317–32.

Taylor, A & Skinner, A 1783 (first edn 1778) *Taylor & Skinner's Maps of the Roads of Ireland, Surveyed 1777.* Dublin.

Waddell, J 1990 *The Bronze Age Burials of Ireland.* Galway Officina Typographica, Galway.

Walsh, C 1997 *Archaeological Excavations at Patrick, Nicholas and Winetavern Streets Dublin.* Brandon Press, Dingle.

Westropp, M S D 1917 'Notes on Irish money weights and foreign coin current in Ireland', *Proceedings of the Royal Irish Academy, Section C, 33 (1916–17),* 43–4.

Zilic, A M 2002 *Discovering the Lost History of Irish Tenant Farmers through Analysis of Historic Earthenware Ceramics.* Unpublished Senior Thesis, Illinois State University.

INDEX